HANGING IN THERE

In Memoriam: *Charlie Bayne*   *1965-1990*
              Ghiţa Ionescu   *1913-1996*
              Mike Hodges   *1945-1998*

The G8 and Global Governance Series

The G8 and Global Governance Series explores the issues, the institutions and the strategies of participants in the G8 network of global governance, as they address the challenges of shaping global order in the new millennium. Intensifying globalization is moving many once domestic issues into the international arena, requiring constant international co-operation, and demanding new collective leadership to direct the galaxy of multilateral institutions created in 1945. In response, the Group of Eight, composed of the world's major market democracies, including Russia and the European Union, is emerging as the effective source of global governance in the new era. This series focuses on the new issues at the centre of global governance, from finance, investment, and trade, through transnational threats to human security, to traditional political and security challenges. It examines the often invisible network of G8 and G7 institutions as they operate within and outside established international organizations to generate desired outcomes. It analyzes how individual G7 members and other international actors, including multinational firms and those from civil society, devise and implement strategies to secure their preferred global order.

Also in the series

The G7/G8 System
Evolution, role and documentation
Peter I. Hajnal
ISBN 1 84014 776 8

The G8's Role in the New Millennium
Edited by
Michael R. Hodges, John J. Kirton and Joseph P. Daniels
ISBN 1 84014 774 1

Hanging In There

The G7 and G8 Summit in Maturity and Renewal

NICHOLAS BAYNE
The London School of Economics and Political Science

Ashgate

Aldershot • Brookfield USA • Singapore • Sydney

Published by
Ashgate Publishing Ltd
Gower House
Croft Road
Aldershot
Hants GU11 3HR
England

Ashgate Publishing Company
Old Post Road
Brookfield
Vermont 05036
USA

Ashgate website: http://www.ashgate.com

British Library Cataloguing in Publication Data
Bayne, Nicholas
    Hanging in there : the G7 and G8 summit in maturity and
    renewal. - (The G8 and global governance)
    1.Group of Seven 2.Group of Eight 3.Summit meetings -
    History 4.International relations 5.International
    organization 6.World politics
    I.Title
    327

Library of Congress Catalog Card Number: 99-85920

ISBN 0 7546 1185 X

Printed and bound by Athenaeum Press, Ltd.,
Gateshead, Tyne & Wear.

Contents

PART III: THE RENEWAL OF THE SUMMIT

CONCLUSION

List of Tables

Foreword

By John J. Kirton

Hanging Together, the classic book written by Nicholas Bayne and Robert Putnam, has stood for decades as the master work for all scholars and practitioners seeking to understand and shape the G7's contribution to the process of international cooperation. Since its most recent edition was published in 1987, however, the major transformations the world has experienced have called for a fresh look at the G7's role and even continuing relevance, amidst the end of the Cold War, the onset of globalisation, and the revival and rise of a host of new international institutions.

No-one is better placed to address this fundamental question than Sir Nicholas Bayne. As a participant in many G7 summits and a close observer of most, he is uniquely positioned to explore the dynamics of continuity and change, in both the G7 itself and in the wide world in which it operates. To this task he brings the sensitive insights of the accomplished insider and the independent vision of a caring but critical outsider. Moreover as one whose scholarly interests and policymaking involvement have extended well beyond the G7 to embrace an array of major international institutions in the economic and political domain, he is able to assess the G7's work against, and see it in relation to, the formidable array of bodies contributing to global governance. Above all, as one of the leading interpreters of the G7 during the period of its birth and early growth, he can distinguish between the ephemeral and the fundamental, and reflect with precision and authority on the degree, form and adequacy of the changes the G7 has undergone.

Hanging In There is the product of his reflections. Developed over the past decade they are now integrated into a major new analysis of the Group of Seven and, with the successful incorporation of Russia, the Group of Eight major industrial democracies. As with its co-authored predecessor, this book provides a close, chronological account of the calculations and contribution of the annual G7 summits. This account is set here within the broader interpretive context of the phases the G7 has passed through in its decade of maturity and renewal from 1987 to 1999. For the first time this book places the work of the G7 and G8 fully in the context of the activity of the other major, but still poorly understood, international organisations, such as the OECD and WTO. Moreover, it does so within a broader, critical examination of the major forces - the end of the Cold War and the onset of intensifying globalisation - that have so changed the world during the 1990s.

In doing so, Nicholas Bayne offers an innovative and compelling examination of the G7 and G8's performance as the twenty first century opens. He emphasises how the end of the Cold War and ensuing advent of globalisation have strengthened international organisations by moving them toward genuine multilateral membership and influence, but at the same time have brought a host of new global human security and once domestic issues that threaten to overwhelm their limited capabilities. In this new world, the G8, through successful experimentation and dogged persistence, has found an enhanced role and relevance in directly providing needed global governance on issues where no other credible institutions exist, and in catalysing and guiding the modernisation of those that do.

Sir Nicholas Bayne has thus provided a powerful new interpretation of how a strengthened G8 is operating effectively within a transformed world. He provides an essential account for all who wish to comprehend and direct the dynamic of global governance in the twentyfirst century.

Preface and Acknowledgements

This book is the fruit of 25 years' fascination with the summits. I was present at the very first of them, at Rambouillet in 1975. I have been conducting research into them since 1982. Over the years they have had many names. They began as 'economic summits'; as their agenda grew, they evolved into 'seven power summits'; by association with their finance ministers they became known as 'G7 summits'; and in 1998 the formal addition of Russia made them 'G8 summits'. I have tried in this book to remain faithful to the nomenclature in use at the time.

Over so long an association I have accumulated many debts, which I here recognise - I can never repay them. My first debt is to my colleagues in the Foreign and Commonwealth Office (FCO) and Her Majesty's Treasury over the years. They first brought me close to the summits and enabled me to remain involved with them throughout the rest of my professional career: as Financial Counsellor at the British Embassy in Paris (1975-79); as Head of Economic Relations Department, FCO (1979-82); as UK Permanent Representative to the OECD (1985-88); as Economic Director of the FCO and sous-Sherpa (1988-92); and as High Commissioner to Canada (1992-96). This sequence explains why I am better informed about some summits than others. This book is mainly about the summits from 1988 to the present. Here I know much more about Paris 1989, Houston 1990, London III 1991, Halifax 1995, Denver 1997 and Birmingham 1998 than I do about Toronto 1988, Munich 1992, Tokyo III 1993, Naples 1994, Lyon 1996 and Cologne 1999.

The FCO and Treasury not only gave me professional involvement in the summits. With rare enlightenment they allowed me to conduct research into the summits and to publish the results, even where I did not agree with government policy. William Wallace, as Director of Studies, invited me to spend a year at the Royal Institute for International Affairs (RIIA) at Chatham House and the FCO agreed to send me. Bob Putnam, Professor of Government at Harvard University, asked me to join him in writing the first full-length book in English on the summits. To both I am indebted for the happiest year of my working life, which led to the production of *Hanging Together; the Seven Power Summits*, published by the RIIA and Harvard University Press in 1984.

Hanging Together is the foundation for all my subsequent work on summitry, including this book, which is intended to bring the summit story up to date. Bob Putnam and I maintained our association over several years, to produce updated versions of our book in German, Japanese and Italian and a new English edition in 1987. He has since gone on to well-deserved fame for his later writings. This book owes much to his sustained inspiration.

My next debt is to those journals and other publishers who provided me with a platform for my subsequent articles on summitry and related economic subjects. The late Ghiţa Ionescu, founder of the journal *Government and Opposition*, was a special source of encouragement. These writings provide the basis for the present book. I formally express my thanks to the following for giving me permission to re-use material which they originally published:-

- SAGE Publications Ltd, in respect of Chapter 3 and part of 4, drawn from Chapters 10 and 7 of Putnam and Bayne, *Hanging Together; Cooperation and Conflict in the Seven Power Summits* (SAGE 1987).
- The Editors of *The World Today*, the monthly journal of the RIIA, in respect of:-

  Chapter 2, drawn from 'Western Economic Summits: Can They Do Better?', *The World Today* vol. 40. no. 1, January 1984;
  Chapter 4, drawn from 'Making Sense of Western Economic Policy; the Role of the OECD', *The World Today*, vol. 43. no. 2, February 1987;
  Chapter 5, drawn from 'The Course of Summitry', *The World Today*, vol. 48. no. 2, February 1992.

- The Editors of *Government and Opposition*, in respect of:-

  Chapter 6, drawn from 'International Economic Relations After the Cold War', *Government and Opposition*, vol. 29. no. 1, Winter 1994;
  Chapter 7, drawn from 'In the Balance: The Uruguay Round of International Trade Negotiations', *Government and Opposition*, vol. 26. no. 3, Summer 1991;
  Chapter 8, drawn from 'The G7 Summit and the Reform of Global Institutions', *Government and Opposition*, vol. 30. no. 4, Autumn 1995;
  Chapter 9, drawn from 'What Governments Want from International Institutions and How They Get It', *Government and Opposition*, vol. 32. no. 3, Summer 1997.

- Taylor and Francis Ltd, in respect of Chapter 9, drawn from 'International Economic Organisations; More Policy Making, Less Autonomy', in Bob Reinalda and Bertjan Verbeek, eds., *Autonomous Policy Making by International Organisations*, (Routledge 1998).
- The Editors of *The Round Table*, in respect of Chapter 11, drawn from 'Globalization and the Commonwealth: International Economic Relations in the Post-Cold War World', *The Round Table*, no. 344, October 1997, and 'Britain, the G8 and the Commonwealth', *The Round Table*, no. 348, October 1998.

From Chapter 8 onwards I have drawn on occasional pieces I have written for the University of Toronto G8 Research Group (see below), while Chapter 12 is an updated and amended version of 'Continuity and Leadership in an Age of Globalisation', published in Michael Hodges, John Kirton and Joseph Daniels, eds., *The G8's Role in the New Millennium* (Ashgate 1999), the first volume in this G8 and Global Governance Series.

Since retiring from the FCO in 1996, I have been fortunate in finding academic colleagues who encouraged my interest in summitry. These are my most recent debts. William Wallace intervened again to introduce me to Mike Hodges, who made me a colleague of his at the International Relations Department of the London School of Economics and Political Science (LSE). We travelled together to the Denver summit of 1997 and helped to set up two conferences before Birmingham in 1998. His tragic death in June 1998 is a bitter loss, but the work which he stimulated still goes on.

John Kirton, founder and director of the G8 Research Group at the University of Toronto, is the proximate cause of this book. I am indebted to him and his colleagues in the Research Group for welcoming me into their midst, especially at Denver and Birmingham. John Kirton persuaded me to create this book out of my writings since *Hanging Together* and to give it a theme and structure beyond a simple collection of occasional pieces. I have enjoyed the process, finding a more coherent story in my earlier writings than I had expected. I have greatly benefitted from the comments of pre-publications reviewers. There are, however, omissions and duplications which would not have occurred if I were starting from scratch. This is a book of observation and reflection, rather than true research, so that it lacks a detailed scholarly apparatus. Despite these and other faults - all my own responsibility - I hope it may prove worthy of the G8 and Global Governance Series.

In addition to those already named, I thank many others to whom I am indebted for intellectual stimulus, moral encouragement or both, especially: Rodric Braithwaite, Colin Budd, Brian Crowe, Chris Cviic, Joe Daniels, Wendy Dobson, David Dodge, Huw Evans, Robin Griffith, Peter Hajnal, David Henderson, Tony Hutton, Graham Ingham, Paul Jacobelli, Michael and Sylvia Jay, Rosalind Jones, DeAnne Julius, Ella Kokotsis, Richard Layard, Peter Lyon, Sylvia Ostry, Geraint Parry, Jean-Claude Paye, David Peretz, Christopher Roberts, Tim Shaw, Gordon Smith, Heidi Ullrich, Bertjan Verbeek, Nick Westcott, Nigel Wicks, Gil Winham, Bob Wolfe, Steve Woolcock and above all my beloved wife Diana.

All their contributions would be in vain without the skill of Christine Hunter, who turned my scrappy manuscript into elegant camera-ready copy, and of Kirstin Howgate and her colleagues at Ashgate, who made it into this book.

Nicholas Bayne,
Hampton Court,
September 1999

List of Abbreviations

AIDS	Acquired Immune Deficiency Syndrome
AMS	Aggregate Measure of Support (for agriculture in GATT)
APEC	Asia-Pacific Economic Cooperation
ASEAN	Association of South-East Asian Nations
Bank	See IBRD
CAP	Common Agriculture Policy (of the EC)
CHOGM	Commonwealth Heads of Government Meeting
CMEA	Council for Mutual Economic Assistance (of communist countries)
COCOM	Coordinating Committee (of NATO on strategic exports)
CSCE	Conference on Security and Cooperation in Europe
CSD	Commission for Sustainable Development (of the UN)
CSE	Consumer Subsidy Equivalent (for agriculture in OECD - see PSE)
EBRD	European Bank for Reconstruction and Development
EC	European Community
ECOSOC	Economic and Social Council (of the UN)
EEC	European Economic Community
EFTA	European Free Trade Area
EMS	European Monetary System
EPC	Economic Policy Committee (of the OECD)
ERM	Exchange Rate Mechanism (of the EMS)
EU	European Union
FATF	Financial Action Task Force
FCO	Foreign and Commonwealth Office
Fund	International Monetary Fund (see also IMF)
GAB	General Agreement to Borrow (of the IMF)
GDR	German Democratic Republic
GMOs	Genetically Modified Organisms
G5	Group of Five (finance ministers)
G7	Group of Seven (summit, finance ministers and other groups)
G8	Group of Eight (summit and other groups)
G10	Group of Ten (finance ministers and officials in the IMF)
G22	Group of Twenty-Two (on new financial architecture)
G24	Group of Twenty-Four (coordinating aid to Eastern Europe)
GATS	General Agreement on Trade in Services (in the WTO)

GATT	General Agreement on Tariffs and Trade
GNP	Gross National Product
HIPC	Heavily Indebted Poor Countries
IBRD	International Bank for Reconstruction and Development, also known as the Bank or the World Bank
IDA	International Development Association
IEA	International Energy Agency (linked to OECD)
ILO	International Labour Organisations
IMF	International Monetary Fund, also known as the Fund
LSE	London School of Economics and Political Science
MAI	Multilateral Agreement on Investment (in OECD)
MFA	Multi-Fibre Agreement (for textiles in GATT)
NAFO	North-West Atlantic Fisheries Organisation
NAFTA	North American Free Trade Area
NATO	North Atlantic Treaty Organisation
NEA	Nuclear Energy Agency (of the OECD)
NGOs	Non Governmental Organisations
OECD	Organisation for Economic Reconstruction and Development
OEEC	Organisation for European Economic Reconstruction
OPEC	Organisation for Petroleum Exporting Countries
OSCE	Organisation for Security and Cooperation in Europe
PSE	Producer Subsidy Equivalent (for agriculture in OECD - see CSE)
Quad	Quadrilateral - of trade ministers (US, EC, Japan, Canada)
RIIA	Royal Institute for International Affairs, also called Chatham House
SDI	Strategic Defence Initiative, also called 'Star Wars'
SDRs	Special Drawing Rights (in the IMF)
STF	Systemic Transformation Facility (of the IMF)
UK	United Kingdom
UN	United Nations
UNCED	United Nations Conference on Environment and Development
UNCTAD	United Nations Conference on Trade and Development
UNEP	United Nations Environment Programme
US	United States of America
USSR	Union of Soviet Socialist Republics - also Soviet Union
WTO	World Trade Organization

Introduction

1 Explaining the Summit Cycle

The G8 summit (as it now is) has become a permanent feature in the international landscape of the final quarter of the 20th century. The Cologne summit of June 18-20, 1999, was the twenty-fifth meeting of heads of state and government, in unbroken sequence from the founding encounter at Rambouillet on 15-17 November, 1975 (see Table 1.1). Rambouillet was an experiment and might have been a single, unrepeated event. Once the second summit was held in Puerto Rico on 27-28 June 1976, the components of the annual cycle were set. From then on the summit met every year for 2-3 days over a weekend in the summer months, between May and July. Each head of state or government in turn acted as host and took the chair, always in the same order: France, United States, Britain, Germany, Japan, Italy and Canada. After 1976 the seven-power membership was modified only twice, once early and once late. The European Community (EC), later European Union (EU), represented by Commission and Presidency, was added in 1977; whenever possible the summit was held in the Presidency of one of the four European summit members. After a long apprenticeship, Russia became a full member on probation at Denver in 1997, called 'the Summit of the Eight', and definitively at Birmingham in 1998, the first G8 summit.

Plan and Purpose of this Book

This book offers a selective analytical history of the summits, in their wider context, up to the time of writing in 1999. The summits are examined for their contribution to the three objectives which stimulated their original creation and determined their roles thereafter. These objectives are:-

- Reconciling the tensions between domestic and international politics which result from economic interdependence;
- Developing collective management to take the place of earlier American hegemony;
- Mobilising the political leadership of heads of state and government to resolve problems beyond the reach of national bureaucracies or international organisations.

Table 1.1:   **The Summit Cycle, 1975-1999**

I   **Innovation and Establishment**

The First Series, 1975-1978	Rambouillet	1975
	Puerto Rico	1976
	London I	1977
	Bonn I	1978
The Second Series, 1979-1982	Tokyo I	1979
	Venice I	1980
	Ottawa	1981
	Versailles	1982
The Third Series, 1983-1988	Williamsburg	1983
	London II	1984
	Bonn II	1985
	Tokyo II	1986
	Venice II	1987
	Toronto	1988

II   **Maturity**

The Fourth Series, 1989-1993	Paris (Arch)	1989
	Houston	1990
	London III	1991
	Munich	1992
	Tokyo III	1993

III   **Renewal**

The Fifth Series, 1994-1997	Naples	1994
	Halifax	1995
	Lyon	1996
	Denver	1997
The Sixth Series, 1998-?	Birmingham	1998
	Cologne	1999

This threefold basis for assessment - reconciling interdependence, collective management and political leadership - will provide the analytical framework for the entire book. Of these three, the greatest attention will be given to the first, in particular in charting the transition from interdependence to globalisation.

This analytical framework is the same as was used in the book *Hanging Together: Cooperation and Conflict in the Seven-Power Summits*, which Bob Putnam and I wrote together in the early 1980s. The first edition, published by Heinemann for the Royal Institute for International Affairs (RIIA) in 1984, brought the story up to the Williamsburg summit of 1983. The second, published by SAGE in 1987, extended it to cover fully Tokyo II 1986 and cursorily also Venice II 1987. Chapters 1 and 2 of the 1987 edition set out the analysis and Chapters 10 and 11 draw conclusions from it, based on the first 13 summits in the cycle. The present book therefore concentrates on the 12 summits from 1988 to 1999, passing rapidly over those earlier in the sequence, since it does not intend to replace the previous work. Those interested in how the summits first began and how they evolved through their earlier years should read *Hanging Together*.

This book is in a sense a sequel to *Hanging Together*, as its title - *Hanging In There* - is intended to convey. But there are important differences between the two books. This book has a single author, unlike the twin authorship of the first. *Hanging Together*, as its preface explained, could benefit from the contrasting perspectives of its two authors - one an academic (Putnam) and the other a practitioner (Bayne). Bob Putnam could bring his penetrating intellect and his command of the theoretical debate to enrich *Hanging Together*. Though the present book has his blessing, I am the only author. It therefore does not attempt to replicate the examination of summitry in the context of theories of international relations, as contained in Chapters 1 and 11 of the earlier volume.

Hanging Together provided a continuous narrative of the summits, usually two to a chapter, going into detail over what happened when the leaders met. This book also contains narrative chapters, but they give a more schematic and impressionistic account, tracing what groups of summits did in their major areas of interest. This account is selective. It seeks to concentrate on the topics which dominated the summits at the time and leaves out subsidiary issues, even those which, like nuclear safety in Ukraine after Chernobyl, were recurrent subjects at the summits. It has a bias towards the economic discussions at the summit, covering political items only where the story would not make sense without them.

Each of the narrative chapters, from Chapter 3 onwards, begins with a section on 'political leadership', discussing the institutional development of the summits. Each of them (except Chapter 10) concludes with a section on 'collective management', tracing the shifts in power and influence between the summit participants. The middle part of the narrative chapters examines the issues treated by the summits, chiefly in the context of reconciling the tensions between domestic and international politics, though this examination can also illuminate the other two elements of the analysis.

This book also follows the structure of *Hanging Together* in that chapters of narrative alternate with essays on more general subjects of relevance to the summits. Indeed, the balance has shifted: in this book there are more general essays in proportion to narrative. This is a consequence of the passage of time since *Hanging Together* was written. The forces at work in shaping the world of the late 20th century are visible now in a way they were not in the mid-1980s. *Hanging Together* was much concerned with the oil crises of 1973-74 and 1978-79; with how the summit members confronted them and finally mastered their consequences. But, like the summit members themselves, the authors did not foresee the collapse of the communist empire and the end of the Cold War, which altered fundamentally the priorities of the summits. *Hanging Together* examined in detail the implications of economic interdependence, the original stimulus for the summits. But up to the mid-1980s interdependence affected mainly the industrial West and the summits concentrated on what they should do among themselves and their closest partners. The end of the Cold War converted interdependence into globalisation, a current embracing the entire world. This forced the summit members into a learning process and re-oriented their concerns outwards, so that they did less for themselves and more for the international system.

The chapters containing general essays thus go deeper into the implications for the entire international system - including the summits - of reconciling the tensions between domestic and international politics resulting not only from interdependence but also from globalisation, whose advance was greatly accelerated by the end of the Cold War.

The longer perspective, spanning 25 years, has prompted the division of the summit cycle into three main periods and six shorter series. The first period, from 1975 to 1988, is the one already analysed in large part by *Hanging Together*. It covers the foundation and establishment of the summits in the context of interdependence. The second period begins in 1989 with the ending of the Cold War, the decisive turning point in the summit cycle so far. During this time the summits confronted the new environment created by the collapse of the communist empire and the end of the East/West division in the world economy. The summit was by now a mature institution and struggled to adapt to new demands at a time when its internal dynamic was slowing down. The third period began as the summit leaders realised the true impact of globalisation on themselves and on the world at large. They embarked on a period of renewal, aimed both at their own procedures and practices and at the larger system of international institutions. This renewal is still in progress.

The rest of this Introduction explains this approach to the summit cycle, going through chapters 2 to 11 which make up the body of this book.

The Summit Cycle, 1975-1999

Chapters 2 and 3, which follow this one, are narrative overview chapters which cover the summits from 1975 to 1988. They are shorter than later chapters as they go over ground already covered in *Hanging Together*. They follow the division of the summits into series as established in Chapter 10 of *Hanging Together* (Putnam and Bayne 1987), on which Chapter 3 is based. The rationale for the division into series of varying length is discussed in more detail below.

The summit cycle began with the members' economies in recession as a result of the oil crisis of 1973-74. The first series followed the summits through four years of giving encouragement to economic recovery, matched by international trade negotiations in the Tokyo Round. The last in this series, Bonn I 1978, concluded the most elaborate set of interlocking commitments in economic policy, trade and energy attempted at any summit. The second oil crisis of 1978-79 broke the sequence and started the next summit series. This again ran for four years of tough, corrective economic policies, which squeezed out the inflation generated by the oil price increase at the cost of severe loss of growth.

When this process was complete, the third summit series began in 1983, like the first in 1975, at the start of a slow but sustained economic recovery. In this series, however, the summits hardly considered measures of macro-economic stimulus, as in the first. Fighting inflation remained the priority. New trade negotiations were considered and finally agreed. Economic policy coordination was largely delegated to finance ministers. The leaders turned increasingly to foreign policy and to non-economic subjects like terrorism. The series continued to 1988, concluding on a note of self-satisfaction with no inkling of the changes coming in Eastern Europe a year ahead.

The essay in Chapter 4 examines the Organisation for Economic Cooperation and Development (OECD), as the organisation which best embodied the spirit and practice of economic interdependence while the Cold War lasted. The OECD developed a great variety of links between the industrial democracies, covering a wide range of subjects of economic policy and engaging the officials responsible in capitals. It worked through informal influence on the domestic policy-making of its members rather than through formal commitments. Its relations with the summit itself were close but often uneasy, because of conflicts of loyalty.

Chapter 5 gives a narrative of the fourth summit series, which embraced the end of the Cold War. This was the decisive event for the summits from 1989 to 1993 and indeed for the whole summit cycle. Summit priorities changed to focus on helping first Central and Eastern Europe and then Russia itself. From 1991 the summit leaders began meeting their counterparts from Russia, first Soviet President Mikhail Gorbachev, then Russian President Boris Yeltsin. On their own economic agenda they dealt with subjects with a wider international reach than before: debt relief for poor countries, the global environment and above all the Uruguay Round of trade negotiations in the General Agreement on Tariffs and Trade (GATT). The Uruguay Round finally concluded in 1993, after a successful push at the Tokyo III summit of that year. But the three previous summits - Houston, London III and Munich - had all pledged to end the Round and failed. Trying to help the Russia economy also led to several failed attempts. While the leaders may have been smug in 1988, when the third series closed, they ended the fourth series feeling frustrated, despite some clear achievements.

Two essays illustrate the forces at work in this period of the summit's maturity. Chapter 6 examines the impact of the end of the Cold War on the international economic system. It is in a sense the hinge of the whole book and introduces the subject of globalisation. It looks at developments from the viewpoint of governments and global institutions. It comes to the summits only at the end and concludes that, unless they changed their ways, their influence would fade away.

Chapter 7 looks in detail at the Uruguay Round of trade negotiations. It analyses the reasons for the new Round, the course of the negotiations and the agreements reached. The end of the Cold War helped to make this Round of worldwide relevance, unlike the Tokyo Round which mainly concerned the industrial West. It also stimulated the conversion of the rather improvised GATT into the firmly-based World Trade Organization (WTO). All these were signs of globalisation beginning to work, if not explicitly recognised.

Chapters 8 and 10 are narrative chapters, explaining how the summit came to renew itself. The critical change was the leaders' realisation of the impact of globalisation. This realisation came in two stages. At first they thought of globalisation as affecting the world at large rather than themselves. They were already the beneficiaries of globalisation, while others needed to adapt so as to gain its advantages. So the fifth summit series, from 1994 to 1997, focused on reforming international institutions, with the summits coming closer to the institutions in the process. But this strategy ran out of steam as the summit leaders realised that they too were deeply affected by globalisation. They had to protect their own peoples from some of its dangers and work through the international system to combat others. This led them to reform the summit process itself in the sixth series, which began in 1998 and is still running. The summits in this series took place among leaders only, as envisaged by the founders, French President Valéry Giscard d'Estaing and German Chancellor Helmut Schmidt, but never achieved till then.

A second feature promoting change, as recorded in these chapters, was the involvement of the Russians in the summit process. The experience of the fourth series in dealing with Russia, up to 1993, was frustrating for all concerned. The fifth series began with the Russians joining the political discussions as full members, but not the economic. This was logical, but not practical, and the Russians still chafed at being half in and half out. So the sixth series inaugurated the G8 summits, with the Russians as full members of everything. This paid immediate political dividends, over NATO enlargement at Denver 1997 and Kosovo at Cologne 1999. But Russia's persistent economic weakness, which led to its near collapse in August 1998, prevented it from full integration into the economic work. Serious economic agreements emerged at Birmingham and Cologne from the G7, not the G8. Russia itself was again in urgent need of Western financial help, just as it was back in the early 1990s as the Cold War ended. The impact of Russia's presence at the summits still remains unpredictable.

The essay in Chapter 9 relates to the institutional review conducted by the fifth summit series. This chapter examines how the G7 governments make use of international institutions: what they want from them and how they get it. It shows how globalisation increases the value of multilateral organisations of worldwide membership. Smaller institutions originally founded to serve their members, like the OECD and the G7 summit itself, are now adapting themselves to act as pressure groups or sources of leadership for the global organisations.

Chapter 11 has an essay on the impact of globalisation on the international financial system, which provided the main subjects of concern for the two summits of the sixth series so far, Birmingham 1998 and Cologne 1999, as well as for some of the previous series, like Halifax 1995. There is both a parallel and a contrast with the trade negotiations discussed in Chapter 8. In trade globalisation served to drive the participants in the Uruguay Round towards their final agreement. But in finance globalisation provoked a serious crisis, beginning in Asia and spreading worldwide. Globalisation, by polarising economic performance, also aggravated the economic problems of the poorest countries, especially those burdened by debt. The work of the G7 and the international institutions - International Monetary Fund (IMF) and World Bank - to devise new financial architecture and to provide genuine relief for the debts of low-income countries has marked some important achievements. But there is no confidence that future crises can be averted.

Chapters 10 and 11 bring the summit story up to the time of writing. The Conclusions in Chapter 12 will be reviewed at the end of this Introduction.

Explaining the Summit Cycle

The previous section went through the summit cycle in relation to Chapters 2-11 of this book. It remains to identify some underlying causes; to explain why the summits have evolved in this way and what determines the change from one summit series to the next.

The first question is: how long is a summit series? Chapters 5 and 10 of *Hanging Together* analysed the summits in groups of four years each - 1975-78, 1979-82, 1983-86 - though Venice 1987 was left hanging off the end. Later articles divided the summits by periods of seven years, with the change coming after each country had chaired a summit in turn and France began a new sequence - in 1982 and 1989.[1] But neither division was satisfactory. The summits do not break down into groups of a fixed number of years. So this book adopts a division of the summits into series of varying length. The first two series ran for four years each - 1975-1978, 1979-1982. The third had six years - 1983-1988; the fourth had five years - 1989-93; the fifth had four again - 1994-97. The sixth series will run at least for three years, from Birmingham 1998 to Okinawa 2000. No one can yet tell when the current series will end.

What determines the transition from one summit series to the next? Why do the summits change direction? This analysis examines a range of possible reasons. One cause could be the previous ministerial experience of the leaders. Early summits were dominated by former finance ministers, who provided six out of eight heads of government (including the European Commission) in 1978. This number dwindled to zero by 1982 and then began to rise again. It reached four out of eight in the early 1990s, only to fall to almost zero again by the end of the decade.[2] This cycle certainly influenced the choice of the summit agenda. Economic issues predominated in the early years, but in the 1980s the leaders preferred foreign policy issues, delegating many economic subjects to their finance ministers.   More economic subjects came back to the summit after the Cold War ended, including the need to help Russia. But often the leaders seemed ill at ease and did little more than endorse what their finance ministers put to them.

Another cause could be the political background of the participating leaders. There is no simple correlation with changes of government. For example, US presidential elections do not provoke changes in the summit series - quite the contrary. The summit did seem to be running down at the end of the Reagan administration. But the third series closed and the fourth began not because of the arrival of President George Bush, but because of the end of the Cold War.

Shifts in political allegiance do, however, have long term effects. At the beginning, there was a mix of left and right-wing governments, which produced a group of active and interventionist leaders. The arrival of Margaret Thatcher as British Prime Minister in 1979 and Ronald Reagan as US President in 1981 heralded a general shift to the right, which made the summits less ambitious and more inclined to follow the movement of the market. This right-wing dominance endured well into the 1990s, as Bush succeeded Reagan, John Major replaced Thatcher and German Chancellor Helmut Kohl outlasted all of them. The pendulum began to move back towards the left with the arrival of US President Bill Clinton and Canadian Prime Minister Jean Chrétien in North America. They were followed, after an interval, by a parallel shift in Europe: Tony Blair in Britain, Gerhard Schroeder in Germany and Massimo D'Alema in Italy, as well as Lionel Jospin as Socialist Prime Minister under President Jacques Chirac in France. This gave the latest summits more of a centre-left leaning than they had had since the 1970s. It made for interventionist leaders, ready to act on their own and with an interest in employment and social issues and the problems of the poorest.

These trends in the leaders' political and career background influence the choice of the summit agenda over time. But they do not on their own cause sharp changes in direction, from one series to the next. They need to be combined with the presence of external events. In the early years the sharpest changes came from economic causes. The first summit series ended as the oil crisis of 1978-79 virtually cut off the economic recovery from the preceding oil crisis of 1973-74. The second summit series lasted till the inflationary effects of the oil crisis had worked through; the third series, like the first, started with the new economic recovery. By the later years of the third series the summits had moved from economics to politics. So the fourth series began fittingly with the decisive political event of the quarter-century - the end of the Cold War.

The dip in the economic cycle came later and was spread over the fourth series, with the US, UK and Canada having negative growth in 1991 and Germany, France and Italy in 1993.[3] This complicated the work of the summits, which had to find help for Russia and keep up the momentum of trade negotiations during an economic slowdown.

The ends of the fourth and fifth cycles owe more to the leaders' own decisions. The conclusion of the Uruguay Round in 1993 coincided with the first realisation of the impact of globalisation and the approach of the 50th anniversaries of international institutions, like the UN, IMF and World Bank. For the first time the leaders themselves took the initiative to move into a new series, in their decision at Naples in 1994 to launch their review of international institutions. This was the beginning of summit renewal, even if unrecognised at the time. During the fifth series the leaders began to refer to globalisation in their documents, especially the preamble to the economic communiqué from Lyon 1996.

The move to the sixth series also came from the leaders themselves. By 1998 they had come to realise that globalisation demanded more than an institutional review; it had to be embedded into all their work. The Asian financial crisis of 1997 increased their awareness of the dark side of globalisation. This made them ready to move to the format of meeting alone, without their ministers, so that they could concentrate better on the issues that required their personal attention, leaving others to their ministers.

The position of Russia was a powerful secondary influence in the change of series both in 1994 and 1998. The fifth series began as Russia obtained a seat at the political table; the sixth as Russia was confirmed at the economic table also. Both moves changed profoundly the way the summits were organised and prepared, as well as the interaction between the leaders themselves. By 1999 everyone was accustomed to the presence of Yeltsin, who had been coming to summits for longer than anyone else present. What would happen after him remains an open question.

Deeper Currents Shaping the System

Behind the changes in the summit cycle, divided into series lasting between four and six years, there are deeper currents shaping the world economic system. The essays which separate the narrative chapters of this book trace the movement of these currents.

The first movement reflects the progression from interdependence to globalisation. Interdependence, the theme of Chapter 4, provided the context for the first three summit series. This involved very intimate links between Western industrial economies and involved some developing countries too. But it did not apply worldwide. The centrally-planned economies of the Communist bloc provided a rival system, while many developing countries tried to get the best of both worlds.

The rising tide of globalisation gradually pervaded the summits from the fourth series onwards and came to dominate their work. After transitional difficulties the success of the Uruguay Round, recorded in Chapter 7, served to mark the establishment of globalisation as a beneficent trend. But this did not endure. The later summits, of the fifth and sixth series, became increasingly concerned about the risks of globalisation, especially the instability of the financial system and the plight of poor, vulnerable countries, as Chapter 11 makes clear.

The second movement concerns the adaptation of the international economic system and its leading institutions to this progression. Chapter 6 - the core of the book - looks at the way the end of the Cold War enabled the whole range of institutions - GATT, IMF and World Bank as well as United Nations - to move to worldwide membership and start building up a universal, rule-based system. Chapter 9 again looks at the institutions collectively and the use governments make of them, in the context of the reforms advocated by the summits from Naples 1994 to Denver 1997.

These two chapters consider economic institutions together. Other essays analyse and contrast specific organisations in the light of their interaction with the summits and the progression from interdependence to globalisation. The OECD, treated in Chapter 4, is the typical institution designed to promote interdependence. With the first phase of globalisation, Chapter 7 concentrates on the GATT and its transformation into the WTO. The existing rule-based system of the GATT and WTO enabled them to establish a firm basis for liberalising trade and investment in ways which spread the benefits of globalisation. Chapter 11 completes the picture with a focus on the work of the IMF and the World Bank. Their response to globalisation is more problematical, as the international system which they seek to manage has become more vulnerable to financial crises and poor countries need even more help than before. The new international financial architecture is intended to provide a more solid rule-based structure for the IMF and World Bank. It is harder in finance, however, than it is in trade to bring under control the negative forces of globalisation.

Conclusion

This book thus tells the story of the G7 and G8 summits, especially those from 1988 onwards, in their wider context. The narrative chapters follow the summits through maturity to renewal, marking the changes of direction as the summit adapted to new demands. The narrative of the summits provides pointers to the deeper currents shaping the world economic system. So this book charts the progression from interdependence past the end of the Cold War to the full development of globalisation, with all its benefits and its dangers. It follows the parallel evolution of global international institutions as they adapt collectively to the changes in the system. It looks in turn at the OECD, the GATT and the WTO, and the IMF and World Bank, as they successively provide the focus for most of the summits' work.

The chapter of Conclusions, Chapter 12, looks back over the cycle. It examines the achievements of the summits in the light of the triple analysis used throughout the book, though in a different order: collective leadership, reconciling interdependence and political leadership. The main findings are:-

- In *collective management,* the declining performance of the summits in the 1980s, as identified in *Hanging Together,* has been halted and gradually reversed. An extended table grading the summits shows levels of cooperation improving, despite variations in performance. The summit no longer relies on the 'subjective hegemony' of the United States. Initiatives now come equally often from the European members, acting together or singly. Canada also contributes, though Japan's influence has fallen back.
- *Reconciling interdependence* has become both more needed and more difficult with the advance of globalisation. The problems coming up to the summits are so intractable that they require continuous or recurrent treatment. Originally created to dispose of issues as they arose, the summit has been transformed by the practice of iteration. This has led inevitably to institutional spread.
- In *political leadership,* the heads of state and government have finally reacted against institutional spread and regained their freedom of action by cutting loose from the lower levels of G7 and G8 government action. The book ends by arguing that the heads should allow the rest of the G7/G8 bureaucracy to continue under its own momentum. They themselves should concentrate on improving direct contact with actors outside government, including business, non-governmental organisations and the people at large, mobilising all the new technology for this purpose.

This book thus aims to use the summits, their achievements and their setbacks, as a guide to how the world economic system has developed in the last quarter of the 20th century. This may provide some clues as to what the new millennium will bring.

Notes

1   Writing after London III 1991, I divided the summits into three 'septennial series' (Bayne 1992) and used the same division before Halifax (Bayne and Putnam 1995). In a later paper for the University of Toronto (Bayne 1997a) I first outlined a scheme of series of different lengths, though that scheme was different from the one adopted in this book.

2   The departure of Japanese Prime Minister Hashimoto in late 1998 left Jean Chrétien of Canada as the only former finance minister among the heads of government at Cologne in 1999 - and his experience was from over 20 years before. At Versailles 1982 and Williamsburg 1983 there had been no ex-finance ministers at all.

3   Annex Table 1(p.227), in the June 1999 *OECD Economic Outlook* (OECD 1999) shows clearly how the economic slowdown and subsequent recovery began first in the 'Anglo-Saxon' economies - US, UK and Canada - followed later by the continental Europeans and Japan.

Part I
Innovation and Establishment

2 Getting Started: The First and Second Summit Series, 1975-82

Summits - that is, multilateral meetings of heads of state and government - were rare events in the first three-quarters of the 20th century. Those that did happen had deep historical roots. One series derived from gatherings of kings and chieftains to plan warlike campaigns or share out the spoils. Thus summits of the North Atlantic Treaty Organisation (NATO) were derived not just from the wartime meetings of Western leaders, at Tehran, Yalta and Potsdam, but far beyond them from the Councils of Greek heroes before Troy recorded in Homer's *Iliad*. A second type evolved from meetings of lesser monarchs to render homage to their overlord. So the Commonwealth Heads of Government Meetings held every second year descended directly from the Imperial Conferences of the 1920s and 1930s. But their origins went much further back, for example to the occasion when King Edgar of the West Saxons was rowed up the River Dee at Chester by four tributary kings in 973.

The last quarter of the 20th century gave birth to a new type of summit meeting, unknown to history. These are the meetings of the leaders of the United States, Japan, Germany, France, Britain, Italy and Canada, plus the European Commission and Presidency, which have been held every year from Rambouillet in 1975 to consider mainly economic subjects. The origins of these summits and the first two series of meetings, from 1975 to 1982, are described in detail in Chapters 2-6 of *Hanging Together* (Putnam and Bayne 1987). This chapter gives only an overview of the rationale for the summits and their early achievements. It establishes from the outset the three distinctive objectives and roles for the summits: reconciling interdependence, collective management and political leadership.[1]

Origins of the Summits

Three reasons, each of a different kind, contributed to the genesis of the summits in 1975.

Reconciling Interdependence. One reason derived from the tensions of economic interdependence. During the 1950s and 1960s the Western economies expanded very rapidly. International activity grew faster than domestic, whether it was trade, investment or financial flows. So governments found that the price of rising prosperity was a loss of national autonomy in domestic decision-making, which now depended far more on what others were doing. This interdependence was acceptable as long as things went well. But in the early 1970s, things began to go badly, with confusion on the monetary scene, the first oil crisis and the recession which followed. Now there was tension between economic interdependence and national sovereignty, which only heads of government seemed likely to resolve.

Collective Management. A second reason flowed from shifts in relative power between the United States, Europe and Japan. In the 1950s and 1960s, the United States was so much stronger than all other countries that it could provide, on its own, leadership for the international economic system. But Japan and the European countries were growing faster than the United States. The accession of Britain made the European Community into a unit comparable to the United States in terms of GNP, with a far larger share of world trade. So, by the early 1970s, the Americans became neither able nor willing to exercise sole leadership. Some new arrangements were needed which would associate the Europeans and Japan with the United States, to undertake together the role which hitherto the Americans had played alone.

Political Leadership. A third reason stemmed simply from the personal inclinations of a new set of Western leaders, particularly French President Giscard and German Chancellor Schmidt. They were both finance ministers in the early 1970s and, with their US and British colleagues, George Shultz and Anthony Barber, they created what was originally called the Library Group. Later, when Japan joined, it became the Group of Five (G5). They met in a very informal and relaxed way on the fringes of wider international meetings and relished their direct exchanges in the small group by contrast with the formal proceedings in the larger conferences. Thus, when Giscard and Schmidt gained supreme office, they were attracted by this format for exchanges at their own level. When President Giscard launched the idea of a limited economic summit in 1975, he had solid backing from Chancellor Schmidt and encouragement from Shultz and Henry Kissinger (then US Secretary of State), who together persuaded President Gerald Ford to join in. By the third summit in 1977, no fewer than six out of the eight leaders - Giscard, Schmidt, Fukuda (Japan), Callaghan (UK), Andreotti (Italy) and Jenkins (European Commission) - were former finance ministers.

The essential feature of these summits was that they should be small, select and personal. They should bring together those directly responsible for policy in a context where they could talk together frankly and without inhibitions. They should be prepared by personal representatives, later to be called 'Sherpas', whose links with the head of government were more important than their place in the hierarchy. Schmidt said: "We want a private, informal meeting of those who really matter in the world".[2] Giscard originally envisaged only four participants, or five at the most, and he resisted for a long time the summit's enlargement to include Italy, then Canada, then the European Community. Even thus extended, the summits were the only series of heads of government meetings to be both selective and free-standing, in the sense that they were detached from any other organisation at lower levels. All other recurrent summits, whether of the Commonwealth, the Non-Aligned Movement, NATO or the European Council for the EC, brought together the leaders of all participating countries, as the apex of an institutional pyramid.

Giscard, Schmidt and the others were convinced that heads of government could bring a unique and essential contribution beyond the capacities of officials and other ministers. This unique contribution could be broken down into three components. First, the heads of government could integrate policies normally treated separately by ministers or departments with specific responsibilities. Second, they were best placed to reconcile the various demands of foreign policy and domestic policy and to work out lines of action where domestic and external considerations could reinforce each other rather than conflict. Third, they carried an authority which other ministers did not have. This authority was constrained in various ways in the different countries - less in France than elsewhere - but it was still real. They guaranteed what was called the 'Rambouillet effect' which enabled international bargaining 'to be prodded forward at intervals by political decisions taken at a high level'.[3]

The First Summit Series: 1975-8

When the leaders first met in November 1975, the recession induced by the first oil crisis had already passed its trough. The concern of the Rambouillet summit and its three successors - Puerto Rico in 1976, London I in 1977, Bonn I in 1978 - was to sustain economic recovery. The summits became the focus of the 'locomotive' controversy, on whether the United States, Germany and Japan could properly stimulate their strong economies to encourage recovery in the weaker ones. The leaders moved from simple statements of intent at first to set growth targets at London and to make commitments on policy measures at Bonn - a progression much encouraged by the arrival of President Jimmy Carter, who favoured a highly organised summit process in which meticulous preparation would enable the leaders, when they assembled, to make specific commitments.

Three lessons emerged clearly from the way this quartet of early summits tackled macro-economic policy. The first lesson was that if all the summit countries adopted the same sort of policies together, the cumulative effect was far stronger than each component country intended. When all decided, at the 1976 summit, to adopt restrictive policies, there was a pause in the recovery which none of them had wanted. Second, it became clear that no single country could successfully maintain a policy against the trend of the others. Even the United States in 1977/8 saw its attempts to act as a locomotive, unsupported by Germany and Japan, frustrated by a widening deficit, a falling dollar and mounting inflation.

Coordination of economic policy thus required the participants concerned to act in harmony, but with different countries doing different things according to their situation and capacities. Even this would not work if the other policies of the participants, e.g. on energy or trade, were inconsistent; this was the third lesson. On the one hand, therefore, the summits from the start helped the participating governments to resist the pressure for inward-looking policies. On the other hand, they gave powerful impulses to wider international negotiations. Rambouillet in 1975 produced the breakthrough which enabled the negotiations on reform of the international monetary system to be completed. London and Bonn in 1977 and 1978 exerted crucial pressure on the Tokyo Round of multilateral trade negotiations in the GATT, to bring these to a substantial conclusion.

The Bonn summit of July 1978 knit together many different strands and used the full potential of the summit process.[4] There was a package of commitments which balanced one field against another: economic stimulus by Germany and Japan; energy saving measures by the United States; forward movement in the Tokyo Round by all, but especially France; and supporting undertakings by the other participants to complete the pattern. However, when the leaders met at Tokyo one year later, the economic environment, and their own attitudes to it, had fundamentally changed. The onset of the second oil crisis meant that the next quartet of summits would take place in much more difficult conditions. Tokyo I in 1979, Venice in 1980, Ottawa in 1981 and Versailles in 1982, instead of promoting recovery, had to concentrate on coping with the immediate oil crisis and bringing inflation under control.

In retrospect, it appeared that the earlier summits had not done enough to keep inflation in check. This became the first priority of all or nearly all the summit governments. At the same time, a reaction set in against the meticulous preparation and specific commitments favoured by Carter, on the grounds that these made the summit process too bureaucratic and stifled the personal contributions of the leaders. This reaction gathered strength once Carter had left office, though it proved very hard to reverse the trend.

The Second Summit Series: 1979-82

Because of all this, the treatment of macro-economic policy in the second series of summits changed fundamentally.[5] The conclusions were simpler and the prescriptions - on checking monetary growth and reducing budget deficits - became more uniform; and this was not all. The first four summits had looked for ways in which the actions of some participants would promote recovery not only for themselves but for others, as growth in domestic demand in the strong economies might encourage export-led growth in the weaker ones. However, the control of inflation required painful measures which each country must take for itself. It was helpful for governments to point to other countries making the same sacrifice; but the actions of others to check inflation could not substitute for the decisions each government must take at home. At times, indeed, others could make these decisions more difficult; if one country drove up its interest rates or exchange rate so as to check inflation, others had to follow suit or they would suffer by comparison. This accounted for the persistent dispute over American interest rates at Ottawa and Versailles.

The lessons of the first series of summits, however, still held good in the second. First, the French tried to go it alone in economic policy in 1981, suffered the same consequences as the United States had done earlier and had to go into reverse. Second, the simultaneous pursuit of restrictive policies to check inflation, calculated in each country on domestic criteria to produce a certain impact, generated a much stronger effect when all put together, so that the recession lasted much longer than anyone had envisaged. Third, the macro-economic strategy and the policies pursued in other areas still needed to be compatible with each other. The oil import targets and other energy measures adopted at Tokyo I in 1979 and Venice I in 1980 assumed an early recovery, which would mean steady pressure on oil supplies and prices throughout the 1980s. In fact, the prolonged recession upset these calculations, so that the energy commitments had a good short-term effect, but proved inappropriate over the longer term.

The first series of summits had done well in giving impulses which brought existing international negotiations to their conclusion, but they did not launch any new ones to take their place. The later summits faced the problem of keeping the international system in good order in much less favourable conditions, without any negotiations already in progress which could serve as the antidote to economic nationalism. The leaders feared that any new process of negotiation, if launched in such conditions, would not get into orbit. They preferred instead to promote single events, like the 1982 ministerial meeting of GATT or the Cancún summit on North-South issues in 1981. As a sort of surrogate for wider negotiations, the summits began to set up their own groups of officials or ministers on particular issues, such as monitoring energy commitments, exchange market intervention or technology. But this tended to clutter up the summit process and to worry non-participating countries and established institutions like the OECD - see Chapter 4 below.

Meanwhile, the summits began to give more attention to non-economic, foreign policy issues, which hitherto they had only discussed on the side. There were two reasons for this. First, the international political context took a sharp turn for the worse in 1979, beginning with the troubles in Iran and ending with the Soviet invasion of Afghanistan. Second, the political summit of four powers (US, Germany, France, UK) called by Giscard at Guadeloupe in January of that year provoked a strong reaction from the countries not invited to it. Japan, Italy and Canada now had an interest in seeing the seven-power summits used for foreign policy exchanges so as to forestall any repetition of Guadeloupe. The Japanese, originally very reluctant to discuss political issues in any formal way, became much keener and only the French continued to resist the idea. The Venice I summit of June 1980 provided an obvious and welcome opportunity for the US and its allies to close ranks over Afghanistan. For the first time, the summit issued a substantial foreign policy declaration, prepared shortly in advance by a special group of officials. The process was repeated in Ottawa in 1981. The French continued to oppose formal sessions on foreign policy issues. There were none at Versailles in 1982, though East-West economic relations - essentially a political subject - dominated much of the proceedings. But Versailles was the last of the summits dedicated wholly to an economic agenda.

The Early Summits: Achievements and Prospects

The first eight summits provided examples of what the heads of government could achieve when working together. But they also illustrated sharp shifts in approaches to policy-making and examples of unfinished business, which would need attention in subsequent summits. The economic conditions confronting the summits from 1983 onwards resembled closely those which faced the earliest meetings. The Rambouillet summit of 1975 took place just as recovery began from the recession following the first oil crisis, with the United States well ahead of Europe. The 1983 Williamsburg summit was held at the corresponding point in the cycle following the second oil crisis. The summits were able once again to concentrate on assuring economic recovery and giving impulses in trade and monetary matters rather than on the austere policies necessary in the early 1980s.

A striking contrast with the earlier meetings was the disappearance of former finance ministers. In 1977 and 1978, as noted, they had provided six out of the eight leaders present. By 1982 there were no former finance ministers among the leaders and none waiting in the wings. The leaders then in office brought political experience, judgement and authority to economic discussions. But they were more likely to look to their fellow ministers and advisers for technical expertise or originality.

The summit leaders had come to draw negative conclusions from their attempts at coordinated economic stimulus. The British, German and Japanese governments of 1982 regarded this as an 'intellectual trap'.[6] On the other hand, discussion of money supply, interest rates and budgetary policy had become rather unrewarding at summit level, because of unresolved differences with the United States. These subjects were being shifted into the more technical and less public discussions among finance ministers, plus the Managing Director of the IMF, which were set up at Versailles in 1982. It was suggested that the summit itself might turn instead to considering the structural changes needed to sustain economic recovery, looking, for example, at obstacles to competition, the shape of the labour market or the pattern of investment. The issues in this field were difficult technically and sensitive politically; this was often because they mixed up the domestic and the external in a way which only heads of government could unravel.

The early summits played a key role in invigorating international trade and monetary negotiations. The second series did less in this field; the leaders needed to return to this role. In trade, they could stimulate further rounds in GATT, to pick up where the Tokyo Round left off. The Americans were ready for this by 1982, as being the best way of counteracting protectionist pressures at home. But there was more caution on the European side. Summit intervention on the monetary scene looked less promising. Progress here needed a fundamental change of heart by the Americans, which was not visible in Reagan's first term, while Donald Regan remained as Secretary of the US Treasury. In 1982 French President François Mitterrand and others called for a new Bretton Woods, but this came too early. Even in the most favourable conditions, powerful pressure from the very top would be essential to make headway against the desperate technical problems in this field, as Giscard and Schmidt demonstrated when they launched the European Monetary System (EMS) in 1978.

Lastly, on the economic side, the summit leaders still needed to come to grips with relations with developing countries. Only heads of government could reconcile the political, economic and humanitarian factors involved. For this reason the subject had been on the agenda for every summit so far. But the results had been disappointing and attempts to invigorate institutions like the World Bank had been frustrated, often by the US Congress. An approach was needed which allowed for more visible personal involvement by the leaders. One idea was that at a future summit the Western heads of government might invite a group of their peers from developing countries to join them. But the leaders were not attracted by it.[7]

Foreign policy discussion at the summit was set to grow. Both the state of the world and the inclinations of the leaders meant that, from now on, foreign policy issues were regularly discussed at future summits, with conclusions reached and made public. Japanese reluctance had all but disappeared and French resistance was not maintained *à l'outrance*. East-West relations required summit attention, in the context of arms control, stationing of missiles and other aspects. Policy in the Middle East likewise merited attention by the leaders, to forestall the differences between the allies which had broken out in the past. Hitherto, summits had tended to treat economic and foreign policy questions in separate compartments. There was merit in trying to combine the two - for example, would political unrest in the Middle East again threaten oil supplies? This approach, however, could lead them into awkward exchanges on how far reciprocal security interests should influence economic policy actions, which was at the root of the dispute at Versailles over the gas pipeline link with Russia.

The leaders in power in 1982 had strong views about future summit format. They reacted strongly against the format favoured by Carter, as making the summits congested, bureaucratic and impersonal. They tried to lighten the preparations and to get back to the direct, spontaneous exchanges of the original aspiration. However, there was a risk that the pendulum might swing back too far. There was no substitute for direct personal exchanges. But experience showed that they had their drawbacks too: they could be inconclusive, transitory and open to misinterpretation. The leaders might understand each other better but they still might not agree, and the mutual influence quickly wore off. The summit needed a format which combined the maximum scope for informal exchange with the incentive to move towards consensus and the means of recording and making public whatever was agreed.

The record of the summits up to 1982 suggested that four changes were needed:-

- *First,* future summits should aspire to visible commitments, but only on a strictly limited number of subjects, with preparations focused accordingly. Past experience had shown that each summit could normally digest only one major issue, or at the most two. Other issues would of course be discussed informally but without the intention of reaching public understandings.
- *Second,* the summits should renounce the practice of setting up their own special groups. All such groups should either be disbanded or plugged into international bodies like the OECD or the IMF. Follow-up work from the summits should in future be entrusted to these organisations; the summit process would be less cluttered and the existing organisations would be encouraged.
- *Third,* preparation for political issues should become much more systematic, matching more closely the economic work of the 'Sherpas'. Complex and sensitive subjects like arms control needed to be carefully thought out in advance. It was highly risky to try to produce conclusions on them without detailed preparation.
- *Fourth,* the summit should be extended by a further twenty-four hours. The leaders would spend two full days of discussion, partly on their own and partly with their supporting ministers, and then break up at noon on the third day after a short final morning on the text of their declaration. This would allow them, for example, to spend one day on economic issues and one on foreign policy, or to invite heads of government from developing countries for the second day. It would also provide more time for the bilateral meetings which were an essential accompaniment to the multilateral summit.

Of these suggestions, only the greater focus on political issues would make any real advance in the third series.

Conclusions

The summits of the first two series had some bad patches, especially around Versailles in 1982. But when considered against the three original reasons for inventing them, they fully justified themselves. Their selective and personal character, as originally envisaged, survived after eight years to a surprising degree. This gave them a flexibility which other more formal bodies could not have. The adaptation to shifts of relative power was uneven. But the summits served as a regular reminder of common interests in transatlantic relations which transcended specific differences; they offered a channel at the highest level between the European Community and the United States; and they helped to guard against a return to the mistrust and the frustration which had marked Kissinger's abortive Year of Europe in 1973. Furthermore, they assisted the emergence of Japan, by slow stages, as a full participant in Western discussions of political as well as economic issues, so that it became sensible to use seven-power summits for foreign policy discussions in a way not envisaged back in 1975.

The management of economic interdependence proved much more difficult than anyone expected. The second oil crisis and the ensuing recession tested the system severely. Sometimes the summits made mistakes and sometimes the participants did not live up to their commitments. But their purpose was always to turn governments away from inward-looking policies and to give impulses to wider international cooperation in very difficult times. The early summits showed that there were certain areas of policy where only the heads of government could generate progress, by virtue of their authority and their comprehensive responsibilities, domestic as well as external.

Notes

1   This chapter is drawn from 'Western Economic Summits: Can They Do Better?', *The World Today*, vol. 40 no. 1, pp. 4-11 (Bayne 1984). This article summarised my conclusions on summitry embodied in the first edition of *Hanging Together* (Putnam and Bayne 1984).
2   See Putnam and Bayne 1987, p. 29. There is no published source for this remark by Helmut Schmidt.
3   The term 'Rambouillet effect' was coined by Andrew Shonfield, then Director of the RIIA. For his favourable assessment of summitry, see Shonfield 1976b.
4   Professor Robert Putnam later used the cooperative achievements of the first Bonn summit as the basis for his work on two-level games. See Putnam 1988, and Putnam and Henning 1989 and Evans, Jacobson and Putnam 1993.
5   This changed approach made Andrew Shonfield much more critical of the summits - see Shonfield 1980.

6   According to Geoffrey Howe, the British finance minister, quoted in *The Guardian,* 19
    April 1983.
7   The idea was revived by Mitterrand when he next hosted a summit, in Paris in 1989,
    and strongly urged by his Sherpa Jacques Attali. But again it made no headway; see
    Chapter 5, n. 5.

3   Settling Down:
The Third Summit Series,
1983-88

The first summit series, of 1975-8, followed an increasingly ambitious path of policy coordination to promote economic recovery. The second series of summits, in 1979-82, reacted against this complexity in their handling of the recession provoked by the second oil crisis. They looked for a simple economic message of mutual support, while giving more weight to foreign policy issues. The third series lasted longer - for six years, from 1983-1988 - as the impetus for innovation slackened. It carried the summits through the rest of the Reagan era to the final stages of the Cold War.

The third series, like the first, once again covered a period of economic recovery. At one level, represented by the heads of government themselves, the summits looked like a prolongation of the second series. They stressed the simple message of prudent fiscal and monetary policies and gave increasing attention to foreign policy. But at the level of the finance ministers ideas and approaches were revived which had been topical in the first series but had disappeared during the austere, recession-dominated years of 1979-82. Economic policy coordination and moves to stabilise exchange rates were again actively discussed.

This series has been described and analysed in detail in Chapters 7-10 of *Hanging Together* (Putnam and Bayne 1987). Once again, this chapter only provides a brief overview, essentially derived from Chapter 10 of *Hanging Together*, though extending this to cover Toronto 1988. It uses the triple analysis defined in Chapter 1. It first considers the summit actors and the summit process, in the context of political leadership versus bureaucratic institutions. Second, it reviews economic and foreign policy issues, in relation to the summits' contribution to reconciling the tensions of interdependence. Third, it examines how the summits influenced relations between Japan, Western Europe and North America, and promoted 'collective management' in place of American hegemony.

Political Leadership: Actors and Process

The leaders who took part in the summits from 1983 to 1988 were marked by three outstanding features. First, there was striking continuity. Kohl, Reagan, Mitterrand and Thatcher all stayed in office throughout the series. Prime Ministers Yasuhiro Nakasone and Bettino Craxi brought unusual stability of office to Japan and Italy. Second, there was a strong political consensus, reinforced during the period. The arrival of Kohl and Nakasone in 1983 and Brian Mulroney in Canada in 1984 pushed the balance towards the right. Mitterrand had changed course since mid-1982, and moved towards market-oriented policies. The socialist Craxi also sought to reduce the role of the public sector. Third, there were no survivors from the Library Group, no founder-members of the summits and no former finance ministers among the heads of government.[1] (Delors, former French finance minister, reappeared as President of the Commission from 1985.) The continuity of the leaders, the convergence of their political approaches and the absence of ex-finance ministers had a series of consequences.

The first consequence was a greater interest in non-economic issues. At Williamsburg and again at Tokyo II the main concern of the leaders focused on a political issue: Euromissiles in 1983, terrorism in 1986. Second, the leaders no longer contributed technical expertise and originality to exchanges on economic policy. They were more concerned with the political impact of the issues treated. Third, the leaders looked chiefly to the summits to give international backing for existing policies. Except for Nakasone, they seldom used them as an external stimulus to promote domestic change. Fourth, as the leaders came to know each other better and as (Mitterrand and Craxi sometimes excepted) they shared the same political opinions, they became more reluctant to create trouble for each other at home. Fifth and last: both the domestic resistance to change and the international reluctance to criticise were intensified in electoral periods. At Williamsburg 1983 the other leaders, and especially the American hosts, sought to be helpful to Thatcher, who went to the polls a few days after the summit. Next year at London II Thatcher and the other leaders did the same for Reagan before his re-election. Electoral influences always inhibited policy adjustments. In 1984 the US resisted pressure to bring in changes in fiscal policy, fearing that flexibility before the elections would look like weakness. The same fear inhibited Mitterrand from concessions over the date for the new GATT round at Bonn II in 1985 and restrained the Japanese from easing macro-economic policy before Tokyo II in 1986.

All the major participants were in favour of making the summits as simple, personal and informal as possible. At Williamsburg the American hosts made a far more determined effort than ever before to simplify procedures and lower expectations, both among participants and in the eyes of the media. This simplified format was a conscious attempt to return to the 'Library Group' spirit of the early summits. But none of the heads of government present from Williamsburg onwards had direct experience of these early summits. They were returning to an idealised format, not to the actual events. The pursuit of this ideal in the conditions of the mid-1980s had unforeseen, even perverse, effects. The three main effects were to make the summits episodic and unpredictable; to weaken the role of the Sherpas; and to expand the rest of the summit apparatus.[2]

Despite strong continuity among the leaders there was much discontinuity between the summits themselves. The issues which commanded the leaders' personal intervention at the summit were different each time. It became more frequent for leaders to provoke spontaneous debate without much benefit of preparation. The second Tokyo summit of 1986 was acclaimed by the veterans Thatcher and Reagan as the best they had attended, largely because there the leaders worked out the results themselves on subjects of their own choosing. Right from the origins of the summits, however, critics had pointed to the risk of misunderstandings from relying too much on personal contacts among the leaders. There were increasing examples of such misunderstandings, when the leaders came to the summit with an incorrect view of the positions of their partners. This could frustrate or undermine agreement at the meeting itself. No one predicted, before Bonn II 1985, how the relative positions of Reagan, Kohl and Mitterrand would frustrate agreement on the date for the new GATT round. Such misunderstandings suggested that there were shortcomings in the preparatory process.

Streamlining the preparations, from 1983 onwards, paradoxically weakened the role of the Sherpas and expanded the rest of the summit apparatus. The role of the Sherpas had been to work over the issues for the summit and try to reconcile the national positions, often using the approach of the summits as a lever on specialist ministries. From Williamsburg onwards the Sherpas lost this role. They prepared a 'thematic paper', but this enumerated national positions with little attempt to reconcile them. The process of reconciling positions and striking deals went on elsewhere; either in wider bodies, like the IMF or the GATT, or in other groups of ministers or officials more or less loosely linked to the summit process. The Sherpas themselves became detached from this process and were no longer able to present the leaders with clear choices.

While the Sherpas' influence weakened, the rest of the summit apparatus grew, quite against the leaders' intentions. The seven summit foreign ministers began the practice of meeting on their own each

September, on the margins of the UN General Assembly. Nevertheless, because the heads of government themselves were increasingly interested in non-economic issues, the activities of the foreign ministers and their officials remained dependent on mandates from the summit. The finance ministers, on the other hand, steadily increased their institutional independence and took over the initiative from the leaders in economic policy-making. Williamsburg 1983 consolidated the group, created at Versailles the year before, to conduct 'multilateral surveillance' of economic policy. This was composed of the G5 finance ministers plus the Managing Director of the IMF. The finance ministers began to recover some of the influence lost when the summit displaced the 'Library Group' in 1975. They gained more ground with the first public appearance by the G5 when they announced the Plaza Agreement of September 1985. By Tokyo II in 1986 the independence of the finance ministers had gone so far that they and their supporting officials carried out all the preparations on economic policy, unknown to the Sherpas. They conducted the negotiations at the summit itself and drafted the relevant passage of the declaration. Italy and Canada, who had thought their interests protected by summit membership, felt obliged to demand entry to the circle of finance ministers, converting G5 into G7.

The rise of the finance ministers was due in part to the advantages they enjoyed, by comparison with the leaders, in discussing sensitive and controversial economic issues. G5 (or G7) ministers could meet several times a year and their officials even more often. Their meetings attracted less media attention. The finance ministers had, or could draw on, technical expertise not possessed by either the current set of leaders or, with few exceptions, their Sherpas.[3]

A further reason for the rise of the finance ministers was that in this third series the summits exercised only intermittently their unique capabilities. The summits had the potential to integrate policies handled by different ministries; to reconcile domestic and international pressures in a mutually reinforcing way; and to exercise high-level political authority. There were some good examples, over this period, of the summits exercising their potential: mainly in political issues, like Euromissiles and terrorism, but also in debt relief at London II 1984 and Toronto 1988. But these examples were few. The leaders welcomed support from their summit partners for their existing policies, especially when they could use this in answer to attacks from their domestic opposition. But they seldom employed international arguments as a lever to encourage internal policy change. On the contrary, sometimes they exported their domestic controversies into the summits in a way which increased international tension.

Reconciling Interdependence

Economic Issues

During the third series of summits the heads of government maintained the same macro-economic policy prescription as in the second, to counter the inflation generated by the oil crisis. Every summit declaration advocated 'prudent monetary and fiscal policies', often in those exact words. The summit conclusions were usually simple and uniform, conveying mutual encouragement and support for separate national policies. The aim was to promote convergence of policy, through each country's own efforts. Only from Venice II 1987 did the idea of active coordination return to the summits.

The collective advocacy of fiscal and monetary austerity after 1979 had prolonged the recession beyond the immediate impact of the oil price increase. But by 1983 the effects of this severe restraint had worked through and, with the policy prescription unchanged, a steady recovery set in, being sustained throughout the six year cycle. Its durability owed much to the continued downward pressure on inflation. But earlier summits had shown that no one country, not even the largest, could successfully sustain policies against the trend of what others were doing. While the other countries were faithfully observing fiscal and monetary discipline, the Reagan Administration had brought in powerful fiscal stimuli soon after taking office and then relaxed monetary control in autumn 1982, partly because of the debt crisis. The American boom set off recovery in the other summit countries. But four elements of the US boom could not be sustained indefinitely: the huge budget deficit; the volume of external funds needed to finance this deficit; the overvalued dollar; and the record current account deficit. The dollar proved the barometer of change. It rose 60 percent from late 1980 to March 1985 and then fell back towards its original level. But as the US Administration did not succeed in reducing their budget deficit, their external deficit was very slow to respond to exchange rate changes.

Earlier summits had shown that macro-economic strategy was ineffective unless reinforced by other compatible policies. The period 1983-88 demonstrated the converse of that principle: other policies were frustrated because they were not sustained by a consistent macro-economic stance. This was most evident in trade policy and resistance to protectionism. The recovery, which began in 1983, should have provided the opportunity to check and reverse the protectionist trends. In fact protectionism grew steadily worse. Bilateral trade restrictions multiplied, many of them evading GATT discipline, and began to bite on trade levels.

Without the correction of macro-economic policies, the summits could do little to stem the tide. Anti-protectionist statements from the summits were undermined by the announcement of further restrictive measures just afterwards. A new round of GATT negotiations, the Uruguay Round, was prepared and launched during this period. But although the summits regularly endorsed this objective, they gave no stimulus to the technical preparations except, indirectly, on agriculture. Even there, the encouragement of more cooperative attitudes on agriculture at Tokyo II 1986 and Venice II 1987 had to be set against the open dispute over the starting date for the new GATT round at Bonn II in 1985.[4]

While heads of government had given few hints of any underlying change in macro-economic strategy, the practice of multilateral surveillance, among the finance ministers proved a first tentative move back towards policy coordination. As long as Regan remained as the US Secretary of the Treasury, the Americans remained impervious to external factors. But the arrival of James Baker at the US Treasury in February 1985 fundamentally changed the objective of surveillance. Baker's concern was to counteract US protectionist pressures and to correct the external and fiscal imbalances. He therefore wanted surveillance not to check inflation but to promote growth. Under Baker, the Americans began recommending to others macro-economic instruments which would stimulate growth. They first focused on tax cuts; later, following a Japanese lead, they added interest rate reductions.

This new approach, however, revived the disputes of the first summit series over the relative priority of growth and inflation. In the course of the summits to date, the Americans had first promoted coordination to stimulate growth, then opposed it and were now promoting it again. But the Germans were always deeply sceptical about policy coordination for growth. They would only tolerate it if control of inflation remained the first priority. The Japanese continued to share the Germans' doubts, as did Thatcher for the UK. Macro-economic policy alone looked an unfruitful field for policy coordination. Baker attempted to break the deadlock by bringing in exchange rate management.

The September 1985 Plaza agreement brought a really fundamental shift in US attitudes to exchange rate management, going back (as Baker recognised) to before the floating of the dollar in 1973. The Americans had always declined any multilateral undertaking to stabilise the dollar. But at the Plaza G5 meeting Baker agreed that the Federal Reserve would intervene with others to keep the dollar moving down. This readiness to cooperate in exchange rate policy was naturally welcomed by France, which became the Americans' closest ally. But exchange rate cooperation did not go far to win over the Germans, who saw only limited merit in currency market intervention unsupported by compatible economic policies.

Baker, however, was prepared to use the exchange rate as a means of pressure on his G5 partners. His assertion that, to correct US imbalances, there must be either faster growth abroad or a further decline in the dollar, sounded at first like a warning. With repetition, it was taken as a threat. Germans and Japanese felt obliged to seek a truce at the Louvre meetings of February 1987. They conceded promises of future fiscal action in return for American agreement that the dollar should not fall further. These policy measures were confirmed at the subsequent Venice II summit. But the upheavals on US and European stock markets in October 1987 brought the practice of economic policy coordination to an abrupt halt. The G7 finance ministers and central banks agreed on short-term measures to loosen monetary policy and counteract the effect of the crash - and the leaders congratulated themselves at Toronto in 1988. But the crash undermined the enthusiasts for coordination and confirmed the sceptics. In the fourth summit series, which began in 1989, it hardly featured at all.

Two other types of economic issue attracted the leaders' attention in the third series: structural adjustment policies and debt relief. In previous summits the stress had been on macro-economic measures, to stimulate growth or squeeze out inflation. From London II 1984 onwards the summits gave far greater emphasis to structural reforms as a source of growth than earlier meetings had done. The Americans in particular argued that their boom was due to the greater vigour and flexibility of their private sector - which was indeed true, though only part of the truth. They criticised the Europeans, with reason, for the 'structural rigidities' of their tax systems and their labour and capital markets and for the excessive government regulation which stifled competition.

The heads of government endorsed the objectives of more competition and less regulation, and thus helped some summit countries to carry through national reforms. But they did not go on to reach conclusions on the sort of measures required, except when they took up agriculture at Tokyo II and Venice II. Yet the addition of structural policy commitments - in tax reform, labour and financial markets and industrial competition - might have provided the key to the consensus which eluded the participants at Bonn II and again after Tokyo II. The Europeans and Japanese were sceptical of American approaches to macro-economic policy and exchange rates. But they all recognised the necessity of structural measures to improve their own economic performance, while similar measures could have countered protectionist pressures in the US. The treatment of structural adjustment policies thus had great potential for the summits, but they seldom addressed the subjects being treated in greater detail in the OECD - see Chapter 4 below.

The second summit series had failed to perceive that the prolonged recession would stimulate a debt crisis among middle-income countries unable to keep up their payments on loans from commercial banks. This crisis broke out in August 1982, soon after Versailles. But the summits of the third series contributed little to resolving it, apart from London II 1984. Baker pursued his new ideas (the Baker Plan of 1985) through the IMF, not the summit. The last summit of the series, Toronto 1988, did make a major advance by agreeing a strategy of debt relief for low-income countries. This was the first time that the summits had made a serious contribution to helping the poorest countries. Toronto terms, as they were called, were only a beginning. But they established debt relief as a recurrent summit issue from then on, as later chapters will show.

Political Issues

From Williamsburg 1983 onwards political issues grew in importance and occupied nearly half the leaders' time. This was partly because of the personal preferences of the leaders; partly because the format rendered the summits episodic, which fitted the unpredictable character of foreign policy better than the continuum of economic policy. Nevertheless, foreign policy discussions remained nominally subordinate to economic and preparations were much less elaborate. Political discussions over this period featured two major themes: East-West relations and arms control; and terrorism and international public order.

In addition, the summits continued to give impromptu but authoritative reactions to crises or major disasters that had flared up before the meeting, like the Iran-Iraq war in 1984 and the Chernobyl nuclear accident in 1986. The summits also experimented with the issue of foreign policy declarations of a general and aspirational character, carefully prepared in advance: the London declaration on democratic values, the Bonn declaration on the 40th anniversary of the end of World War II in Europe and the 'general political declaration' at Tokyo. In public relations terms, however, they were a failure. The media either ignored them or referred cynically to 'the technique of tossing out declarations on the first day in order to keep the journalistic wolves away from the statesmen's sledges'.[5]

The Williamsburg statement on arms control was arguably the most important foreign policy achievement of the entire summit series. It successfully resolved the multiple tensions that threatened to divide the participants in at least three ways, all of which the Russians were seeking to exploit. The assertion that 'the security of our countries is indivisible' skilfully enabled Nakasone to bring Japan into security discussions for the first time, since Japan was threatened by Soviet medium-range missiles just as much as Western Europe. Williamsburg was an excellent example of the summit leaders exercising their collective authority.

But agreement at Williamsburg was reached only after heated discussion. It was a 'nail-biting' business, as one Sherpa noted afterwards, to entrust so sensitive an issue to spontaneous discussion, without the careful preparation which would have preceded a comparable debate in NATO. But the summits never developed a systematic procedure for preparing these issues for summit treatment; and they rarely attempted a common assessment of Soviet motives and tactics to form the basis of the allied response.

After Williamsburg the Strategic Defence Initiative (SDI) shifted US priorities towards an issue which aroused the anxieties of the Europeans and Japan but nonetheless came to dominate Reagan's approach to arms control. The summits, with their compact and informal structure, could have provided good opportunities to build up allied confidence and to avert unsettling surprises, notably when Reagan met Gorbachev at Reykjavik in November 1986. But these opportunities were largely not taken.

As a result, none of the following summits gave the same concentrated attention to East-West relations and arms control as Williamsburg. Bonn II avoided open disagreement on the Strategic Defence Initiative only by the expedient of having an American presentation but no debate. At Venice II the leaders did have a concentrated debate about political developments in the Soviet Union. But in spite of this, the third series ended without any sign of awareness that the Soviet empire would start to crumble from 1989 onwards.

Hijacking, terrorism, hostage-taking and related subjects had occasionally come to the summits before. They appeared with renewed vigour at London II 1984, which first addressed Libyan terrorism, and at Tokyo II 1986. These subjects were highly suitable for the summits, as they involved a complicated interaction of domestic and external factors. Domestic public opinion reacted strongly against terrorist attacks, hijackings or drug abuse, and looked for decisive action. The international aspects, however, were often complex. It was easy to condemn terrorist groups. But the governments that protected them might have influence over the release of hostages or over conditions of life for all foreigners in their country. While these aspects concerned foreign ministers, interior and justice ministers were equally involved, being responsible for police matters, immigration control and extradition. The increasing ability of terrorists to move unchecked across national frontiers strengthened the arguments for international cooperation. There was thus a clear role for heads of government to reconcile all these factors.

The Tokyo II terrorism declaration of 1986 proved the main test so far of the summits' effectiveness in this field. The Tokyo summit was successful in restoring unity. The outcome patched up the transatlantic differences and quelled the media storm. The summit also created a useful, if cumbersome, network of official groups on terrorism, hijacking and drugs, capable of effective preparation and follow-up. Foreign policy analysis was less successful. The US concentration on retaliation and obsession with Libya prevented a serious debate on the political roots of terrorism in Lebanon and the Iran-Iraq confrontation. Finally, the outcome revealed a sharp contrast between Europe and the United States. The approach of the Tokyo summit encouraged the Europeans to cooperate internationally. They adopted a series of concrete measures against Libya, which found favour with the Americans at Tokyo, thanks to Thatcher's vigorous advocacy, and formed the basis of the summit declaration. This helped the Europeans, later in 1986, to take similar measures against Syria. For the Americans, on the other hand, the over-riding objective of their strategy was to protect or, if need be, to rescue their own citizens. This led them simultaneously to promote overt retaliation and to strike clandestine deals to release American hostages. Such an approach could not be reconciled with good faith towards their allies.

By the agreements reached at Williamsburg and Tokyo, in East-West relations and terrorism, the summits showed a potential for effective action that no other international body could match. But these successes were not repeated. Part of the difficulty lay in the preparatory process. While in economic issues the summit apparatus was becoming unwieldy, on political issues (terrorism excepted) it was still too light, not being capable of sustained and recurrent preparation of complex and sensitive issues. Slender preparation in turn encouraged the leaders to leave foreign policy over for mealtime discussion, which was good for informality but less good for reaching and recording firm conclusions. Ever since 1980 outside commentators had been recommending that, while economic issues should remain the major focus, the political structure should be strengthened so as to improve the balance with the economic and promote better interaction between the two.[6] This was still unfinished business in 1988.

Collective Management: North America, Europe and Japan

The creation of the summits in 1975 reflected the emergence, at least in the perceptions of the founders, of a 'trilateral' world. The undisputed hegemony of the United States was past. The European Community and Japan now shared the ability to influence economic and even political events; they should also share responsibility for 'collective management'. It is therefore worth looking back to see how far their relative positions had altered since the summits began and whether the requirements for collective management had changed by 1988.[7]

Japan

Japan's relative position improved in every way, both in economic and political relations. The most durable achievement of the summits was to bring Japan firmly into the circle of Western consultation and cooperative action.

The advance in political relations was the most striking. In the mid-1970's Japan's foreign policy was hesitant and withdrawn. But summit participation gave the Japanese new confidence. When the Guadeloupe four-power summit of 1979 threatened to exclude them from the inner circle they became keen to see regional political issues treated at the seven-power summits. When Nakasone arrived in 1983, he welcomed the discussion of security and NATO issues as well.

Up to 1988 Japan had the most successful economy of all the summit countries. It regularly outperformed the European countries and usually the US as well. The Japanese economy, however, was strongly oriented to penetrating foreign markets and this created difficulties for the other summit partners. The Japanese authorities recognised their danger and took pre-emptive action, which always served to avert collective criticism. This action was at first wholly defensive, taking the form of packages of unilateral measures of economic stimulus or trade liberalisation, announced just before each summit. Nakasone supplemented these by more active involvement in cooperative actions, taking the initiative at London II 1984 in promoting a new GATT round.

The summit was used by successive Japanese leaders, especially by Nakasone, to exert pressure on their sluggish bureaucracy to bring about policy change. There were examples of summit-induced policy advances in Japan virtually every year, more often than in any other country. Nakasone consciously used the summit to build up his personal prestige in a way that was unfamiliar in Japanese politics. Under him a breed of Japanese ministers and senior officials developed who were far removed from their self-effacing counterparts of the 1970s and could be just as decisive and assertive as their American and European colleagues.

This third series was a golden age for Japan at the summits. Nakasone was followed by a series of short-lived leaders and political instability. From 1991 the Japanese economy went into a decline which lasted the rest of the decade.

Europe

The Europeans gained fewer advantages from the summit process than they had hoped at first, despite the presence of four national participants out of seven, plus the Commission and occasionally a fifth European country as EC Presidency.[8] One basic premise behind the summits' creation was that Western Europe was steadily overhauling the US in economic strength. The relative weight of the European Community was increased in 1986, by a stroke of the pen, by the accession of Spain and Portugal. But otherwise the sluggish performance of the European economies was a disappointment. The European countries grew more slowly than both Japan and the United States. Their economies proved less able to adapt to external shocks, to stimulate new business activity and, most of all, to create new jobs.

The European Community was intended to give the member states the ability to exert their collective influence, at the summits as elsewhere. The EC made some effective contributions early on, after it won access to the summit itself in 1977. But European initiatives in economic fields petered out after 1980, while divisions persisted even on subjects like trade policy, where Community rules required a common position. National economic and monetary policies diverged, so that from 1981 to 1985 the Germans, tacitly at least, supported the Americans against the French. After the Plaza agreement the French moved closer to the Americans just as the Germans moved apart. The Commission's role in economic and monetary policy was weakened, so that by Tokyo II the Americans vetoed their inclusion in the new G7 finance ministers.

In contrast to the economic divisions, there was some evidence of effective European solidarity on foreign policy issues. In 1986, the Europeans, under extreme pressure, produced an alternative set of anti-terrorist measures, based on diplomatic and police action, to set against the US preference for economic sanctions or military attack. This was translated virtually unchanged into the Tokyo summit declaration. Terrorism at Tokyo II demonstrated that whenever the EC could agree on an effective joint position its views would largely prevail. This argued for a more conscious effort by the Community in summit preparation, especially the holding of a European Council shortly before the summit itself. The next series of summits began to show some progress towards this goal.

The United States

For the Europeans and Japan the advent of summitry was a sign of growing relative power. For the Americans, however, it was the opposite. The adjustment from hegemony to collective management was bound to be uneasy. To be successful the summit process required a US administration, and a president, that was both domestically strong and responsive to international cooperation. But this combination was likely to be rare. A strong president would be tempted to try to re-establish American hegemony. A weak one would find his efforts at cooperation frustrated by other forces, especially by Congress.

President Reagan was domestically more strongly based than Carter, his predecessor. But this led him to attempt to re-establish American leadership. Reagan's initial strategy produced Versailles, an ambitious summit which ended with open discord. As the third summit series began, the Americans still pressed ahead with economic 'leadership', brushing aside warnings from their summit partners. But events showed that the United States was no longer strong enough to act as sole leader. An astounding surge in US domestic demand and in the value of the dollar had beneficial effects on the rest of the world while it lasted; but it could not be sustained. Treasury Secretary Baker looked for outside cooperation as the US position weakened. America's summit partners welcomed this change of heart at first, at the time of the Plaza agreement. But they reacted against US pressure for policy coordination.

In foreign policy matters the Americans moved to a more cooperative attitude. The summit produced its most lasting political achievement to date: the Williamsburg statement on arms control, which reconciled US, European and Japanese positions. But this skilful balance of internal strength and international cooperation was upset by US policies which gave undue priority to national concerns, first on SDI and then on terrorism and hostages.

Summitry had so far produced imperfect results as regards the United States. Carter had been responsive to international cooperation but domestically weak; Reagan had been much stronger but also much less responsive. But even the Reagan Administration was shaken by economic and political setbacks and the rise of protectionist pressures. The United States was becoming more exposed to external pressures and needed the support of its summit partners to achieve its international objectives.

Conclusion

The summits of the third series tried to recapture political leadership, but adopted methods which weakened the summit process and inhibited its full potential.   Reconciling the tensions of interdependence yielded mixed results: there was greater focus on non-economic issues, while on economic subjects power shifted to the finance ministers.   Collective management made only uncertain progress, but revealed that Western stability could never be taken for granted.   The United States might no longer be 'hegemon' and now needed the support of Europe and Japan.   But the Europeans and Japanese even more needed the full international involvement of the United States to ensure a secure and prosperous Western world. Summitry was therefore just as necessary in 1988 as it had been in 1975.

Notes

1   There were, however, two notable survivors among the foreign ministers.   One was George Shultz, US Secretary of State from 1982, who, as Secretary of the Treasury, had helped to found the Library Group and had been President Ford's Sherpa.   The second was Hans Dietrich Genscher for Germany, who was present at every summit from the beginning up to London III 1991, a remarkable record.

2   The episodic character of the summits of this series emerges from Artis and Ostry, pp. 70-76. Sylvia Ostry wrote this book while she was Canadian Sherpa.

3   Among the Sherpas only Hans Tietmeyer (state secretary in the German finance ministry) and Sylvia Ostry (Canadian international trade negotiator and former head of the OECD Economics and Statistics Department) were involved in current economic policy-making. The others had a political or diplomatic background.

4   On these summits' role in agriculture, see especially Wolfe 1998, p. 80.

5   Sarah Hogg, *The Times,* 3 May 1986.

6   This was one of the recommendations made by David Watt, Director of the RIIA, in his report commissioned by the Twentieth Century Fund; see Watt 1984.

7   This trilateral analysis leaves no clear place for Canada, the seventh summit member. Sometimes Canada gains a place of its own, as in the 'Quadrilateral' of trade ministers created by the Ottawa 1981 summit. Sometimes it is combined with the United States to form 'North America'. At other times it prefers to join the Europeans to resist being overwhelmed by the US. See Chapter 5 below.

8   When the summit is held during the EC (now EU) Presidency of a member state other than Germany, France, Italy or the UK, that country forms part of the European delegation to the summit, together with the Commission.   This first happened at Versailles in 1982, when Belgium held the Presidency. For more details, see Putnam and Bayne 1987, pp. 150-154.

4 Economic Interdependence: The OECD

Reconciling the tensions between domestic and international politics created by economic interdependence was the principal reason for creating the economic summits. During the first three summit series, before the end of the Cold War, the most active management of interdependence took place in the Paris-based Organisation for Economic Cooperation and Development - the OECD. Since its creation in 1961, as the heir to the Marshall Plan, the OECD had built up a series of procedures for reconciling domestic and international pressures across a wide range of economic issues. These procedures were based on technical discussions among permanent officials, with rare intervention by ministers. They ensured continuous close contacts between the 24 industrial democracies which made up the OECD's membership.

This chapter examines the activities and achievements of the OECD and its relationship with the summits during their first three series.[1] The OECD covered all the economic subjects of concern to the summits and included all the summit participants. But the political objectives of the leaders and their reaction against bureaucratic procedures made it difficult for the summits and the OECD to work together. Their relations were often tense or distant. The OECD, instead of being encouraged by the summits, at times came to feel threatened by them. While these tensions did not endure, the end of the Cold War and the advance of globalisation shifted the summits' attention to institutions of wider membership.

The Origin and Nature of the OECD

The nature and membership of the OECD owed more to history than to logic. The history went back to the founding of the Organisation for European Economic Cooperation (the OEEC) in 1947, more than 50 years ago. The OEEC was created as the collective European response to the Marshall Plan. It embraced 18 states of Western Europe, with the United States and Canada as associates. During its 12-year life it worked out the

European recovery programme after World War II and brought about the removal of the many controls and restrictions imposed by the war.

Oliver Franks, who headed the committee which drew up the joint European programme, later recorded that there were two conflicting concepts at work in the OEEC: one French and one British. The French wished the OEEC to have supranational authority, with limits on the sovereignty of its members. The British wished the OEEC to be an instrument of international cooperation under the control of the participating governments.[2]

The OEEC was in fact created largely on the British model. In consequence, French supranational energies were transferred to creating the European Economic Community. Around the time when the EEC was established, with its customs union and its other common policies, the OEEC began its transformation into the OECD. The new Organisation, launched in 1961, retained no trace of supranational aspirations; only the more modest intergovernmental concept survived. Both British and French attitudes to limits of sovereign independence have moved a long way since then. But the OECD was the inheritor of these original British ideas and approaches.

The United States also had a major hand in the transformation of OEEC into OECD.[3] The OEEC reflected the asymmetrical post-war relationship of donor and recipient. By 1960 the Europeans had grown prosperous; and the Americans wanted a forum where they, the Europeans and other 'industrial democracies' could sit down together on equal terms. So the OECD included the United States and Canada as full members from the outset, to be joined shortly by Japan, Australia and New Zealand. This took the membership up to 24 countries, as Finland had joined the original 18 Europeans, and it remained stable till the mid-1990s. The result was a grouping which did not include all the largest or all the richest countries in the world of the 1980s. But the membership was reasonably homogeneous in economic structure and political system; and it was just small enough to allow every member to take a full part.

The OEEC had covered a wide range of economic issues and this multi-disciplinary character persisted in the OECD and its associated bodies. Macro-economic policies were always at the centre of OECD's work; but that was far from all. The A-Z of OECD activity encompassed agriculture, competition, development, education, employment, energy (including nuclear energy), environment, financial markets, industry, investment, public management, science and technology, services, social affairs, taxation, trade and transport. In this range of subject matter, the OECD resembled the European Community and differed from bodies such as the IMF or the GATT, which treated more closely defined subjects for a larger membership.

While it is easy to list the members and the activities of the OECD, it is harder to explain its nature. One way to define the OECD is by contrasting it with the European Community, to which half of OECD's members belonged by the mid-1980s. The EC, for example, was a progressive organisation in that it focused on a series of targets and goals. If one was achieved, then others were set. The OECD was not progressive in this sense. It adapted, of course, to the manifold changes in conditions since its creation in 1960. But its aims remained the same as defined then: economic growth, rising living standards, financial stability, expanding trade. To take a mundane analogy, OECD membership was like marriage; EC membership was more like parenthood.

The EC had European integration as its rationale. It created common policies in successive areas, in which each member state did more or less the same thing. The drive for so-called 'harmonisation' persisted at least until the Single Market campaign of the late 1980s. But the OECD (unlike its predecessor) did not start from the objective of integration. It started from the fact, or rather the ineluctable trend of interdependence. Its aim was to reconcile the policies of its members: to render them consistent and compatible and where possible mutually reinforcing. This did not necessarily mean all members doing the same thing. It could often mean some doing one thing and some another.

The EC possessed extensive mandatory powers. Its regulations and decisions had the force of law. Increasingly, it took decisions by majority vote. The OECD had very few mandatory powers. Votes were virtually unknown. Nor could it offer tangible inducements, in the way that IMF members could obtain drawings from the Fund if they accepted its disciplines. The OECD had no carrots and no sticks. It had to achieve its results by persuasion; by convincing its member governments to adapt their perceptions of their own self-interest.

A parallel from ancient Greece may be enlightening. The OECD sometimes calls to mind the Delphic oracle: as being an institution wholly maintained by its members' subscriptions, whose neutrality was recognised by all and which offered advice for the present and forecasts for the future. There was no compulsion on the members to follow the advice given. They did so because they realised the consequences of going against a body with such a solid reputation for accurate forecasts. Two slogans were displayed in the temple of the oracle at Delphi: 'Know yourself' and 'Nothing in excess'. These could be suitable mottoes for the OECD as well.

Know Yourself

Accurate and objective data were the foundation of all the OECD's work. The OECD produced a very wide range of statistics and technical assessments. Member governments often regarded these as being more reliable than what they produced themselves. They also provided a wealth of information about what their other partners were doing. But information was only the starting point. The greatest part of the OECD's work in which governments took part consisted of policy comparison, assessment and mutual criticism. This was done through a dense network of committees, to which responsible officials and sometimes ministers came from capitals.

In each of these groups, each member could learn from the others' experience, which could help in their own policy formation. Each member had to present its own policies in a way which was comprehensible and convincing to the others - in itself a useful discipline. Each member had to respond to probing questions from fellow members. Mostly this was done by exchanges among all the members, who alternated in explaining their own policies and criticising others. But there were also national examinations, leading for example to the issue of Economic Surveys for each member country. The result was a subtle discipline, which could be quietly effective. Governments could be induced to adapt their policies in practice, when they would never accept a formal obligation to do so. The OECD could supply governments with good ideas that they could later claim as their own.

Persuasion and pressure for change was naturally applied discreetly. In public exchanges governments would dig their toes in to defend their chosen policies. In informal debate, out of the public eye, they would often be more flexible. This was one reason why the OECD deliberately kept a rather low profile. But once the discussions were completed and a consensus was reached, as much as possible of OECD's work was published. Sometimes the need to agree led to rather dense and oracular prose, with criticism expressed in coded language which had to be read between the lines. But the OECD could state critical views trenchantly if the need arose.

Nothing In Excess

What were the arguments by which governments might be induced to adapt their policies? Outright opposition was seldom voiced, as it was not usually likely to succeed, on the terms in which the OECD operated. The OECD was more likely to suggest shifts in the balance of policy and the moderation of extremes.

The OECD could point out that policies which might make sense if adopted by one country could be self-defeating if widely followed by others. Agricultural subsidies provided a good example. The OECD could demonstrate that the aims of one country's fiscal or monetary policy could be frustrated if its partners were doing the opposite or the effects exaggerated if others were all doing the same. The Organisation developed its own model of the world economy, precisely to show how these interactions worked and to measure their consequences.[4]

Again, the OECD by its multi-disciplinary character could examine the effects of policy in one area on other policy objectives - and encourage this sort of process within its member governments. It could show how national policies could produce wider effects than originally expected, which might undermine the basic intention. Its 1985 study on the Costs and Benefits of Protection, for example, showed that measures to restrict imports by OECD countries were beginning to become effective in the early 1980s. But while jobs might be saved in the industries protected, these were often offset by viable jobs foregone elsewhere in the economy, usually in more dynamic sectors. Import restrictions, like quotas, gave bigger profits to established foreign firms, since they could sell at higher prices. But they aggravated the problems of developing countries, which depended on expanding their sales to OECD countries for servicing their debts, and this helped to provoke the international debt crisis from 1982 onwards.[5]

The OECD in the Early Summit Period

It is instructive to review the range of OECD activity in the late 1970s and the 1980s, and to compare that with what the summits were doing at this time, as described in the previous chapter.

Macro-economic Policy

Macro-economic forecasting and policy consultation had always been at the core of the OECD's work. This was the field where OECD's work was best known, not only through the Country Economic Surveys, but also its twice-yearly *Economic Outlook*. It became, however, an area where many other bodies were active: the IMF, the G5, the G7, the G10 and of course the summits themselves. The OECD was only one actor on a crowded stage. Furthermore, macro-economic policy coordination was proving increasingly controversial from the late 1970s onwards. There was unresolved dispute about the impact of fiscal and monetary policies both within and between governments, especially the prolonged debate about the American budget deficit noted in Chapter 3. This controversy complicated the relationship between the OECD and the summits, as described later in this chapter.

Structural Policies

One consequence was that the OECD concluded that macro-economics was not enough. If the vehicle of the world economy no longer responded predictably to the accelerator or the brake, perhaps it was time to look at the engine. Once that conclusion was drawn and governments were looking less at the running of economies and more at their structure, then the OECD emerged with comparative advantage because of its wide multi-disciplinary coverage. The OECD's Country Economic Surveys no longer looked just at macro-economic prospects. They also chose a structural subject for examination in each country under review. For example, the United Kingdom survey looked at employment in 1986 and at the financial markets in 1987.

At the same time, the OECD prepared an overall study of structural adjustment, submitted to its annual ministerial meeting in May 1987. This examined the whole range of areas where structural policies were relevant: education and training; research; labour and financial markets; adjustment in manufacturing industry and in agriculture; the size of the public sector; the impact of taxation. The study drew general conclusions on what sorts of structural policies worked best and on how they influenced economic performance. The OECD went much deeper into these structural issues than the summits ever achieved up to that time.

Alongside this horizontal study, the OECD was specially active in four specific areas of structural adjustment: energy; employment; agriculture; and services.

Energy

Issues in energy policy were handled mainly by the International Energy Agency (IEA), founded in 1974 after the first oil crisis, while more technical nuclear matters fell to the Nuclear Energy Agency (NEA), which went back further. The IEA worked closely with the Tokyo I summit in 1979 and the Venice I summit in 1980, after the second oil crisis. Thereafter energy issues ceased to engage the summits much. But from 1986 the sharp drop in oil prices and the nuclear disaster at Chernobyl greatly increased the requirements placed on both IEA and NEA. The NEA had a wealth of expertise in reactor safety which was much in demand as OECD countries reviewed their nuclear generation programmes after Chernobyl. The IEA had a more complex task. First, together with the OECD economists, it tried to assess the short-term impact of lower oil prices on inflation, growth and external balances and to draw out the policy implications. Second, the IEA prepared advice to its members on how lower oil prices and public concern about nuclear power might affect investment decisions in all forms of energy and the consequences for energy supply five or ten years hence.

Employment

Sustaining employment was a major preoccupation of all OECD members, but particularly in Europe where unemployment was rising even at a time of economic recovery. The question was how to increase 'the employment content of growth'. With that aim the OECD developed a range of ideas mainly under the heading of 'labour market flexibility'. This did not just mean moderation in wages, where most OECD countries could show good results. It also meant encouraging the creation of new firms, reducing non-wage costs of employment and increasing mobility of labour both between and within enterprises.[6]

Agriculture

Support policies for agriculture were becoming an increasing source of tension between OECD members. To tackle some of the underlying problems, the OECD worked up a method for calculating in a neutral way the impact of the various forms of agricultural support practised by its members: price maintenance; deficiency payments; import quotas; domestic and export subsidies and so on.[7] The units of measurement were called Producer Subsidy Equivalents (PSE) and Consumer Subsidy Equivalents (CSE). With an agreed method of measurement, it should be possible to envisage multilateral reductions of support, which would be less painful and more effective than unilateral action. The work showed that virtually all agricultural markets were distorted by oversupply and by self-defeating competitive subsidy. It was too late for any country to escape by putting the blame on others or exporting itself out of trouble. When OECD ministers met in April 1986 they recognised that fundamental changes were needed. The same message came from the Tokyo II Summit and this gave high-level impetus to the OECD's work, which was endorsed by the summits of the next two years. This was highly relevant for the Uruguay Round of the trade negotiations in the GATT, which recognised from the outset that agricultural protection went far deeper than trade measures or subsidies - see Chapter 7 below.

Services

Trade in services was also a key part of the new Uruguay Round, as the GATT prepared to look at services for the first time. The OECD however had been concerned with trade in services since its foundation, through two little-known instruments called the Codes of Liberalisation - one on Current Invisible Operations and the other on Capital Movements. The original impetus to liberalisation had grown rather attenuated. But the OECD had built up an unrivalled store of information both about services in general and about specific sectors; about traditional sectors like insurance and new ones like international information flows. Though the OECD would not take part in the new GATT negotiations on services as such, it sought to illuminate the issues and point the way towards the solutions finally adopted (as described in Chapter 7). For example, liberalisation of services required the easing of government regulations. Ways had to be found to distinguish regulations which were legitimate, e.g. for prudential purposes, from those which were essentially protectionist.[8]

The Operation of Markets

One common theme in the work on employment, agriculture and services was the removal of obstacles, restrictions and distortions to the operation of markets. The work on energy, too, had been stimulated by the break-up of the cartel in the oil market. This market-oriented approach became increasingly prevalent across the whole range of OECD's work as the 1980s progressed. The role of governments was seen less as the 'fine-tuning' of policy and more as 'framework-setting': that meant defining the rules within which markets could operate with the greatest freedom consistent with the prevention of abuses. Historically this theme recalled the original task of the OEEC in removing wartime controls. But it also reflected the OECD's response to the dilemma between the national responsibilities of governments and the international nature of so much economic and financial activity - i.e. the management of interdependence.

External Relations

The OECD was also concerned with the world outside the circle of its membership: with the centrally planned economics and particularly the developing countries. Two fundamental points determined the OECD's approach.   First, the OECD gave much thought to the impact of its members' policies on developing countries, especially as regards aid, trade, export credit and financial flows.   Second, the OECD seldom acted collectively in wider international contexts.   It provided an intellectual contribution when Western countries were obliged by convention to present a common position, for example in UN meetings.   But OECD members believed that acting together in the name of the Organisation when dealing with developing countries could create a sense of 'them and us' which could provoke resentment rather than cooperation.   This cautious approach was influenced by the confrontational atmosphere which prevailed in North-South relations after the first and second oil crises, though this eased in the course of the 1980s.

The Summits and the OECD

As this review shows, the OECD was involved with all the economic subjects considered at the summits and had the same capacity to treat them in relation to one another.   It sought to influence policy in a variety of ways: by supplying its members with comprehensive high-quality data and careful analysis of policy issues; and by mutual persuasion and argument, conducted mainly among national officials and the OECD Secretariat, with foreign and finance ministers meeting only once a year.   In principle, the summits and the OECD ought to dovetail together neatly, with the former providing occasional, high-level political impulses to move forward the continuous, highly professional work of the latter.   In practice, however, the relationship proved uneasy.

The OECD faced a difficult choice: to seek close links with the summits, at the risk of losing its independence; or to remain detached, at the risk of being bypassed.   If the summits had limited themselves to political impulses, that would have been easier for the OECD to accept. But the summits soon moved on to adopt precise commitments, notably in economic policy, with direct consequences for the OECD. Sometimes the summits went in directions with which the OECD disagreed.   This active summit strategy could justify a more organic link between the two, for example with the Secretary-General attending the summits and summit country representatives forming a nucleus at the OECD.   In fact neither side developed this approach.   The summit leaders preferred a compact, personal format, where each spoke for himself, not for others.   They did not seriously consider inviting the OECD Secretary-General to join their circle. The OECD, for its part, found it hard to accommodate new groups which were not open to the entire membership.

Macro-economic Policy Coordination

In these conditions different procedures were developed to keep the summits and the OECD together. The most visible of these was the practice, from 1976 onwards, of holding the annual OECD Council, attended by foreign and finance ministers, shortly before the summit. This practice has continued to this day. Informal links also operated for a time in summit preparations. From 1977 to 1980 the representatives of the seven summit countries in the OECD's Economic Policy Committee (EPC) met for the express purpose of preparing the macro-economic policy part of the summit's discussion.[9] The chairman of this group would send forward a report to the Sherpas. Even so, the OECD Secretariat was not actually present at the meeting and had to exert its influence at one remove.

This osmotic arrangement worked best during the first two summit series when there was consensus between the summit countries and the OECD Secretariat on the direction of economic policy. For example, the first Bonn summit provided the keystone to the OECD's 'concerted action' strategy of 1978; and during the period of 'non-accommodating' policies in 1979-80 the summits and the OECD were able to reinforce each other effectively. Thereafter, however, the policy prescriptions began to diverge. Reagan, on taking office, suspected the OECD of being too 'Keynesian' and Thatcher tended to agree with him. The summit countries continued with restrictive policies, giving absolute priority to fighting inflation. The OECD Secretariat, however, began to worry about the effect of these policies on the severity of the recession. The informal collaboration over summit preparations did not survive this strain. The group formed of EPC members ceased to handle preparations for the summit after 1981. The summit countries turned instead to the IMF, associating the Managing Director with the practice of policy surveillance agreed at Versailles in 1982, which has proved remarkably durable.

Follow-up proved another source of tension. After the summit, the Sherpa of the host country would come and give a report to the Organisation, but there were no more systematic arrangements for associating the OECD with the consequences of the summits. Thus other OECD countries and the Secretariat began to feel that they were being starved of information and that summit proceedings had become furtive, ambiguous and obscure. The Versailles summit of 1982 left the worst impression in this respect. Thereafter the tension between the summits and OECD eased, though the earlier preparatory activities were not resumed. In the central field of macro-economic policy, therefore, the summits gradually took the limelight away from the OECD, possibly thereby weakening it.

Structural and Other Issues

There was not the same tension between summits and OECD in other economic subjects. But the relationship was often distant. Early summits endorsed OECD work to combat protectionism, especially its 'trade pledge' against import restrictions. The IEA provided input to the summit's work on energy policy at Tokyo I in 1979 and Venice I in 1980 and carried out the decisions from these summits, despite some misgivings. Thereafter, however, energy dropped off the summit agenda. The summits of the third series, as noted in Chapter 3, began to devote much more attention to structural adjustment from 1984 onwards. But apart from agriculture, these summits did not provide a collective stimulus to OECD work in structural issues. The summits only seriously addressed structural adjustment in the 1990s, when they began to focus on topics like environment, employment and the policy content of the Uruguay Round.

Conclusion

By the late 1980s, when the fourth summit series began, the tension between the OECD and the summits was receding into the past. The summits were turning more to structural issues, where the OECD had comparative advantage. The OECD continued to hold its annual ministerial meeting about six weeks before the summit, where non-summit OECD members had an opportunity to influence the summit process.

At this time, however, the end of the Cold War began to change the institutional balance in the management of interdependence. The OECD was well-placed to promote cooperation between its limited membership of industrial democracies. But as interdependence gave way to globalisation, more could be achieved in institutions of worldwide membership. The summits shifted their attention and the OECD lost its central position. It became more important to its members as a place for mobilising ideas to deploy in wider institutions. These issues will be explored later in this book, especially in Chapters 6 and 9.

Notes

1   This chapter is drawn mainly from 'Making Sense of Western Economic Policies: the Role of the OECD', *The World Today*, vol. 43 no. 2, pp. 27-29 (Bayne 1987). This article was written while I was UK Representative to the OECD. The final section of the chapter is drawn from Chapter 7 of *Hanging Together* (Putnam and Bayne 1987).

2   This emerges from his account in Franks 1978 and meshes precisely with the French view set out in the memoirs of Robert Marjolin, the first OEEC Secretary General (Marjolin 1989).

3   Camps 1975 gives a highly perceptive analysis of the OECD, from an American viewpoint, which remained valid throughout the 1980s.

4   The INTERLINK forecasting model then used by the OECD is described in Llewellyn, Potter and Samuelson 1985.

5   This study (OECD 1985) was influential both as regards the policies of member countries and in making the case for a new round of GATT negotiations.

6   The key document was the report of the Dahrendorf group called *Labour Market Flexibility* (OECD 1986).

7   This was first set out in OECD 1987. For more data on the crippling costs of agricultural support, see OECD 1991. See also Wolfe 1998.

8   The role of the OECD and its Secretariat in preparing for the treatment of trade in services in the Uruguay Round is analysed in Drake and Nicolaidis 1992.

9   The summit countries already used to meet on occasion as the EPC's 'bureau'; see Camps and Gwin 1981, p. 236 n. 39 and de Menil and Solomon 1983, p. 16 n. 11.

Part II
The Mature Summit

5 Progress and Frustration: The Fourth Summit Series, 1989-93

The 1988 Toronto summit said goodbye to Ronald Reagan on a rather self-congratulatory note. The leaders showed no inkling of the momentous changes in store, which would fix 1989 as the year when the Cold War ended. Even the Paris Arch summit of July 1989 was almost taken unawares; the historic shifts then beginning in Poland and Hungary only caught the leaders' attention at the last moment. But Paris 1989 clearly marks the start of a new summit series. The five summits of 1989-1993 were dominated by the consequences of the end of the Cold War and the entirely new task of encouraging working democracies and market economies in the former Communist countries, first in Central Europe and then in Russia itself. This chapter applies the familiar triple analysis - political leadership, reconciling interdependence and collective management - to the summits of this series.[1]

Political Leadership: Pressures on the Summit Process

The third summit series had been distinguished by a striking continuity of leaders in power, a general consensus of centre-right policies and the disappearance of former finance ministers. In the new series, the personal continuity among the leaders was soon broken, with Reagan giving way to George Bush and Thatcher to John Major. There was a rapid turnover of Japanese leaders, which weakened Japan's role in the summits by comparison with Nakasone's long tenure in the mid-1980s. The same discontinuity prevailed in Italy. Political continuity lasted much longer, with a Conservative leader still in London and a Republican President in Washington. Both Kohl and Mulroney were renewed in office early in the series, the former becoming leader of a reunited Germany. But by the end this was broken too, with the Democrat Bill Clinton as US President at Tokyo III in June 1993 and the Liberal Jean Chrétien becoming Canadian Prime Minister only weeks after the summit. Former finance ministers were re-appearing among the leaders. These had provided six out of eight in 1978 but dwindled to zero by 1982. They were back at four again in 1992, with Jacques Delors, Giulio Andreotti, John Major and Kiichi Miyazawa.

Nevertheless, the G7 finance ministers retained their grip on economic policy coordination. The summits reviewed the issues, but added little of their own.   The seven finance ministers took over all the responsibility for dealing with the economic slowdown, which during this series affected first the US, UK and Canada and later the continental Europeans and Japan. The ministers now met regularly three to four times a year and in between their deputies met much more often. There was an element of tension here, in that the European Community (Commission and Presidency) were part of the summit process but not in the G7 finance ministers' group.[2]

The non-economic, foreign policy elements in the summit process continued to gain ground. The key decisions on helping Poland and Hungary taken at the Paris 1989 summit emerged from the political preparations, not the economic ones. The spread of democracy all over Central and Eastern Europe gave the political theme for Houston in 1990. The Gulf crisis exerted a powerful influence over the preparations in 1991, stimulating the key political decisions at London III: on strengthening international discipline over conventional arms transfers; and on improving the UN's capacity to respond to humanitarian crises. Yugoslavia similarly dominated political discussion at Munich in 1992.   An important innovation was to extend the role of the Political Directors of foreign ministries, alongside the Sherpa teams, in addressing the foreign policy issues of concern to the summit leaders. This was particularly welcome to the Japanese, who were not involved in political consultations conducted in NATO or the Conference on Security and Cooperation in Europe (CSCE). It facilitated the systematic preparation and follow-up of the foreign policy exchanges at the summit, correcting a besetting weakness of earlier series.

Overloading the Agenda and the Leaders' Response

The traditional economic agenda for the summits had been economic policy, monetary issues, trade, energy and relations with developing countries. By the fourth series, only one and a half of these traditional items regularly occupied the leaders themselves: first, international trade and, second, debt problems, a specific aspect of relations with the third world. The leaders' attention had shifted to a different range of issues, which were still very suitable for summit treatment, in that they combined political and economic elements.

The first category of these was *transnational issues*, where effective solutions required truly worldwide cooperation. Among these, the environment and drugs emerged as major subjects during this series, to join terrorism, especially hijacking and hostage-taking, already a regular summit item. The second category could best be called *historic changes*. These might be regional in scope but called for a collective international response, both economic and political, to encourage and support fundamental change. The examples were, naturally, first Central and Eastern Europe and then the Soviet Union and its successors.

The introduction of new issues, while the old ones were still nominally on the agenda, weighed heavily upon the summit process. The Sherpas had to meet more often; the economic declarations grew longer. The Toronto declaration of 1988 had 11 pages; the Paris 1989 declaration had 17; the Houston 1990 document came out with 20. The numbers and length of non-economic documents were also increasing. In preparing for the London III 1991 summit, John Major instructed his Sherpa team to check these inflationary trends. But they made only limited progress, as circumstances were against them. The uncertainties of the Gulf crisis and of developments in the Soviet Union brought new items onto the agenda and there was the further complication of inviting Gorbachev. The economic declaration was shorter than the Paris and Houston documents. But, at 64 paragraphs, it was still too long and only the Sherpas really understood what it meant.[3] The pressure from the leaders for simpler procedures and shorter documents was gathering strength.

Munich 1992 was another summit where a congested agenda and too much ceremony frustrated the leaders. Shortly afterwards Major wrote to his colleagues with a programme of summit reform. He proposed that the leaders should meet alone, without supporting ministers. There should be lighter preparation, shorter documents and less ceremony. Most of the other leaders applauded the spirit of this approach, but concrete progress was slow. Countries like Germany and Japan whose governments were overt or implicit coalitions clung to the idea of supporting ministers. Major's proposals had the beneficial effect at Tokyo III 1993 of reducing the economic declaration to six pages and 16 paragraphs, the last of which read, in part

> We believe summits should be less ceremonial, with fewer people, documents and declarations and with more time devoted to informal discussion......We intend to conduct future summits in this spirit.[4]

But substantial progress in this direction had to wait until Britain was the host again, as recorded in Chapter 10 below.

**Reconciling Interdependence: the Evolution of Summit Themes
Traditional and Transnational Issues**

Leaving aside foreign policy issues, six themes dominated the subject matter treated in the fourth summit series. There were two traditional themes - trade and debt; two transnational issues - the environment and drugs; and two historic changes - Eastern Europe and the Soviet Union. These were the subjects on which the summits had devoted most effort or had most impact.

Trade

International trade had been discussed at every summit since 1975. Helmut Schmidt, one of the founding fathers, saw the main rationale of the summits as deterring the leaders from protectionist policies. The general obligation on the leaders, when they met, to recognise the external impact of their domestic policies had certainly been beneficial in this area. But the summits found it harder to exert direct influence on the outcome of the successive negotiations in the GATT to remove trade restrictions. The gap between the high-level strategic exchanges at the summit and the complex, detailed and technical discussions in Geneva often proved too wide to bridge.

The first Bonn summit in 1978 had been able to give a vital impetus to the closing stages of the Tokyo Round, with trade negotiators meeting on the margins. But a similar impact on the Uruguay Round 12 years later proved elusive. The timing was unhelpful, with the summits in mid-year trying to influence negotiations which tended to reach their climax six months later. There were far more key players in the Uruguay Round than in the Tokyo Round. The agenda was much wider and included agriculture which, though long overdue, made agreement far more difficult.

At Houston 1990 the leaders made great efforts to ensure a successful conclusion and especially to overcome the problems with agriculture. They managed to agree on a formula for launching the agriculture negotiations, which had eluded the OECD ministers meeting six weeks before. But the formula proved too ambiguous and the agreement too fragile to survive further treatment at Geneva. Continued differences over agriculture frustrated the conclusion of the Round in 1990 and prolonged it into 1991.

At London III the British hosts wanted to avoid the mistakes of the previous year and provided time for a full debate of all the issues, not just agriculture, among the leaders. They did not seek to solve specific problems, but stressed the importance of concluding by the end of 1991.

With this in mind, the leaders committed themselves to remain personally involved and to intervene with each other to resolve differences. This provision was fully used in the closing months of 1991, with frequent contacts, both face-to-face and by telephone, between Major (as G7 chair), Bush, Kohl, Mitterrand, Delors and Dutch Prime Minister Ruud Lubbers (for the EC Presidency). But these did not suffice to bridge the gaps, especially on agriculture, and the Round once again went into extra time.

By Munich 1992 the leaders were distracted by the claims of Russia; the Europeans were preoccupied by reform of the Common Agricultural Policy; and President Bush was facing elections. So Munich did no more than set a new deadline for the end of the year. This again failed, in part because of Bush's electoral defeat. In the closing weeks of his Administration the EC/US Blair House Agreement essentially struck the deal needed in agriculture. But agriculture was not the only issue holding up the Round.

1993 looked like the GATT's last chance. Clinton came to the Tokyo III summit determined to succeed where Bush had failed. The trade ministers of the Quad (US, Japan, Canada and European Commission) met in Tokyo shortly before and reached agreement on tariff cuts which cracked the final major obstacle. By December 1993 the GATT's dynamic new Director General, Peter Sutherland, had driven the round to its conclusion.

Trade and the Uruguay Round was the major economic issue between the G7 in the four summits from 1990 to 1993. At each the leaders pledged themselves to action to bring the Uruguay Round to a successful conclusion that year. Each time except the last they failed, because of disputes among themselves. The summit lost much credibility and reputation from these broken promises.

These failures, however, obscure the extent of what summits did to advance the Round in those four years. The failure to conclude the Round, at least in 1990 and 1991, was indeed because of deep US/European differences over agriculture. But on other things, the summits contributed greatly to the final outcome. They kept the negotiations going through recession and held protectionism at bay. They pushed for a solid and binding dispute settlement mechanism - the centrepiece of the new World Trade Organization (WTO). They gave high-level backing to the idea of the WTO itself, which ensured that this institutional innovation took root. They provided in 1993, the final year of the negotiations, the pressure at the Tokyo summit which drove their trade ministers to strike the essential deal on market access.

Where did they go wrong? A deadline seemed obvious in 1990, as the US Administration's fast-track authority was running out. The Europeans gained a tactical victory on agriculture at Houston in July 1990.

But they were unable to exploit it and ended up with all the blame for failure at the Brussels Conference in December, which was meant to conclude the Round. In retrospect the EC needed longer to bring in its internal reforms in agriculture before it could accept substantial commitments in the GATT. So even in 1990 a deadline was a long shot. Having missed the first, would it have been wiser not to set others? At the time deadlines looked like the best way of keeping up pressure for results. It is hard to see what alternative pressure might have worked better. It may be that a loss of summit prestige was the price of a successful Round and a strong WTO. Whatever the earlier failures, the conclusion of the Uruguay Round in 1993 restored the summit's morale and prepared for the move to a new summit series in 1994. Chapter 7 will look at the trade issues in more detail, while Chapter 8 deals with the new series.

Debt

International debt issues came onto the summit agenda in the 1980s. At first sight, there was no reason why they should not have passed to the G7 finance ministers, as economic policy coordination had done. But summit timing worked in favour of influencing debt issues, just as it had worked against influencing the GATT Round. The summit fell halfway between the IMF's spring Interim Committee and its autumn Annual Meeting. It therefore provided a good occasion for giving an impetus to proposals launched over the previous year and intended for conclusion at the autumn meetings.

This had already happened at the Toronto summit in 1988, which gave a key push to debt relief proposals for the poorest countries, known as 'Toronto terms'. Early in 1989 Nicholas Brady, the US Treasury Secretary, launched the 'Brady Plan', promoting debt reduction for countries heavily in debt to commercial banks. The idea of debt reduction - i.e. that debts might not be repaid in full - was highly contentious at the IMF spring meetings. But the differences among the G7 were ironed out in time for the Paris summit to give its blessing. This ensured the adoption of the Brady Plan by the Fund in the autumn.

By the middle of 1990 it was clear that the relief provided by the Toronto terms was inadequate for the poorest debtors. John Major, as British finance minister, proposed an enhanced package at the Commonwealth Finance Ministers' meeting in September - immediately christened 'Trinidad terms'. As prime minister and host to the 1991 summit he had an excellent opportunity to move these proposals forward. The London III summit encouraged the Paris Club of creditor governments to work for prompt implementation of measures going well beyond Toronto terms. Although the Americans had serious difficulties, the Paris Club was able, before the end of 1991, to agree on 'Trinidad' packages for Nicaragua and Benin. In practice, the US problems proved hard to resolve and even Trinidad terms were not generous enough to rescue some countries. A new, improved package was agreed at the Naples summit of 1994 (called, inevitably, 'Naples terms'); and a new initiative was needed immediately thereafter. Chapter 11 examines this subject in more detail, which remained a persistent item on the summit agenda.

Environment

Since the second Bonn summit of 1985, environmental issues had begun to find a place in the leaders' discussions and a brief mention in the declaration. But the French decided to make the environment a principal theme of the Paris Arch summit of 1989, where it occupied two full sessions of debate and a third of the very long economic declaration.[5]

The Paris 1989 summit identified the environment as a long-term challenge facing Western governments, which affected all areas of policy-making. It raised the priority of environmental protection in domestic policies and encouraged work by international institutions, notably the OECD. The Houston 1990 summit carried the debate into specific international issues, such as global warming, bio-diversity and the preservation of both forests and oceans. London III 1991 concentrated the debate yet further, by focusing the leaders' attention on the UN Conference on Environment and Development (UNCED), due in Rio in June 1992. It prepared the way for several of the achievements of UNCED, including the conclusion of framework conventions on climate change and bio-diversity.

The environment was clearly a worthy summit subject. The leaders could give impulses to domestic policy, which involved the whole range of government. They could stimulate international institutions, especially in the UN family, to develop the cooperative solutions required by global environmental problems. These summits of 1989-1991 did much to focus world attention on the environment. They promoted basic concepts: environment policies should be based on sound economics and work with markets; global issues must involve all countries, so that developing countries are helped to avoid the errors of the industrial world. They also identified key subjects - the ozone layer, climate change, bio-diversity, conservation of forests and oceans - which came together at Rio.

The exchanges at the summits were not easy. The Europeans, especially Germany, as well as Canada, were ambitious, while the US was often sceptical. As summit discussions moved from the general to the specific, they revealed underlying differences between the Europeans and the Americans on the nature of the problem and the urgency of action, especially on global warming. Furthermore, the summits did not focus on the tangle of international institutions in this field. In consequence, there was a loss of momentum after UNCED, with commitments not being met. Environmental institutions remained fragmented. Meanwhile the G7 leaders seemed rather to have lost interest, except in the special issue of nuclear safety in East Europe and particularly Ukraine. Though G7 environment ministers began meeting regularly each year, this was not due to instructions from the summit, and it was not clear that the leaders paid much attention to their findings.[6]

Drugs

The fight against illegal drug trafficking and addiction had begun to concern the summit leaders in the late 1980s, especially as the international effort did not seem well organised. Each of the summits from 1989 to 1991 addressed the subject, developing innovative solutions to specific problems. The Paris summit established a Financial Action Task Force (FATF) against the laundering of drug money. The FATF drew up disciplines that came to apply in all major financial centres. Houston was most concerned at the cocaine threat from the Western hemisphere and launched a new task force to check the movement of chemical pre-cursors used in drug manufacture. London shifted attention to heroin, the main hard drug of abuse in Europe and Asia, and asked the Customs Cooperation Council to improve methods of intercepting drugs in transit. All three summits encouraged the creation of better anti-drug cooperative machinery, especially in the UN. While the drug menace continued unabated, the summits served to mobilise international action against it.

Thereafter there was a lull in the summits' attention; but drugs returned to the agenda later in the 1990s as the leaders turned to international crime in its wider forms. As with the environment, the weakness of international institutions had blunted some of the summits' impulses. In issues such as terrorism, drugs, money laundering and international crime, the summits attracted attention to the problems and made some short-term impact. But only money laundering found an effective institutional home in the Financial Action Task Force. The others tended to come back to the summit again in times of crisis.

Historic Changes: Ending the Cold War

Central and Eastern Europe

The summits had not treated East-West relations since the pipeline dispute of the early Reagan years which dominated Versailles 1982. The easing of Soviet policy towards Eastern Europe, and the consequent moves towards democracy in Poland and Hungary, brought these issues onto the agenda of the 1989 Paris summit at the last moment. They were discussed only at the final Sherpa meetings, a week before the summit, as part of the non-economic preparations, and featured in the political rather than the economic declaration. The key decision of the Paris summit was to create the 'Group of 24' to coordinate assistance to Poland and Hungary, with all OECD countries as members and the European Commission in the chair. This was the first time the Commission had been given such responsibility in a group going wider than the EC member states. After some initial uncertainty over relations with other institutions, such as the IMF and World Bank, the G24 became an established and valued part of the machinery for mobilising help for Eastern Europe.

When the leaders met again at Houston a year later, the scene in Eastern Europe was transformed. All the former Warsaw Pact countries were moving towards democracy and market economies and were being brought into the ambit of the G24. The European Bank for Reconstruction and Development (EBRD) had been created and most East European countries were building up relations with the IMF.[7] The Houston summit celebrated the return of democracy and pledged financial and technical support for reforming countries.

By the London III summit of 1991 the Central and East European countries were into the hard task of transforming their economies. In spite of support from the G24, the fiscal and monetary stabilisation needed in these countries had led to unemployment and loss of growth, aggravated by the collapse of their markets in the Soviet Union. Their first concern, therefore, was to improve their access to Western markets, seen also as a condition for attracting direct investment. The leaders at London committed themselves to this; and the EC, after difficult negotiations, concluded Association Agreements for this purpose with Poland, Hungary and Czechoslovakia later in the year.

The process of absorbing the Central and East European countries into the international economy continued in subsequent years, with many ups and downs. But after this initial impulse over 1989-91, their economic problems did not require summit treatment. The leaders' attention shifted further East.

The Soviet Union - and Russia

A letter from Soviet President Mikhail Gorbachev was delivered in the middle of the 1989 Paris summit. It appeared to be a bid to take part, on equal terms.[8] But between the lines, as Geoffrey Howe, the British foreign minister, remarked, it read more like a cry for help. Mitterrand returned a courteous, non-committal reply, on behalf of all. But from then on the idea was born that Gorbachev might one day sit down with the G7 leaders.

Over the next 12 months Gorbachev's foreign policy was helpful to the West, facilitating the spread of democracy in Eastern Europe and the unification of Germany. Economic reform was also gathering pace in the Soviet Union, though the economy itself was deteriorating. There was a strong political disposition in Europe, and especially in Germany, to offer the same sort of help to Gorbachev as had been given to Poland and Hungary in 1989. But doubts remained, especially in the United States, about both the political and the economic commitment to reform in the Soviet Union. The Americans covered Eastern Europe but not the Soviet Union in the Houston 1990 summit preparations. They were therefore taken aback when the European Council in June, under German and French encouragement, invited the Commission to draw up plans for helping the Soviet Union and expected the other G7 summit participants to join in.

At Houston itself a compromise was found by asking the IMF, the World Bank, the OECD and the EBRD, in consultation with the European Commission, to draw up a study on the Soviet economy, the measures needed for reform and the criteria for Western assistance. The study was completed by the end of the year and presented a coherent set of reform policies, though based on the assumption that the USSR would hold together. The parallel EC study, commissioned in June, looked more deeply into the relations between Soviet republics. The December 1990 European Council, in Rome, made commitments of food aid and technical assistance for the Soviet Union as its economic problems worsened. Meanwhile, in a speech at Aspen, Colorado, on 5 August 1990, Margaret Thatcher suggested 'bringing the Soviet Union gradually into closer association with the economic summit'. Next year's summit, which Britain would host, could take a first step along that road.[9] Thus she introduced the major innovation of the British G7 chairmanship - an unprecedented meeting initiated by the summit participants with a third party.

Early in 1991 an invitation to Gorbachev looked unlikely. Gorbachev was going backwards over economic reform, bringing in the conservative Valentin Pavlov as prime minister and doing nothing to implement the policies in the Houston study. Politically he was moving to more authoritarian measures, notably in the Baltic States. At the Sherpa meeting in early May there was no decision to invite Gorbachev to London.

Gorbachev then launched a diplomatic offensive. He revived a series of economic reform proposals, some sponsored by Pavlov, others put together by Grigory Yavlinsky, with advice from a group from Harvard. Gorbachev wavered between first one and then the other, while all the time power was shifting from him to Yeltsin and the other republican leaders. In these conditions, the G7 heads decided that an invitation to meet them in London was the best way to encourage Gorbachev's own commitment to implement genuine, workable reforms. But the encounter was clearly separated from the main summit, to remove any suggestion that a 'G8' was being created.[10]

There was even less disposition than in 1989 to offer Gorbachev massive financial assistance while his reform plans remained so inchoate. The intention was to inaugurate a process of economic cooperation which would encourage reform and could be adapted in the light of events. The shape of this was much debated in the preparations and at the summit itself and some quite elaborate plans were drawn up. But the approach finally agreed on had a simple structure, as outlined publicly by Major. It focused on 'association' of the Soviet Union with the IMF; technical assistance from the other institutions and the summit participants; better trade access; and the involvement of G7 finance ministers and ministers for small business creation in helping Soviet reform.

In the event, what mattered were not the details of this structure but the manifest involvement of the G7 in the economic fate of the Soviet Union and its republics. Some argued, at the time of the coup against Gorbachev in August 1991, that a more generous response from the G7 would have prevented the coup from happening. This seemed improbable. The coup leaders disliked Gorbachev's links with the West; to avert the coup, Gorbachev should not have gone to London at all. In any case, the coup leaders' real worry was about the shift of power to the republics. The London visit was irrelevant to that, but the coup itself made the shift irreversible.

Of the points agreed at London, association of the Soviet Union with the IMF, rather than membership, proved of particular value. It enabled the Fund staff to develop links and offer advice not only to the Union authorities but also to the Russians and other republics, without blocking the republics' route to full membership, which was able to move forward after the Soviet Union collapsed. The two issues of greatest concern to the G7 leaders as the year ended did not in fact feature at the summit at all. One was the debt problems of the Soviet Union and its republics, which involved the deputies of the G7 finance ministers in the complex negotiation of a debt deferral. The other was emergency assistance, especially food supplies to relieve shortages that winter which could have undermined efforts at reform. The coordination of this assistance was addressed by ad hoc meetings of officials from the G7 countries plus the EC, an exceptional use of the summit machinery in the latter part of the year. Emergency assistance and debt deferral brought the Soviet republics some $15bn by the end of the year, including amounts committed earlier by G7 participants. Action by the G7 formed the basis for wider measures, through both the Paris Club and the Washington conference on humanitarian aid for the republics in late January 1992.

The prospects for economic reform in Russia and the other republics, and the nature of Western support for these reform efforts, inevitably became the first item on the agenda for the Munich summit of 1992. By then the Soviet Union had collapsed, but Yeltsin was firmly in charge in Russia. Yegor Gaidar, his prime minister, had begun the first stage of the transformation of the Russian economy, concentrating on abolishing price controls. Yeltsin and Gaidar impressed the G7 leaders and the IMF with their commitment to reform. Yeltsin was invited to Munich and the IMF agreed a programme for Russia shortly before the summit met.

Both the process of reform itself and the construction of Western aid packages were far harder than anything done in Eastern Europe. The Russian economy was much bigger and in a much worse state. Disentangling Russia from the wreckage of the Soviet Union added great complications, especially as regards external debt. The G7 had some guilt feelings about Gorbachev and over-compensated at Munich 1992. They promised Yeltsin too much - $24bn - little of which could be disbursed once the IMF programme began to run into trouble. Yeltsin removed Gaidar and replaced him as prime minister with Victor Chernomyrdin.

Before Tokyo III in 1993 the G7 preparations were more systematic. Clinton, as the new US President, had an early meeting with Yeltsin in Vancouver, which established Yeltsin's need to preserve his political authority and not look like a suppliant. G7 foreign and finance ministers had a joint meeting in April, which produced a more coherent programme of support for Russian reforms. The IMF created its Systemic Transformation Facility (STF), especially to help Russia and other ex-communist states, and disbursed a first tranche of $1.5bn to Russia.

As a result, the summit could agree on an impressive but more realistic set of measures to help Russia. At the time, the Russian economy looked on the mend, but the improvement was not sustained. Both monetary and fiscal policy soon began to get out of control and out of line with IMF commitments again. For all the effort and resources committed by the G7 to Russia, the results must be regarded as disappointing.[11]

Yeltsin's relationship to the summit was also sensitive. Like Gorbachev before him, he aspired to equal status with the G7 leaders. They were hesitant over converting the G7 into G8, especially in economic issues where Russia had no claim to summit status. Japan was the most reserved, because of an unresolved territorial dispute. As against this, the G7 recognised the Russians' political weight in the world and wanted them to exert a helpful influence. This issue was still unresolved at Tokyo III in 1993. But the change in the treatment of Russia between Tokyo and Naples in 1994 marks the end of the fourth summit series and the start of the fifth.

Collective Management under Increasing Strain

A review of the relative positions of the G7 members during the fourth series reveals uneasy shifts and growing tensions, as compared with earlier summits.

Japan

During the fourth series Japan essentially marked time and did not improve on the advances made up to 1988. After a rapid succession of short-lived prime ministers, the Japanese political system began to show signs of strain. Japan, like all G7 economies, endured a recession. But while the others soon recovered, the Japanese economy entered a period of weakness which was to endure throughout the 1990s. From being the most buoyant G7 economy it became the least. Japan was also unenthusiastic about the attention showed to the Soviet Union and then Russia. Thus, while the officials concerned did not lose the self-confidence gained in earlier years, the Japanese were mainly spectators and not initiators in this summit series.

Europe

The European Community (which became the European Union at the end of this series) was more successful than before in deploying its collective weight at the summits. There were none of the open disagreements within the EC such as were seen, for example, at Bonn II in 1985. At the same time, relations between European and non-European summit participants were well managed in the years when the summits met in Europe. The host country could ensure that EC and G7 summit processes moved on consistent lines. This was less successful in 1990 when the Americans preparing for Houston were taken by surprise by European Council decisions concerning the Soviet Union and Brazilian forests. The European Commission achieved its greatest success of the entire series when the 1989 Paris Summit made it responsible for coordinating Western aid to Central and Eastern Europe, as Chair of the G24.

The United States

When Bush succeeded Reagan, it looked as if the summits might at last get the sort of US President it needed; domestically strong but open to international influence. Bush had previous experience of national office, as Reagan's Vice-President, and a known reputation in foreign affairs. His Administration had some undoubted achievements. Bush, well advised by James Baker, now Secretary of State, showed a more enlightened attitude to German reunification than several European leaders did, notably Thatcher and Mitterrand. Stiffened by Thatcher, Bush mobilised an impressive operation against Saddam Hussein in the Gulf, where Europe in general did not distinguish itself. But for all this, Bush was never at ease in the summit process and suffered from lack of purpose and clear objectives. He remained in control neither of Congressional opinion nor of the disparate elements of his own Administration. Clinton, on his first appearance, was a much more assured summit performer, despite his professed lack of interest in international issues.

Conclusion: Hopes and Frustrations

Contrary to expectation, the fourth summit series was a period of unusually difficult relations between the G7 members, especially between Europe and the United States. (Canada got closer to the US but had more trouble with Europe, while Japan had more trouble with the US.) For various reasons, the end of the Cold War, which should have been a time of successful joint endeavour, revealed serious sources of transatlantic discord, all the worse because they were unexpected. One can identify four such sources, which persisted well beyond 1993:-

- *First,* the Cold War had been a factor inducing the members of the Atlantic Alliance to settle their disputes and remain united before their common enemy. Without this constraint, countries were tempted to push disputes and differences further before accepting a settlement. Thus the Uruguay Round ran three years over time; the US had persistent trade disputes with Japan; Canada's quarrel with the EC over fisheries festered unresolved.

- *Second,* the end of the Cold War coincided awkwardly with a period of recession and low growth. Before the events in Eastern Europe, the Anglo-Saxon economies - US, UK, Canada - went into a recession caused by asset-based inflation. The continental European economies went down after them into a recession provoked by the strain of absorbing the Eastern *laender* into Germany. Recession fed protectionism and inhibited economic reform. This delayed progress in the Uruguay Round and reform of the EC's Common Agricultural Policy.
- *Third,* the end of the communist empire and the unification of Germany caused the Europeans to go further than originally intended in their new round of integration, adding elements of European political union to economic and monetary union. Negotiating the Maastricht treaty and getting it accepted preoccupied the Europeans and made them also rather arrogant. Other G7 partners felt neglected and patronised.
- *Fourth,* the end of the Cold War gave a strong boost to the UN, as the Security Council could now reach agreement. There were many more peace-keeping and humanitarian operations, more than the machinery could bear. Late in 1992 the US decided, exceptionally, to send troops on the UN operation in Somalia. This was a bad experience for them, which made them refuse to send ground troops to the UN operation in Bosnia. Their refusal to do this, while urging NATO air strikes endangering the European and Canadian troops that were on the ground, caused deep resentment in Europe and Canada.

The mature summits of the fourth series tried to tackle a growing agenda; of traditional economic subjects; of transnational issues; and of entirely new subjects generated by the collapse of the Soviet empire. The leaders urgently desired to help Eastern Europe and the former Soviet Union escape from the errors of the past. The period began in a spirit of dynamism and hope, symbolised by the fall of the Berlin Wall in November 1989. But it ended with the G7 leaders often at loggerheads among themselves and frustrated that the summits were not producing the results they wanted.

The summit process was unable to prevent these tensions, nor could it always resolve them. But the G7 summits proved their worth; they encouraged the practice of consultation, inhibited disagreement from turning to conflict and produced some useful results. In particular, after three years of failure, the summit encouraged the successful conclusion of the Uruguay Round, with much richer results than originally foreseen. The narrative in this chapter of what the summits did (or failed to do) does not reveal the more profound changes in the international system set in motion by the end of the Cold War. These changes are the subject of the next chapter, which forms, in a sense, the nucleus of this entire book.

Notes

1   This chapter is largely drawn from the 'The Course of Summitry', *The World Today*, vol. 48 no. 2, pp. 27-29 (Bayne 1992). I wrote this article as I came to the end of over three years as Economic Director of the FCO and sous-Sherpa for the summits of 1989-1991. The chapter, however, extends also to cover Munich 1992 and Tokyo III 1993, on which my sources are much less full.

2   At the Tokyo II 1986 summit Reagan had refused to allow the Commission into the G7 finance ministers - see Putnam and Bayne 1987, p. 217.

3   Chancellor Kohl made this point himself to the Sherpas on the margins of the London III summit in 1991.

4   The text of the Tokyo III 1993 declaration (like other summit documents) is available on the website of the University of Toronto G8 Research Group, www.g7.utoronto.ca.

5   The details of the preparations for the Paris Arch summit of 1989 are given in the full account by Jacques Attali, the French Sherpa, in his *Verbatim III* (Attali 1995). This also describes his long but vain struggle to get the G7 members to sit down with the leaders of selected developing countries.

6   My judgement differs somewhat from that of Dr Ella Kokotsis, who sees a rise in compliance by G7 countries with their environment commitments after 1992 (Kokotsis and Daniels 1999). However, the disappointing results on the environment from the Denver 1997 summit contrast with the degree of cooperation in 1989-91. See Chapter 8 below.

7   Jacques Attali used the G7 machinery without scruple in the creation of the EBRD, of which he became the first President; see Attali 1995, entries from 6 January 1990 onwards.

8   It was later revealed that Attali had supplied a draft for this letter to Gorbachev's emissary Zagladin; see Attali 1995, pp. 284-5.

9   The full text of Thatcher's speech is in the London Press Service Verbatim no. VS 039/90.

10   The invitation to Gorbachev in 1991 was supported by all the G7 members, though Japan was the most reserved. This was in contrast to their reluctant acquiescence in Mitterrand's plan to have them meet leaders from developing countries before the Paris 1989 summit.

11   Brigitte Granville has a hostile critique of G7 help for Russia, as an example of what not to do for the Balkans, in Granville 1999.

6 The End of the Cold War and its Impact

When the Berlin Wall came down, on 10 November 1989, and communist regimes crumbled first in Central Europe, then in the Balkans, finally in the Soviet Union, everyone hoped that a new era of peace and prosperity would begin. It would clearly be hard and painful for working democracies and effective market economies to be established in the former Warsaw Pact countries. But there was confidence that this could be achieved: and that the West could provide not only material help, but also the valuable example of the successful economic system practised by the G7 and the other OECD countries. This system had finally triumphed over the rival, centrally-planned approach. Moreover, it was not just in Central and Eastern Europe that the open market economic system was prevailing, but all over the world. China was transforming its economy, with conspicuous success. The 'little dragons' of East Asia were reaching economic standards close to those of OECD; and their neighbours in the Association of South-East Asian Nations (ASEAN) were following in their wake. In Latin America new open economic and trade policies were being brought in, notably in Mexico. The worldwide prospects had never looked better.

By the end of 1993, these early hopes had given way to a more sombre mood.[1] The political dangers and disappointments are beyond the scope of this book. In economic affairs the West had had many unpleasant surprises. The Anglo-Saxon members of OECD - the US, Britain, Canada, Australia and New Zealand - were the first to go into a recession they found hard to shake off. As those countries recovered, recession attacked continental Europe and separately Japan. The Exchange Rate Mechanism (ERM) of the European Monetary System (EMS) suffered unparalleled turbulence and only survived by drastically loosening its disciplines. Most serious of all the Uruguay Round of multilateral trade negotiations, which should have ended in 1990, ran on three years beyond its deadline. Meanwhile, everywhere in the West, governments became unpopular and electorates dissatisfied with their political elites. What had gone wrong? What would be needed to put things right?

This chapter offers a first analysis of these developments and some tentative recommendations, to be explored further in later parts of this book. It argues that the Cold War, while it lasted, encouraged some helpful attitudes which ceased to apply; it masked or distracted from some trends which could no longer be ignored; and it created some weaknesses, not evident in a divided world, but which became troublesome in the new conditions. A better understanding of these should lead to improved performance in the future. In particular, the end of the Cold War had accelerated the transition from interdependence to globalisation. This had implications for the entire international system, as this chapter explains. These implications embraced the G7 summits, whose task of reconciling the tensions between domestic and international pressures became even more necessary under globalisation.

The Cold War, Interdependence and Globalisation

To state the obvious, the Cold War was not a war. Indeed for Europe it was the alternative to war. The awful consequences of nuclear war deterred lesser conflicts. Few of the economic restraints common in war were applied, except for the COCOM limits on strategic exports. The Cold War was instead a contest between ideas and systems. It was a struggle of the open system, in which governments encouraged competition, the private sector and freedom of choice, against the centrally-planned system where everything was done by government direction. The most warlike thing was that communist governments sought economic success by prolonging into peacetime the practices used in wartime. They encouraged ever greater volumes of output, with no thought of cost or concern for the consumer. The West did exactly the opposite.

The economic rivalry between East and West was much less tense than the strategic confrontation. The fear of Soviet aggression drove most countries of the West into a defensive alliance. They took care to maintain solidarity among themselves and present a common front to the enemy. The Western economic system, which encouraged competition, especially international competition, was bound to give rise to disputes. But Western countries never allowed their trade or other economic disputes to damage the unity induced by the external strategic threat. This was one positive influence of the Cold War, while it lasted. Now that the threat from the Soviet superpower had disappeared, that pressure to resolve economic disputes was removed. The three-year delay in concluding the Uruguay Round appeared as the first evidence of this.

The Cold War had another positive influence on international economic relations, linked to the first. Especially in the early years, the Western democracies sought actively to demonstrate that their open economic system worked better than the closed, state-controlled system of the East. Rivalry with the East drove them to enhance the openness of their economies to the outside world and to resist pressures to impose government controls or limit freedom of choice. Domestic pressures for such controls were often extremely strong, from those whose jobs or businesses were put at risk by external competition. But the dislike of using measures similar to those practised by the communist countries was a powerful inhibition on Western governments. This inhibition was reinforced by the superior performance, in growth and consumer satisfaction, delivered by the open system. By resisting protection against competition, Western governments allowed the weaker parts of their economies to wither but enabled the stronger parts to flourish. The consequence was vigorous, healthy growth in the West, as against increasing distortions in the East.

In the process, however, Western governments encountered increasing limits on their economic power. Within national boundaries, governments would like to be independent, able to take measures to direct the public sector or to regulate private business, with some confidence that they alone determined the outcome. But they could no longer do so. That was the price they had paid for the unparalleled economic advance of the 45 years since World War II. Not a single area of economic activity was immune from international influence. It was not just macro-economic matters, trade policy, exchange rates and financial flows which were subject to international pressures. It was all what are called structural policies as well, as described in Chapter 4 of this book: labour markets, agriculture, environment, education and training, investment, competition policy, taxation, transport - the list went on and on.[2]

This process, which was formerly called 'interdependence', shifted to become 'globalisation' with the end of the Cold War. It upset the relative roles of governments and private companies. Governments' powers, however great, extended only to their borders. Multinational companies could ignore boundaries and move wherever they found conditions of operation were best - the most skilled and industrious workforce, the best facilities for research, the most favourable tax regime. A government, in these conditions, might increase its tax revenue by lowering taxes on business and attracting foreign investment away from its neighbours.

This trend to globalisation was sparked off by the Cold War but had long since acquired its own momentum. Even so, the Cold War, while it lasted, had masked it and distracted from it. Governments were in full control of security policy. While there was still a military threat from superpower confrontation, their responsibility was clear and their electorates were reassured by this. But with the military threat passing, economic policies took predominance. Electorates discovered that here their governments could not take independent decisions and found that deeply unsettling. In consequence all Western governments and political elites became unpopular and distrusted.

The European Community provided a special case of this. Since its creation, the Community had been seen as the great alternative vision to the communist domination of Eastern Europe. Despite its ups and downs, the success of economic integration in the European Community had been in striking contrast to the dilapidation and discontent of Eastern Europe. The peoples of Western Europe thus took great pride in the success of integration while the Cold War was on. But once the Communist threat was gone, the citizens of each member state found that the external influences on their economies, through the Community, were greater than anywhere else in the world. They reacted against this loss of economic independence by turning against their elites. This manifested itself in different ways, for example in the popular criticism of the Maastricht Treaty concluded in 1991, not only in Britain but also in Denmark, France, Italy, and Germany. Economic recession sharpened this popular criticism. In Britain, as in all the OECD economies outside Europe, the recession of the early 1990s was largely caused by bursting the bubble of asset price inflation, in property and financial markets. In continental Europe the recession was directly due to the strains created by the end of the Cold War itself, specifically the abrupt absorption of the former German Democratic Republic (GDR) into Federal Germany.

Governments, like their citizens, found the loss of control in areas where they were held responsible to be no less unsettling. Their traditional economic instruments no longer seemed to work; their forecasts gave deceptive messages. Some of them looked around for ways to regain control over economic activity and to give their electorates the same reassurance which they could provide in security issues. Concepts like 'economic security' thus became popular. Different regimes of protection against external competition were examined. In the United States, the focus was strongest on the relationship with Japan, which was accused of unfair competition. In Europe, France revived the idea of a self-sufficient Community, shutting out unwelcome competition from low-cost producers, especially in Asia.

But despite these dilemmas of globalisation, there could be no going back. The genie was out of the bottle. Like the invention of printing and the industrial revolution, the changes in economic behaviour produced by the open international system were permanent. During the Cold War, the Soviet Union and its allies tried to maintain a regime of 'economic security' and to protect themselves from outside competition. Their attempt collapsed because, in the end, their populations would not accept living standards which steadily fell behind those achieved in the West. The same would happen to any other country or group of countries which tried to maintain a protected system in this competitive world. Electorates might not like the pressures of competition, but they would like the dead hand of protection even less.

The Cold War and the International Economic System

As noted, multinational companies could ignore national boundaries, while the powers of governments were limited by them. But governments too, if they chose, could operate internationally, through institutions providing for collective action. This section examines how international economic structures and institutions evolved during and immediately after the Cold War.

For a very brief period, as World War II ended, one could speak of a truly worldwide economic system. But very soon, at least from the Soviet refusal in 1947 to let Eastern Europe benefit from the Marshall Plan, this worldwide economy was split apart. The open system of the West struggled against the communist centrally-planned system, and each competed to extend its influence over the developing countries of the Third World, which grew in numbers as former colonies achieved independence.

In this competition, the West in general had the advantage. It could always offer more in financial aid and, naturally enough, had a far wider circle of trading partners. But the extent of communist influence was not negligible, even into the 1970s. Beyond the Soviet Union and Eastern Europe, China was solidly committed to central planning. The Indian economy was largely closed and did more trade with Russia than with the West. Many Latin American countries had heavy government controls over trade and investment. Even so, in the decade of the 1970s the main challenge to the open economies of the West did not come from the East but was provoked by the oil crises of 1973 and 1978. These put a negotiating lever into the hand of some oil-producing countries and their allies and gave a sense of solidarity to the Group of 77 developing countries in United Nations contexts. It looked as though the worldwide economy might be fragmented into three conflicting approaches, not just two.

In the decade of the 1980s these divisive trends were reversed. Falling oil prices weakened the negotiating position of the oil-producers. First in East Asia, then in Latin America, more developing countries opened up their economies. Finally, from 1989 onwards, the Central and East Europeans, followed by Russia and the other states of the former Soviet Union, abandoned their closed circle and wanted equal partnership with the West. So a truly global economic system was once more a real prospect. Did the institutions required for such a system exist?

In the short period at the end of World War II, before the Cold War began, there was a tremendous burst of international institution-building, both political and economic. The key pillars then established were: the United Nations and its family; the Bretton Woods institutions of the IMF and the IBRD or World Bank; and the GATT, only survivor of the abortive International Trade Organization. All these were intended as fully universal institutions. But not all achieved that goal and the advent of the Cold War frustrated many of their objectives.

During the 40 years of the Cold War a hierarchy of institutions emerged:-

- At the top, the United Nations and its agencies remained the only truly *global* institutions, to which all countries, even the communist states, belonged. Some new UN bodies were created, notably the United Nations Conference on Trade and Development (UNCTAD) and the United Nations Environment Programme (UNEP). But their efficiency was hampered by the presence of two, later three, rival approaches.
- The IMF, World Bank and GATT did not achieve worldwide membership. The communist countries in general stayed out. Many developing countries likewise did not join the GATT. So these bodies were at best *sub-global* institutions, for want of a better name. They attracted more support from the West than the UN did.
- Next came the smaller, selective bodies which might be called *plurilateral* or *trans-regional* institutions. These brought together countries from different areas of the world, chosen on specific criteria. For example, the OECD grouped the industrial democracies. The CMEA, while it lasted, brought together the centrally-planned economies. OPEC served the main oil exporters. The Commonwealth had its economic aspect. UNCTAD, though universal in membership, in fact functioned for many years as a trans-regional body, supporting the developing countries of the UN in rivalry with the West. Of all these bodies of restricted membership, the G7 summit attracted the most attention.
- Finally there were the *regional* institutions. The European Community was by far the most ambitious. For many years no comparable economic grouping existed elsewhere. Then its example

was followed in the Western hemisphere by the North American Free Trade Area (NAFTA), and by various Latin American groups. In Asia, ASEAN was adapted to take on economic functions, while Asia-Pacific Economic Cooperation (APEC) spanned the Pacific with a loose grouping of large membership.

The end of the Cold War provoked changes in both the shape and the functions of all these organisations. After 1989 the sub-global bodies - IMF, World Bank and GATT - were able to achieve at last truly universal membership. Virtually all countries became members of the Fund and the Bank. A score of developing and East European countries joined the GATT, while the Uruguay Round was in progress. Russian and Chinese membership was under active discussion.

For the trans-regional and regional institutions too the end of the Cold War often reopened the basis of membership. For example, the OECD admitted Mexico, followed by three Central European countries and South Korea. The European Community, even while negotiating to admit the EFTA countries, was looking beyond them towards Poland, Hungary, the Czech Republic and others. These pressures for enlargement were not without problems. Formerly compact bodies had to change their procedures as they grew bigger.

The changing functions of these institutions can be illustrated by a distinction earlier used by Andrew Shonfield. He contrasted 'administrative discretion in collective management' with 'tightening the rules governing international relations and increasing the power-load on the machinery for their enforcement'.[3] This contrast was between discretionary collective management, which was flexible but depended on consent and voluntary commitments, and the setting and enforcing of rules, which was predictable at the risk of rigidity.

The post-war economic institutions largely focused on making and keeping rules. The GATT did this for trade and the IMF for monetary relations. The UN itself was more a deliberative body but facilitated binding international conventions in various subjects. But this worldwide rule-making capacity went into abeyance during the Cold War. The GATT survived, but lagged behind the increasing complexity of world trade. The IMF's capacity for rule-making was reduced with the loosening of exchange rate regimes.

The most striking innovations in rule-making were thus at the regional level and particularly in the European Community. The EC developed the most extensive and ambitious set of rules on record to apply between its members. But a system of tight regional rules in a loose international context was always liable to create friction and suspicion with non-members of the regional body. The EC, for example, was hard put to reassure others that its campaign to complete the Single Market did not mean Fortress Europe.[4]

In contrast the trans-regional institutions which grew up during the Cold War focused not on rule-making but on discretionary collective management. The OECD pursued this task with admirable tact, being the more successful by staying out of the limelight. The G7 summits also focused on discretionary management and voluntary commitments. Inevitably, they became more prominent and controversial. The summits had some notable successes. But their promise of collective management sometimes took authority away from wider, more established bodies. They were confronted with an ever increasing agenda of problems which had defied treatment elsewhere.

With the range of new issues which surfaced as the Cold War ended, the load on the summits became intolerable, as the previous chapter showed. The 1991 London III summit, for example, had at least five major problems on its plate: sluggish growth in the West; the economic consequences of the Gulf crisis; the approach of the UN Environment Conference (UNCED) in Rio; the failure to complete the Uruguay Round; and the economic disintegration of the USSR. This was clearly too much for the leaders to settle in a two-day meeting, however good the preparations. Much the same happened at Munich in 1992. By the Tokyo summit of July 1993 all the leaders were fully aware of the overload on the summit's apparatus and were looking for a way out. The time was thus ripe for a new look at international institutions and their responsibilities.

Moving to a Rule-Based International System

The main conclusions of this analysis are:-

- The Western alliance against the Soviet military threat helped to dampen economic disputes. This ceased to apply once the Cold War ended.
- Rivalry with the East encouraged international competition in the West, with good effects on growth.
- In the process, national governments steadily lost control over economic policies. This was exposed once security policies, which they could control, became less important.
- The Cold War had split apart the international economic system. It could now come together again, with the open liberal approach prevailing.

- International rule-making institutions, except at regional level, had tended to lose authority during the Cold War. But the alternative institutions of discretionary collective management could no longer stand the strain.

The rest of this chapter examines how the end of the Cold War opened new prospects for:-

- First, restoring a rule-based system of international economic relations.
- Second, creating a network of truly universal international economic institutions.

The Merit of Rules

Governments had, for the best of reasons, given up most of their independence of action in economic policy. They could no longer claim to manage their economics, because anything they did could be upset by actions outside their borders. In these conditions, what should governments do to exercise the responsibility laid on them by their voters?

At one extreme, governments could try to reassert control by shutting out unwelcome international competition, especially from those who seemed the greatest threat. This could provide temporary relief. But inevitably firms sheltered from competition let prices rise and quality fall. Jobs would be protected which should be shifted into more efficient sectors. Over time this would be no solution.

At the other extreme, governments could withdraw altogether and leave everything to the market, on the grounds that markets were self-regulating. But this too would be dangerous. All markets, including international markets, were subject to abuse, of which the most damaging was abuse by predatory monopolies. Markets too worked in a Darwinian way, by survival of the fittest. But governments rightly felt a responsibility towards those in difficulty.

A third approach would focus on international economic policy coordination - a form of discretionary collective management. The aim would be for governments, acting in concert, to ensure that their powers applied internationally rather than stopping at their borders. But experience, especially at the G7 summits, showed that the world was not ready for this. Systematic coordination demanded greater commitments than governments could deliver and a greater surrender of independence than they could tolerate. Ad hoc voluntary coordination proved to be very laborious and to exert inadequate pressure on the participants. The prospects of success receded as more and more countries became active in the world economy and needed to take part. Policy coordination was a valuable discipline, but it was yielding diminishing returns.[5]

Governments, however, did not need to be economic actors or managers; they could instead be umpires or judges. They could no longer wholly determine whether their economies achieved less or more, but they could determine right and wrong. They could promote and apply a system of international economic rules which sustained and extended open competition, but would check and penalise abuses, provide safety-valves and help those in difficulty. Such rules would deter any government from tolerating on its territory economic practices which were unacceptable elsewhere. They would determine conditions under which governments could take temporary relief if competitive pressures became intolerable. Such a system would not require the international community to intervene constantly, but only when needed to enforce the rules and resolve disputes.

Trade and the GATT

The best way of explaining this approach is to look at the GATT, the only part of the post-war rule-making apparatus to survive intact and in good order. The GATT could provide the pattern for a rule-based system covering other economic subjects. As founded in 1948 and developed thereafter, it consisted of two elements.

The first element comprised a set of rules governing trade restrictions between members, plus a mechanism for settling disputes. The GATT accepted that restrictions existed, but it required that they should be non-discriminatory between members. Likewise, trade preferences were permitted only under certain conditions. The basic principle was that trade worked best when conditions of competition were equal.

The second element was a mechanism for the progressive removal of trade restrictions, on a reciprocal basis. The removal of restrictions should be permanent, but they could be put back temporarily, without discrimination, in case of severe need. The GATT did not oblige its members to conduct unrequited trade liberalisation, even though many did this and benefitted from it. The GATT's approach reassured its members that, as the world trading system became progressively more open and free from restrictions, the conditions of competition would remain equal.

The GATT first concentrated on bringing down tariffs from the high levels reached during World War II and had great success in this, up to 1980. Thereafter the issues became much more complex. Governments were resorting to other forms of trade restrictions than tariffs. Entire areas of trade were escaping GATT rules, both traditional areas, such as agriculture and textiles, and new areas, notably trade in services and intellectual property. Many more countries became active in world trade and in the GATT itself. These included both developing countries and, most recently, East European countries, for whom rising trade with new partners offered the best route to a prosperous market economy. Finally, the GATT's own institutions needed strengthening, particularly to make its dispute settlement more effective. The objective of the Uruguay Round of trade negotiations, which began in 1986, was to bring the GATT up to date by extending it and strengthening it in all these ways.

The Uruguay Round was meant to finish in December 1990. In fact, it was only completed three years later after two extensions of the United States' negotiating authority. Its completion gave a strong non-inflationary boost to the world economy. This was not only from the progressive removal of trade restrictions, but also from the return to a regime of certainty in world trade. This stimulus to the world economy was not the greatest benefit of completing the successful Round. At a late stage negotiators decided to transform the GATT into the World Trade Organization (WTO). The WTO would provide the first and strongest pillar of a rule-based international system adapted to post-Cold War economic conditions. It would maintain international disciplines which bore directly on domestic policies and compensated for governments' loss of economic independence. Such disciplines would apply, for example, to industrial subsidies. They would apply to agriculture, in order to break down the opaque and Byzantine methods used to support agriculture by almost all governments. They would apply very much to trade in services, such as banking, insurance and telecommunications, and to intellectual property, which were all subject to domestic regulation rather than to border restrictions. The significance of the Uruguay Round and its results will be examined in detail in the next chapter.

Investment

The Uruguay Round was intended to create or reinforce rules for trade in both goods and services. But other areas demanded similar attention. Two examples were foreign direct investment and the environment.

While cross-border trade grew very strongly in the 1960s and 1970s as tariffs came down, in the 1980s the most vigorous advance was in foreign direct investment. This became one of the most striking indicators of interdependence. In 1990 the stock of foreign investment was three times its level in 1980, while merchandise trade had only grown by 75 per cent. Already in the mid-1980s, foreign sales by American, Japanese and European companies established abroad were well in excess of national exports - for the United States they were four times greater. Cross-border trade or investment with local production had become equal alternatives for transnational companies.[6]

Direct investment was put on the agenda for the Uruguay Round in 1986. The same sort of international rules were needed for investment as the GATT applied for trade. Any new regime should provide for a standstill on existing restrictions, for non-discrimination, for dispute settlement, and for the reciprocal removal of obstacles to investment in a way which could not be reversed. But the climate was much less welcoming in many countries for investment than for trade, so that progress in the Round was limited. The need for such rules did not diminish during the 1990s, as foreign direct investment continued to grow strongly, but negotiating them would not prove easy. A move to conclude a Multilateral Agreement on Investment in the OECD collapsed in 1998, while progress in the WTO was very slow.[7]

Environment

The creation of international instruments for the environment only began in the late 1980s. But there were some encouraging pointers that a rule-based system for handling global environmental issues was emerging. With some environmental issues, like river pollution, international damage was confined to close neighbours. But many problems affected the ecological balance of the entire planet: damage to the ozone layer; climate change; and loss of biodiversity. The international response to these global problems, much of which came together at the Rio UNCED Conference of June 1992, laid the foundations of a system which reflected the changes in the post-Cold War world.

The main aspects were:-

- The new regimes were truly universal, in a way which would have been impossible while the Cold War was on. It was recognised that all countries must take part, or the global response would be ineffective. The active involvement of large, populous but poor countries, like China, India and Brazil, was encouraging. Russia and the East Europeans, whose environmental record had been lamentable, were fully engaged. There was also a new stimulus to UN bodies, notably the UN Environment Programme (UNEP).
- For each global issue the international system was based on a set of rules and commitments embodied in binding conventions - the Montreal protocol for the ozone layer and the two Rio conventions for climate change and biodiversity. In due course further

conventions, for example on forest management and deserts, would follow.

- The commitments in these conventions were not expected to be achieved by controls and regulations alone. Such a restrictive approach would not be tolerable for developing countries seeking to expand their economic output and their energy use as they aspired to Western levels of prosperity. So there was a premium on environmental policies which also made good economic sense and would work with markets. Partly through financial assistance and partly through the application of new technology, countries were encouraged to economise in energy and the use of resources.

These instruments, though only a beginning, moved the international environmental system in a good direction. Though there were subsequent setbacks and disappointments, the underlying principles were maintained and were not called in question.[8]

Monetary and Financial Relations

International monetary and financial relations were much more intractable. In some financial areas the development of open and rule-based regimes made good progress, for example in banking supervision and in the fight against money laundering. But in the international monetary and exchange rate regime there was no early advance, as a result of the end of the Cold War, which matched the progress in trade or the environment.

Since the introduction of floating regimes in the 1970s, the volume of transactions on the foreign exchange markets had risen inexorably. By 1993 it was estimated at about $1 trillion per day, having increased three-fold over the previous six years.[9] This was a rate of growth which far exceeded international trade or investment. With this enormous volume of daily transactions, governments and monetary authorities were becoming the prisoners of unwelcome market movements. Private companies were likewise victims - an unforeseen shift overnight in relative currency values could reverse the profits earned by a year's hard work. In trade, the greatest danger was from protectionism which made markets harden and contract. With monetary and financial transactions, the danger was the opposite - an unstoppable inflation, which no system of rules could withstand.

Only one international monetary arrangement sought to counter this accelerating volatility - the Exchange Rate Mechanism (ERM) of the European Monetary System. The ERM only covered all the key European currencies after Britain joined in 1990. When the UK was forced out after two years, it looked at first like a failure for British policy. In fact it was the first evidence of failure in the ERM itself, which proved unable to hold the European currencies together in a narrow band.

The end of the Cold War itself proved fatal for the ERM. As German policy for absorbing the GDR caused the Deutschemark to rise, other currencies could not respect the rules and the margins had to be widened. The ERM had always been vulnerable to external pressures, because it set rules only for relations between member currencies and not with others. When people moved out of US dollars into DM but not into other European currencies, that created severe tension within the ERM. This happened often in the early 1980s and contributed to the troubles of 1992. Any European monetary instrument which linked national currencies would need not just internal rules but a common attitude to other major currencies, notably the dollar and the yen. But if the European currencies were to take a common position against the dollar and the yen, it would not be desirable for them to act alone. Compatible moves by the Americans and the Japanese would be required. This would entail a system of international discipline on exchange rates, very different from what prevailed in the early 1990s. The attempts at exchange rate coordination at the Plaza and Louvre meetings of 1985-87 had been short-lived and led to disappointment.

The Europeans, in the Maastricht treaty of 1991, decided to move from linking national currencies to a single currency, which could not be split apart by external pressures. By 1993 the prospects for a rule-based international monetary system seemed to be receding. In fact, the pressures of international financial crises, first in Latin America and then in Asia, forced a reform of the system in the direction of tighter rules, as later chapters will describe.

Post -Cold War International Institutions

In the post-Cold War world there would be a single international economic system, not two or three rival systems. To handle that system the worldwide economic institutions needed to be capable both of meeting the requirements of larger membership and of dealing with a more demanding agenda.

In trade, as the next chapter explains, the GATT had been in training for this role throughout the Uruguay Round, leading up to its transformation into the WTO, with greatly enlarged responsibilities. These would encompass the agreed measures both in traditional GATT subjects and in the new ones like services and intellectual property. The WTO would bring together and reinforce the machinery for settling disputes in all these areas. The WTO would have virtually universal membership, lacking only Russia, China and Taiwan among major trading partners. There was no intention to dilute the contractual nature of GATT obligations for these and other new members. But the WTO would need to show itself as effective in enlarging market access for developing countries and for East Europeans as it had been for OECD members.

In the financial field, the Fund and the Bank together achieved worldwide membership by 1993. They were fully occupied in devising innovative programmes and facilities, such as the Systemic Transformation Facility (STF) to help the new members from the former Soviet Union and Eastern Europe establish market economies. That would be a major task and would take time. But it was similar to what the Fund and Bank had been doing in recent decades - i.e. providing assistance to economies in trouble. Economies not in trouble got much less evident benefit out of Fund membership. It would be a healthy development if the IMF went back to the rule-making and supervisory functions it filled up to 1970, as well as tightening its policy surveillance. This would be particularly helpful now that far more of its members were participating in the open economic and monetary system. It took the financial crises of the late 1990s to stimulate this sort of institutional reform in the Fund and Bank, leading to the 'new financial architecture' discussed in Chapter 11 below.

Specific parts of the UN family soon emerged as important players in the post-Cold War economic world. The institutions responsible for the environment did this. So too did those concerned with specific issues like population and drugs. But the UN itself found it hard to develop a coherent economic role. In contrast with its political side, centred on the Security Council, the economic and social side of the UN had no mandatory powers. Many of the things the UN might aspire to do would be better handled by the WTO, the Fund or the Bank, given that they now had universal membership. But there was one area where the UN itself could develop a useful economic role, thanks to its widening programme of peace-keeping operations. Peace-keeping and peace-making now involved humanitarian operations. Humanitarian aid in turn led to rehabilitation, while peace-making involved rebuilding the civil authority. The UN would be the best place to develop guidelines for this progression from conflict to civil peace, up to the point at which the traditional instruments of economic and technical assistance could take over.

There would thus be plenty of work for the global institutions to do, both on their own agenda and in providing the right framework for regional organisations to operate without creating suspicion. But what about the trans-regional bodies hitherto engaged in discretionary management? In particular, what would be the best contribution which the G7 summit could make?

New Directions for the Summits

Earlier analyses distinguished three approaches by the summit to the wider international context: as catalyst - exerting influence for change but remaining unaffected itself; as core group within wider organisations; or as giving parallel treatment to issues handled by other bodies. All three approaches persisted side-by-side up to the late 1980s and could never wholly be reconciled.[10] In the changed international context each of three approaches had to be reconsidered.

The attempt to give parallel treatment to issues had already contributed to the overload on the summits. It had led the summits to make commitments that later they were unable to deliver. This approach was defensible only in those cases where there was no competent international institution of wide membership to handle the issue.

The G7 as core group was also under challenge. The seven summit countries were no longer the undisputed leaders of the world economy. The 1993 World Development Report showed the G7 members losing ground to the growing economic weight of large populous countries like China, India, Brazil and Mexico, especially as they opened up their economies.[11]

The best approach for the summits from now on would be closest to that of catalyst. The summits should provide impulses to wider international institutions but should not dictate to them or try to do their work for them. This would allow for lighter preparation of the summits and for a more informal atmosphere at the meetings themselves. This was what the current generation of summit leaders wanted, as they demonstrated at Tokyo III in 1993 by their support for the ideas launched by John Major. It was what the founding fathers, Giscard and Schmidt, hoped for too, when they tried to rediscover their experience in the Library Group of finance ministers. Even in the 1970s, however, the leaders could not really expect to give directions to international bodies, while themselves remaining aloof and unaffected. This was even less credible in post-Cold War conditions. The G7 leaders would have to become less conscious of their own importance and more sensitive to the institutions they sought to influence. They would need to exercise tact and restraint to achieve and maintain this more austere approach to summitry.

Conclusion

This chapter has argued that the fundamental shifts generated and revealed by the end of the Cold War called for a network of international economic organisations of universal membership. Through these, governments could work to apply rules which would encourage the open economy, rather than trying to manage it collectively themselves. This process would help them reconcile international pressures with domestic responsibilities. The successful conclusion of the Uruguay Round (analysed further in the next chapter) could be the starting-point, which would provide hope for a prosperous world economy benefitting from the lessons of the Cold War. In this changed context the G7 summits could not expect to provide leadership through discretionary management, nor to stimulate the international system while remaining detached themselves. They would have to get closer to the global institutions and be more responsive to the concerns of their other members.

The conclusion of the Uruguay Round did indeed mark a change in the pattern of the summits, following some of the trends and recommendations identified here. From 1994 onwards, the summits began to give much more systematic attention to their contribution to the work of other institutions. They began to focus on the implications of globalisation, both for themselves and other players in the world economy. While the fourth summit series generated mounting frustration among the leaders, the fifth series, starting in 1994, marked a revival of the G7 process. This will be explored from Chapter 8 onwards.

Notes

1 This chapter is drawn from 'International Relations after the Cold War', *Government and Opposition,* vol. 29 no. 1 (Bayne 1994). This article was an edited version of my *Government and Opposition*/Leonard Schapiro lecture, given at the LSE in November 1993 as the Uruguay Round was approaching its climax.

2 The breadth of structural policy discussion, especially in the OECD, is well brought out in Henderson 1993.

3 The distinction is spelt out in Shonfield 1976a, pp. 131-136.

4 Tensions between regional trading arrangements and the global system are analysed in Cable and Henderson 1994; see also Chapter 7 below.

5 Two contrasting views of economic policy coordination around this time are given in Dobson 1991 and Bergsten and Henning 1996. Wendy Dobson, drawing on her experience in government, gives a balanced judgement of what can and cannot be done. Fred Bergsten and Randall Henning have higher expectations and are more critical of lack of achievement.

6 Julius 1990 gives a good analysis of these trends in the 1980s, especially Chapter 4 and Table 4.4.

7 . Despite the problems on agreeing on a WTO regime for all investment, the provisions of the General Agreement on Trade in Services (GATS) concluded in the Uruguay Round cover investment as well as trade. Many countries are readier to make commitments in investment than in cross-border services trade.

8   Kokotsis 1999 gives useful background to the growth of international action on the environment, in the context of G7 summit compliance in this field.

9   Estimates given in *Financial Times,* 26 May 1993, Survey on Foreign Exchange, p. 1.

10 This analysis is developed in Putnam and Bayne 1987, pp. 155-158.

11 See World Development Report 1993, Table 30. The argument about G7 membership is developed in *The Economist,* 10 July 1993, p. 67.

7 Internationalising Domestic Policy: The Uruguay Round

The removal of barriers to international trade was a powerful stimulus to economic growth in the period since World War II. World trade grew on average two per cent faster than GNP throughout this period. Countries which deliberately sought to make themselves competitive externally grew much faster than countries which relied on their domestic market. By contrast, communist countries, where the system discouraged external trade, fell steadily behind. The consequence for most countries was that a steadily growing share of their economy was exposed to international competition.

But because trade was a competitive activity, the contest between 'winners' and 'losers' all too easily obscured the general benefit of removing trade barriers. Governments would intervene at home to save potential losers or support potential winners. They would complain abroad if they thought their trading partners were acting unfairly, either to discriminate against imports or to boost exports. As the scope of international competition increased, so did the potential for trade disputes. Policies formerly determined wholly by domestic factors now came under international scrutiny.

Removing barriers to trade had also been a force for creating closer political links between countries. The most striking evidence of this was in the development of the European Community (EC), which began with the Common Commercial Tariff and followed it with the Single Market campaign. In international trade the competence of the Community was undisputed and national 'sovereignty' had largely disappeared. Removing trade barriers was also used worldwide as an instrument of foreign policy as, for example, the EC sought closer relations with Mediterranean countries or the United States with its Latin American neighbours.

Yet while trade relations could bind countries together politically, they could also divide them. Trade disputes could infect the overall relationship between countries, and the risk of this increased as trade and domestic economic policies became harder to disentangle. Furthermore, if countries saw less need to unite against a common adversary, that removed a constraint on allowing trade disputes to spill over into political relations.

The General Agreement on Tariffs and Trade (GATT), based in Geneva, had been at the centre of these currents since its foundation in 1948. It was responsible for setting and keeping the rules of international trade and promoting the removal of barriers to trade on a worldwide scale. It pursued the task of trade liberalisation by successive rounds of multilateral negotiations among its members. The eighth such round was launched at Punta del Este in Uruguay in 1986 and was thus called 'the Uruguay Round'. It should have been completed at a ministerial conference in Brussels in December 1990. But that conference broke up without reaching agreement. The Round had to be extended for another three years of often tense negotiation before finally concluding in December 1993. In the process the GATT decided to convert itself into the World Trade Organization (WTO).

This chapter looks at the Uruguay Round as an example of the growing internationalisation of domestic economic policy.[1] The Round served as a bridge between the limited interdependence possible while the Cold War lasted and the full globalisation which developed once it was over. The G7 summits contributed to the outcome of the Round, as Chapter 4 has shown, in pursuit of their aim of reconciling domestic and international pressures. The summits had not yet recognised the advance of globalisation, first evoked explicitly by the Naples summit of 1994. This chapter concludes, however, that the successful completion of the Uruguay Round was an early example of the beneficial impact of globalisation.

How the GATT worked

The GATT, like the IMF and the World Bank, was born from the great post-war surge in international institution-building. As outlined in the previous chapter, it combined two roles. First, it embodied a set of rules, to which all its members subscribed, together with procedures for settlement of disputes. The dominant principle was non-discrimination. The GATT did not prevent its members from maintaining trade restrictions, provided they applied to all trading partners and did not discriminate against any of them. It allowed trade preferences to be given to some countries and not others only on certain conditions, to ensure that such arrangements expanded trade overall and did not raise new barriers. The underlying conviction was that trade was encouraged most when conditions of competition were equal.[2]

Secondly, the GATT provided a mechanism for lowering barriers to trade. For this role, the GATT's basic principle was active reciprocity. The preamble to the Treaty spoke of 'entering into reciprocal and mutually advantageous arrangements directed to the substantial reduction of tariffs and other barriers to trade'. The GATT did not make much of the argument that the removal of trade restrictions brought economic benefit to a country even if unrequited by others. It recognised that, while many governments would accept that argument as true, few would base their policy upon it. Most would only lower their barriers if they saw their other partners doing the same.

In its early years, the GATT concentrated on lowering tariffs, on a reciprocal basis, and 'binding' those that remained. Binding tariffs at the lower level prevented countries from raising them again. Seven rounds of tariff-cutting negotiations, held between 1947 and 1979, brought the average level of tariffs in industrial countries down to only 4.5 per cent. Tariffs were no longer the principal obstacle to trade. So, in the seventh of these rounds, the Tokyo Round which ran from 1973 to 1979, the GATT began to address a wider range of issues. It tried to discipline other government actions affecting trade, such as export subsidies, standards and government procurement. It sought to strengthen its own rules permitting trade restrictions in certain conditions: safeguards against sudden import surges; and action against the dumping of exports at below their domestic price.

The Tokyo Round expanded the GATT's responsibilities. But it was not adequate to counter the serious challenge to the GATT which developed during the turbulent 1970s and continued to grow in the recession of the early 1980s. This challenge had several sources:-

- Now that tariffs were bound at such low levels, governments under pressure were tempted to use other measures of protection less compatible with GATT rules.
- The Tokyo Round and its predecessors were largely concerned with trade in manufactured goods and non-agricultural commodities, leaving aside the controversial area of agriculture and the growing sector of trade in services.
- The developing countries played little part in the Tokyo Round. But certain of these countries, especially in the Far East, were becoming highly competitive participants in world trade.

Therefore, once the world economy began to recover from recession, the pressure mounted for a new, more comprehensive round. This would have four broad aims: to close, or at least to control, the loopholes by which trade restrictions escaped the authority of the GATT; to continue liberalising trade in goods, bringing fully under GATT discipline the two key areas of agriculture and textiles; to extend GATT rules and liberalisation to new areas - trade in services, intellectual property, investment; and to strengthen the GATT as an institution.

The Uruguay Round, after a difficult gestation, was launched in September 1986 with a far-reaching agenda and a four-year timetable. The US Trade Act of 1988, which gave the Administration its negotiating authority, reinforced this timetable. Provided an agreement was laid before Congress by 1 March 1991, Congress was obliged either to accept or to refuse this agreement, and could not modify it. This was the so-called 'fast-track' authority. Because the Round ran so much over time, this authority had to be extended twice - once by Bush and again by Clinton - before the final conclusion in December 1993.

Internationalising Domestic Policy

The tensions between domestic and external economic policy generated by the negotiations did much to explain why the Round took so long to complete. As trade grew faster than output over the post-war period, the price of greater prosperity was a loss of direct control by national governments over the levers of policy. Even while the Cold War persisted, the interdependence of the industrial economies meant that domestic decisions were constrained by events in the wider world. The more competitive parts of economies thrived in this situation. But the weaker parts suffered and looked to their governments for help. Governments recognised the benefits of free trade but faced growing demands for protection from sectoral lobbies, often with great political power. In these conditions the GATT had to go beyond reducing tariffs. It had to tighten its own rules; induce the reform of domestic regulation; and overcome the pressure of special interests.

Tightening the Rules

The GATT sanctioned two forms of exceptional protection. *Safeguards* might be applied against sudden import surges, but only against all importers, not against a specific country. They were therefore rarely used. (During the Tokyo Round the EC had argued for a 'selective safeguard', but others resisted so open an exception to the principle of non-discrimination.) *Anti-dumping* action might be taken against specific countries, if dumping by them could be proved. Such action was widely used by the US and the EC against their Far Eastern competitors, but only affected a small fraction of trade - about one per cent for the EC.

Since these permitted loopholes were inadequate, governments resorted widely to 'grey area measures' of protection, contrary to the spirit of GATT if not expressly forbidden. These were quantitative restrictions or market-sharing arrangements, often introduced by non-governmental bodies or adopted voluntarily by exporting governments for fear of something worse. By 1985 products affected by such measures accounted for around 30 per cent of the consumption of manufactures in industrial countries. Steel, cars, textiles, footwear and consumer electronics were particularly affected.[3]

Both the growth of trade and the authority of GATT were undermined by the spread of this kind of protection. The Uruguay Round needed to bring large areas of trade back under open, non-discriminatory rules and to ensure that these rules were respected. The negotiators had to strike a balance between rules so strict that governments looked for ways to avoid their GATT obligations and loopholes so wide that the value of the GATT discipline was eroded.

Reforming Domestic Regulation.

As international competition spread, more domestic policies affected trade and thus came under the eye of the GATT. In contrast to tariffs, applied in percentage terms to a standard classification of goods, these policies differed widely between countries and their impact on trade was often contested. Even where admitted, this impact was difficult to measure, as the trade barriers created were qualitative, not quantitative. Their removal was not easily phased, as tariff cuts could be. All this made it hard to construct reciprocal packages of liberalising measures which each party would regard as having equal value.

The new areas like services illustrated the problem. Services had come to provide 50 to 70 per cent of economic activity in developed countries, far more than manufacturing. International trade in services was estimated at about 25 per cent of trade in goods, but could well be more, as services statistics were very unreliable. Service activities were very varied, embracing banking, insurance, transport, tourism, telecommunications and professional services. In every sector restrictions to external competition were applied through the regulations for doing business, such as rights of establishment or the acceptance of professional qualifications. The regulations were normally justified in terms of domestic objectives, such as the sound prudential supervision of banks or the protection of consumers. But they could still clearly discriminate against foreign suppliers.

Agriculture presented special difficulty, not only from the nature of the domestic regulations but from their extent. Virtually all developed countries supported and protected their agriculture extensively and all in different ways. The result was chronic over-supply and depressed prices in the world market. The cost of government intervention, to consumers and taxpayers in the OECD countries, had risen through the 1980s to come close to $300 billion in 1990. But little of this was actually reaching the farmers it was intended to help.[4]

Though a few countries provided even higher levels of protection, the most controversial system was the Common Agricultural Policy (CAP) of the European Community. For the most important products this had three main elements:-

- Controlled internal prices, usually well above world prices, with an obligation on the Community to buy products into stock unsold at this price.
- Community preference, using levies which varied with the world price to bring the cost of imports to the level of internal prices.
- Export restitutions, which offset the difference between EC and world prices so that EC exports remained competitive in world markets.

Action to lower import protection or export subsidy tended to increase the amount the EC had to buy into stock, so that any benefit to consumers was balanced by a loss to taxpayers. This meant that simply addressing trade barriers would be ineffective in attacking agricultural protection. The Uruguay Round negotiators had to address the domestic support measures themselves.

Overcoming special interests

The GATT negotiations were also vulnerable to the dilemma which affects so many reform programmes: the asymmetrical distribution of benefits and costs. The benefits of removing protection and increasing competition were greater in aggregate: lower prices and public spending; and a shift of labour and capital from inefficient to efficient sectors. But these benefits were spread widely through the economy as a whole. The advantages of protection were concentrated in the sector being protected. So the lobbies in favour of protection were more vocal and better organised, because their very livelihood might be at stake.

One method used to resolve this dilemma was to raise the political level of the international debate. Heads of government could combine to assert the benefits of the open trading system and together resist the pressures which ministers with sectoral responsibilities find hard to escape.

This was part of the original rationale for the G7 summits. The summits regularly asserted their resistance to protectionism and sought to encourage any GATT negotiations in progress. But even heads of government were not immune from the political tensions between external and domestic policies - between promoting competition and protecting specific sectors.

The record of the summits was positive, but uneven. The Bonn I summit of 1978 had given a successful impulse to the closing stages of the Tokyo Round. The 1986 Tokyo II summit was influential in ensuring that agriculture found its place in the Uruguay Round and Venice II 1987 and Toronto 1988 maintained the pressure. By contrast the second Bonn summit of 1985 was spoiled by an argument about when the Uruguay Round should begin.

As the Uruguay Round moved towards its planned completion, the Houston summit, in July 1990, sought to give a strong impetus to the Uruguay Round, to bring it to a successful conclusion by the end of the year. But the summit's message, especially in agriculture, contained too much ambiguity and was inadequate to avert the breakdown in December. The Uruguay Round was back on the agenda for the London III summit in 1991 and the Munich summit in 1992. Each time the leaders again pledged themselves to complete the Round by the year's end; and each time they failed because of disputes between the G7 members. Only in 1993 did the Tokyo III summit exert enough pressure to clinch a G7 deal on market access and create the momentum for the final conclusion.

Strengthening the Multilateral System

By the time of the Uruguay Round, the GATT was not only threatened by unilateral measures of domestic protection. It was also at risk when major trading powers conducted their trading relations on a bilateral or a regional basis, in opposition to the multilateral system. Both bilateralism and regionalism could depress world trade, as either single countries or whole regions became embroiled in disputes and raised barriers against each other. However, the end of the Cold War created a new opportunity to restore the GATT at the centre of a truly global system for rule-based international trade.

Bilateralism

The country most strongly tempted by bilateralism was the United States. The Administration was traditionally committed to the open trading system, but was obliged to respond to protectionist pressure from Congress, which in turn was exposed to local, sectoral lobbies. Congress argued that certain other countries unfairly kept out American products and services and that the GATT was powerless to prevent this. So the 1988 Trade Act gave the Administration much stronger powers to identify countries restricting access to specific US products and services and to insist that these countries provide redress within a fixed timetable or face retaliation. The Act increased the obligation on the Administration to make use of these powers.

This bilateral approach was arguably better than unilateral protection. It invoked the principle of reciprocity enshrined in the GATT. The intention was to force other countries to reduce their barriers. The Americans could point to some success in this direction, which had sometimes benefitted not just the US but other trading partners too. But GATT's multilateral reciprocity worked only one way, to reduce protection. Bilateral reciprocity could work both ways. It could equally well lead to higher trade barriers and less trade. It put the decision in the hands of a single power, acting as both judge and prosecutor, rather than a multilateral process. If others were to follow the US example, it would undermine the GATT and depress world trade. It was therefore necessary to strengthen the GATT as a rule-making and dispute-resolving body, to reduce the incentive to resort to bilateralism.

Regionalism

Regional trade arrangements were widespread and growing by the late 1980s; for example, in Europe between the EC and EFTA and in North America between the US, Canada and Mexico. Malaysia proposed a new regional grouping for East Asia. These trends were sometimes used to justify the claim that the world trading system was splitting into three rival regional blocs, one based on Europe, one on the US and one on Japan.

If the threat of bilateralism was greatest from the US, the danger of regionalism was most plausibly attributed to the European Community. During the 1960s and 1970s the EC did adopt something of a regional approach, which relied heavily on preferential trade agreements and led to some difficult negotiations in the GATT. But as overall tariff levels came down, these agreements became much less of a cause of friction.

The campaign to complete the Single European Market aroused new fears that as the barriers came down within Europe they would be raised against the rest of the world, to create a 'Fortress Europe'. In fact, the development of the single market largely removed the grounds for these fears. The removal of barriers within Europe was making it easier to do business there, not just for European firms, but for all firms present in the Community. In banking, for example, foreign banks established in one member state could obtain a 'passport' to operate elsewhere in the Community, like European banks. Residual bilateral trade restrictions were being removed, as being incompatible with the single market. The coincidence of the single market campaign and the Uruguay Round proved helpful, in both directions. It reminded the EC of the need to respect its wider multilateral obligations; and it enabled the Community to contribute to the liberalising process, notably in services.

Regional trading arrangements were unlikely to turn into exclusive rival blocs as long as the multilateral system was in good condition. The rules of the GATT required that such arrangements were trade-creating and did not raise new barriers. A successful Uruguay Round, which strengthened the authority of the GATT, was needed to keep regional arrangements benign.

The Merits of Multilateralism

There were wider economic and political advantages in preserving and strengthening the multilateral trading system. Developing countries took little part in the earlier GATT rounds. The Tokyo Round coincided with the heyday of the New International Economic Order, when some developing countries sought to advocate a rival system, based on government intervention and regulation. But during the 1980s many developing countries moved to adopt more liberal trade and investment policies. The dynamic economies of East Asia were followed by countries in Latin America and Africa, on the advice of the World Bank. The developing countries played an active and influential part in the Uruguay Round. This was to the mutual interest of all GATT members. The developing countries themselves saw improved access to Western markets for their products as the key to their future prosperity. As for the industrial nations, they sought to convince the developing countries to observe international rules in the new areas of services, investment and intellectual property.

Hitherto the states of Eastern Europe had been outside GATT or, if inside, gained little benefit because of their distorted trading patterns and special terms of membership. But as part of their political and economic reforms they needed to re-orient their trade so as to escape from the old CMEA regime, which was fast collapsing. They therefore moved to become active GATT members. Behind them, China and Russia also looked forward to membership, though both had further to go. The completion of the Uruguay Round therefore encouraged the shift, by developing countries and East European states alike, towards more open, market-based economies and more democratic political systems, expanding their common interest with the industrialised West.

The Uruguay Round Agreements

If the Round had concluded in December 1990, the agreements struck would have had many loose ends. As it was, the extension into 1991 allowed many of these to be tied down, so that the GATT Director-General, Arthur Dunkel, could produce a consolidated text by the end of the year. But the Uruguay Round envisaged a single undertaking, so that nothing was agreed until everything was agreed. Other subjects were placed in suspense until the US and EC could strike a deal on agriculture. On this the breakthrough came at the Blair House agreement of November 1992. The Tokyo market access deal of June 1993 removed the last major obstacle. The final spurt of negotiations up until December 1993, driven on by Dunkel's successor Peter Sutherland, yielded some substantial advances, especially in institutional matters. As a result, the final package was much richer than anything envisaged in 1990. The agreements which GATT ministers signed in Marrakesh in April 1994 covered 26,000 pages and weighed 200 kilos.[5]

Some of the agreements covered GATT subjects familiar from the Tokyo Round and earlier, such as market access and trade rules. Others dealt with areas which penetrated deep into domestic policy: subsidies, agriculture and the new issues of services and intellectual property. A third group concerned the future institutions responsible for world trade.

Market Access and Trade Rules

These issues covered the GATT's traditional area of trade in goods, where the developing countries especially looked for movement from their Western partners. The most important advance in market access was the agreement on restoring trade in *textiles* to normal GATT rules. Imports of textiles and clothing from developing into developed countries had been governed for many years by a rigid and discriminatory system of quotas under the Multi-Fibre Arrangement (MFA). This reduced the prospects for efficient producers in the developing world to expand their trade. The new agreement provided for the MFA to be phased out over a long transitional period, with a special safeguard against sudden import surges. This was intended to allow time for adjustment for those developed countries that still had large textile industries. Studies of the textile industry in the UK showed that protection preserved jobs only at considerable cost.[6] Useful progress was also made in improving access for *tropical products* of interest to developing countries.

In *tariffs*, the results were disappointing until the final year. Since average tariffs were so low, the EC proposed deep cuts in the remaining high tariff peaks. But the US preferred to advocate zero tariffs for some major industrial products. A combination of these two approaches was only achieved at the meeting of the Quad (the trade ministers of US, Japan, Canada and European Commission) in Tokyo in June 1993, when the need to report a successful deal to the G7 summit a few days later concentrated their minds.[7] In consequence, tariffs were cut by an average of one-third (bringing the mean tariff in industrial countries down to 3.5 per cent) and reduced to zero for some key categories, like chemicals.

The GATT's rules were strengthened and given more authority to check abuses by a new agreement on *safeguards*. The EC abandoned its demands for selective application in return for a renunciation by all of 'grey area measures'. Progress on *anti-dumping* action was less decisive. But a deal was struck which enabled anti-dumping action to be somewhat more tightly controlled and harder to circumvent.

Disciplining Domestic Policy:
A   Subsidies

The agreement on *industrial subsidies* was a great advance. Unlike the voluntary code produced by the Tokyo Round, it applied to all GATT members. It established a classification of subsidies in the light of their impact on trade, using the analogy of traffic lights. 'Green' subsidies were permitted as supporting policies like regional development; 'red' subsidies, with clear trade-distorting effects, were forbidden; and 'amber' subsidies were permitted but open to challenge. If another GATT member could show that its trade was damaged, the subsidy had to be amended.

B   New Areas: Services, Intellectual Property, Investment

Services, intellectual property and - to a certain extent - investment were being brought under GATT for the first time. The first objective was to formulate multilateral rules and to provide for the settlement of disputes. Good progress was made in this for services and intellectual property. The second objective was to begin removing barriers to trade. This inevitably made less progress, since it depended on the rules being in place. In each area the US was the strongest advocate. Many developing countries were initially nervous about what they were expected to take on, but recognised the merits of including these subjects as the negotiations progressed.

In *services*, a wide consensus was reached on a 'General Agreement on Trade in Services' (GATS), containing a framework of rules based on the central GATT concept of non-discrimination. The framework covered investment as well as cross-border trade in services, but needed to be supplemented by provisions for specific sectors, with no service sector excluded *a priori*. As the negotiations approached their conclusion, the Americans became worried that in offering access to their market on a non-discriminatory basis they would give away too much when other countries' regimes were less liberal than their own. They argued that new rules were inadequate without more progress in removing restrictions on services trade; and that non-discriminatory access should only be extended conditionally. In order to reassure them, others began to offer initial commitments to open their markets in specific sectors. But the Americans were not wholly convinced of the value of the offers on the table by December 1993. The negotiations in three important sectors - basic telecommunications, financial services and maritime transport - were continued after the conclusion of the Round.[8]

The aim of the negotiations on *intellectual property* was to obtain better protection for copyright, trademarks and patents. Here too the negotiators came to an accord on new rules which would define common standards, provide for action against abuses and set up machinery for dispute settlement. In itself the agreement would not remove restrictions on trade. But the new rules could serve to encourage both trade and investment. Negotiations on *investment* rules as such, however, made only limited progress, going little beyond what was already in the original GATT Treaty.

C   Agriculture

Though not a new subject for the GATT, like services or intellectual property, agriculture had never come fully under GATT disciplines. It was always expected to be the most difficult issue, and so it proved. But many countries saw little merit in the Round without an agreement on agriculture. This especially applied to the Cairns Group of agricultural exporters, which linked Australia, Canada and New Zealand with a range of developing and East European countries.

A successful negotiation on agriculture had to address domestic support measures as well as agricultural trade policies. As the Round began, the OECD developed a new technique for calculating agricultural support from all sources on the basis of common units of measurement called 'Producer Subsidy Equivalent' (PSE) and 'Consumer Subsidy Equivalent' (CSE). This permitted comparisons to be made between countries, despite the differences in their support policies. It made it easier to envisage concerted reductions in support and protection, to which all could contribute equitably.

The EC combined and adapted the PSE and CSE into an Aggregate Measure of Support (AMS) to form the basis for its proposal in the GATT for domestic price reductions. Other major participants were prepared to do the same. Though positions were divided on the depth of cut in domestic support and the duration of the agreement, it looked as if conditions existed for striking a deal. The Houston summit of July 1990, with great difficulty, hammered out a formula intended to advance the negotiations on this basis.

But serious problems emerged when the EC argued against separate commitments on imports and exports. Because lower prices would mean reduced output, the EC claimed that this of itself would expand the market for imports and reduce the amounts attracting export refunds, as well as the scale of the refunds themselves. This was a logical position, given the structure of the CAP. But it did not meet the expectations of agricultural-exporting countries, which had suffered too long from barriers to the EC market and competition from subsidised European exports. The offer prepared by the EC, with intense difficulty, was rejected by the other parties at the Brussels conference in December 1990, which broke up in disorder.

In the hectic conditions at Brussels the EC had been brought to add some initial proposals on imports and exports. Early in 1991, with an eye to ensuring that the US Administration renewed its fast-track authority, the EC went further and agreed, with others, to negotiate specific commitments in each of the three areas of domestic support, import access and export subsidies. The separate decision by the European Commission to initiate a fundamental reform of the CAP also greatly improved the atmosphere.

It still took two more years before the agriculture agreement took shape. Import and export regimes were relatively straightforward. Import barriers were converted to tariff equivalents - a familiar GATT technique - and then had to be reduced progressively over time. Export subsidies likewise had to be reduced progressively - both the cost of subsidies and the volume of subsidised exports. But progress in these two areas only made the EC more concerned about the structure of the agreement on domestic support. An EC/US deal - the Blair House agreement - was only struck in November 1992, once the shape of the reformed CAP was clear. Even then France delayed its approval for many months.

The domestic support agreement, still based on the Aggregate Measure of Support, made use of the same technique as the subsidies agreement. Some types of support were 'red' and had to be reduced; this applied to export subsidies.   Some support was 'green' and could be maintained; this applied to income support for farmers and to 'set-aside', which were considered not to affect trade.   Other policies supporting prices or production were 'amber' and had to be reduced unless they could be shown not to distort trade.   This structure was compatible with the new CAP reforms, which would shift support from farm prices to farmers' incomes.   But as this would take time, a further category was needed.   Price support ('amber') policies which were due to be converted into income support or other 'green' policies were placed in a 'blue' box and were exempt from the obligation to reduce them.   This arrangement was not subject to challenge for nine years, while the other reductions required by the agreement would take place over six years.[9]

After their abortive intervention in 1990, the G7 summits never again ventured into the details of the agriculture negotiations.   But, on balance, their regular deadlines for concluding the Round, even if not met, prevented the negotiations from total impasse.   Bilateral exchanges between the G7 leaders often addressed GATT agriculture, right up to the end.

Institutional Issues

These became more important as the Round progressed and the summit provided essential impetus during this process.   The most important single achievement was agreement on strengthening the capacity of GATT in the *settlement of disputes*.   Hitherto the results of panels set up to resolve disputes had to be adopted by consensus, enabling the parties to the dispute to frustrate the outcome.   Under the new dispute settlement mechanism this possibility was removed and replaced by a limited right of appeal.   The US, at an early stage, associated itself with commitments to operate under the multilateral rules.   These commitments were regularly renewed by the G7 summits.   A stronger GATT dispute settlement mechanism would reduce the need for bilateral action and render superfluous the national powers given by the US Trade Acts.   In addition the GATT began holding regular reviews of national trade policies and developed closer contacts with the IMF and the World Bank.   All these decisions enhanced both the standing and the effectiveness of the GATT.

The Houston summit of 1990 first endorsed the idea of giving the GATT more solid legal foundations, converting it into a 'Multilateral Trade Organization' closer to the intentions of its post-war founders.   This process should ensure that all the agreements reached - those on trade in goods in the existing GATT plus the new agreements in services and intellectual property - would be brought together in a single coherent framework. Initially this institutional move was expected to follow the completion of the Round. But as time went by, it became incorporated in the final package. The negotiations therefore agreed in December 1993 to convert the GATT into the World Trade Organization (WTO). This embraced the agreements on the different subjects, both traditional and new. It incorporated features common to all, in particular the dispute settlement mechanism and provision for regular ministerial meetings. All WTO members had to subscribe to all the agreements. There were no special provisions exempting developing countries and no voluntary agreements except on government purchasing and civil aircraft. It was a complete transformation of the GATT.[10]

Conclusion: The Benefits of the Uruguay Round Agreements

The Uruguay Round proved by far the most significant advance in the international trading system. Each of the agreements reached had its imperfections and was the result of compromise. But together they added up to a very substantial and wide-ranging package. They restored the authority of the GATT and checked the erosion of its rules. They reduced trade barriers across a range of products. They brought important areas of trade and economic activity under international discipline for the first time, opening the prospect of reciprocal removal of restrictions in the years ahead. They had far greater participation than before of developing and former communist countries. The GATT, greatly strengthened as an institution, was transformed into the firmly based World Trade Organization, which would preside over a truly worldwide system.[11]

The benefits of this successful outcome spread more widely than the GATT, the WTO and the international trading system:-

- Increased trade, encouraged by the more effective rules and the removal of barriers achieved in the Round, could stimulate more growth with less inflation in the world economy. It would help to sustain a healthy recovery from the economic slowdown.

- The GATT had been the only international system of contractual economic obligations to survive the Cold War. Strengthening the GATT system and creating the WTO would encourage the treatment of other economic issues by reference to established rules rather than by discretionary management.

- A stronger international trading system would expand the growth potential for both developing countries and the former communist states of Eastern Europe. It would encourage them to adopt liberal economic policies internally, reinforce their political links with the industrial nations and strengthen their attachment to democracy and human rights.

- A successful Round would provide a useful component in a strong, cooperative relationship among the Western industrial democracies, a relationship based on the perception of shared interests rather than an alliance against an external threat.

Despite these manifest benefits, it often looked likely that the Round would collapse or suffer gradual erosion without final agreement, which would have been a serious setback. It would have opened the prospects of regional rivalries, of obstacles to growth and of trade disputes spilling over into political frictions. That governments would run these risks was evidence of the difficulty created by the internationalisation of domestic policy. The greatest problems in the negotiations arose between the G7 members, especially the US and the EC. The intervention of heads of government often failed to break the deadlock and sometimes even made things worse. But the practice of the leaders meeting together regularly, developed since 1975, made them understand the external consequences of their domestic positions and the damage done by protectionist policies. This helped to keep the Uruguay Round alive until the final conclusion could be reached.

The successful completion of the Uruguay Round was an example of the benign operation of globalisation following the end of the Cold War. The widespread adoption of open market-oriented policies and the extensive participation in the negotiations led to the conclusion of a much richer package of agreements than expected when the Round began in 1986. The opening of markets brought opportunities of greater prosperity to countries at all stages of development, by lowering costs, improving quality and choice and spreading the advantages of new technology. All this, though hard-won, demonstrated the beneficial side of globalisation. Later summits had to grapple with its darker side, especially in the financial system, as Chapter 11 will explain.

Notes

1   This chapter is drawn from 'In the Balance; the Uruguay Round of International Trade Negotiations', in *Government and Opposition*, vol. 26 no. 3, (Bayne 1991). This article was written while I was Economic Director at the FCO, when the fate of the Round was still uncertain. The chapter has been updated to reflect the full outcome of the negotiations as concluded in December 1993.

2   A brief account of the foundation and early years of the GATT is in Jackson 1998, chapter 2.

3   OECD 1985 gives details of the extent of protection in these manufacturing sectors.
4   The scale of support and over-supply is documented in OECD 1991.
5   A complete history of the Uruguay Round is in Croome 1995. The texts of the Agreements are accessible through the WTO's website, www.wto.org.
6   The key document was the Silberston report, produced for the British government in 1984 (Silberston 1984).
7   The Quadrilateral or 'Quad' of trade ministers was created by the Ottawa summit back in 1981. Because of Community competence in trade, only the European Commission took part, not the G7 European member governments. It became a useful instrument of coordination, at ministerial and official level, and its summit origins were largely forgotten.
8   For a detailed analysis of the results of the Round in services, see Hoekman 1995.
9   The course and outcome of the agriculture negotiations and the resulting agreement are explained fully in Wolfe 1998.
10   The institutional shape of the new WTO, including its dispute settlement mechanism, owes much to the sustained intellectual stimulus of Professor John Jackson of the University of Michigan (and lately Georgetown). See especially Jackson 1990, Jackson 1994 and Jackson 1998.
11   For an assessment of the results of the Round as a whole, see Schott 1994.

Part III
The Renewal of The Summit

8 The Reform of Other Institutions: The Fifth Series, 1994-97

At the time, the Naples summit of 1994 did not seem very different from its predecessors. Only with the passage of time can Naples be identified as a turning-point. It launched two trends of such importance that this summit must stand as the start of a new series:-

- The *first* trend was the gradual involvement of Russia as a participant, and not merely as a visitor to the summit.
- The *second* was the recognition of the impact of globalisation and an initial response. The Naples summit declaration contained the first reference to globalisation. The institutional review launched there was directly stimulated by it.

In fact, by turning their attention to other international bodies, the G7 leaders started to generate the renewal of their own institution. This renewal of the summit was not completed during the fifth series and continued during the sixth which began with Birmingham in 1998. A further innovation was the start of systematic treatment of structural economic and social issues, prepared before the summit by meetings of specialist ministers. These issues had long seemed suitable for summit treatment but tangible results were slow in coming.[1]

Political Leadership: Reshaping the Summit

The political shifts and realignments which began at the end of the fourth summit series (see Chapter 5) gathered pace in 1994-1997. Clinton was a much more active summit player than his predecessor Bush. His fortunes suffered in the Congressional elections of 1994, when the Republicans gained control of both houses of Congress. But they revived with his own re-election in 1996 and with sustained growth in the US economy. When Clinton hosted the 1997 summit in Denver the Americans adopted a tone of triumphalism which irritated the Europeans especially. The energetic Gaullist Jacques Chirac replaced the ailing Socialist Mitterrand as President of France in 1995, though Chirac had to accept a Socialist prime minister, Lionel Jospin, in 1997. Tony Blair arrived also in 1997 as the first Labour prime minister in Britain for 18 years. His centrist views brought him close to Clinton and Chrétien of Canada. Political upheavals persisted in Japan and Italy, though by the end Ryutaro Hashimoto and Romano Prodi looked well established. As the series concluded, Helmut Kohl was the last surviving G7 veteran and his days were numbered. The political balance of the group had moved further to the left and the newcomers were ready for innovation in the summit process.

The summit continued to be at the same time an institution and an anti-institution. This made it hard to pin down, but provided the secret of its survival. It had many of the attributes of established inter-governmental organisations meeting at head of government level, such as NATO or the European Union. But the summit was meant to be quite different from such meetings. It had been invented by Giscard and Schmidt, twenty years before, in rebellion against the formality of large international meetings, which had frustrated them when they were finance ministers. The founders wanted instead a direct, unscripted, unbureaucratic exchange between a few heads of government. Even in the 1990s, after many disappointments, the G7 heads of government longed for such a refreshing and stimulating encounter, of a kind they would never expect from a NATO summit or a European Council.

By 1994, however, the summit had moved a long way from this ideal. The fundamental reason for heads of government to meet had always been that they could reconcile the domestic and external pressures of national policy, in a way that other ministers could not. As the overlap between domestic and external policies increased with globalisation, so the requirement to reconcile conflicting pressures had grown, dragging heads of government into international disputes. But as economic levers passed from the hands of government into the private sector, so the ability of heads of government to determine policy and resolve disputes was eroded.

In consequence the agenda of the G7 summit had become hopelessly overloaded. The original list of topics was expanded to cover a growing range of new ones. An extra day of non-economic, foreign policy discussions had been added, complicated by the requirement to accommodate the presence of the visiting Russians. With this mass of intractable problems, it was hardly surprising if the summit leaders failed to agree or if understandings reached at the summit came apart later. But if the leaders tried to resolve matters and failed, this damaged their reputation and discredited the summit process.

The G7 heads of government began to share the dissatisfaction with the summit process already widespread in the media. John Major had started a movement to retrieve the informal, personal origins of the summit, which was strongly endorsed by the leaders in Tokyo in 1993 - see Chapter 5 above. Its three objectives were:-

- More informal and spontaneous discussions at the summit, with less ceremony;
- Lighter preparations and a shorter agenda;
- Shorter and simpler summit documents.

Considerable progress was made with the first objective, especially on reducing ceremonial. Though Silvio Berlusconi held the 1994 summit in a Renaissance palazzo in the major city of Naples, Chrétien in 1995 chose the medium-sized harbour town of Halifax, Nova Scotia, where the leaders, on their way to meetings, mingled with the local citizens and holiday makers, which they had never done before. They had one evening at the circus, but otherwise every minute spent together was used for discussion and every meal was a working meal. Chirac and Clinton maintained the pattern in the next two years. In particular Chirac abandoned the spectacle of the Mitterrand summits and moved from Paris to the provincial centre of Lyon.[2]

The leaders appreciated the growth of informal, spontaneous exchanges. But they carried two risks. The first was that the leaders simply focused on the crisis of the moment. At Halifax 1995, Bosnia dominated the political exchanges and even threatened to drive everything else off the summit agenda. Chechnya took up most of the time with Yeltsin, as Chechen terrorists had seized hostages in Boudonnovsk, though the G7 leaders wanted to express their anxieties about Russian policy in any event. Another terrorism crisis distracted Lyon in 1996, as US troops in Saudi Arabia had been attacked just before the summit. The planned conclusions on crime were diverted to provide a response to terrorism.

The second risk was that the leaders simply concluded their discussions by proposing more meetings in the G7 format. Both Chirac in 1995 and Blair in 1997 proposed more G7 ministerial meetings on job creation, following on from the one held in Detroit in 1994 which Clinton had launched at the Tokyo III summit. Yeltsin proposed a special G7 summit on nuclear safety, which was held in Moscow in 1996. Other such meetings were initiated on terrorism and crime. These extra meetings appeared to clutter up the G7 apparatus, against the professed intentions of the leaders, and to siphon issues away from the wider international institutions competent to handle them. While these ministerial meetings often produced useful conclusions, e.g. on employment at Detroit (1994) and Lille (1996), the summits themselves added little new.

As a result, no progress at all was made in the other two objectives of summit reform - lighter preparations and shorter documents. The need to absorb the results of additional ministerial meetings added to the burden on the Sherpas. Hitherto, the Sherpa teams met collectively, with the lead Sherpa flanked by sous-Sherpas from foreign and finance ministries. From now on they separated into three distinct cycles, dividing up the agenda between them. The agenda grew even longer: by Denver in 1997 it embraced economic subjects, global issues (as transnational issues were now called), foreign policy and institutional reform.

The progress made in shortening the summit documents, which had been registered at Tokyo III 1993, all disappeared. Denver produced 29 pages of documents endorsed by the leaders - 18 from the G7 plus Russia, nine from the G7 alone, plus separate statements on Bosnia and Cambodia. The foreign ministers produced a further eight pages and the finance ministers another seven. Little of this reflected decisions by the leaders themselves. Most of it was a report on 'work in progress' in various G7 contexts. Some of this work included the Russians, while some did not. Absorbing the Russians, whatever its political benefits, greatly complicated the summit process and its reform.

Absorbing the Russians

Ever since the G7 leaders had invited Gorbachev to meet them in London in 1991, they had wrestled with their precise relationship with the Russian President. Associating the Russians with the summit helped to reconcile them to the loss of their superpower status and encouraged them to persist in economic and political reform. But the Russians always disliked coming to the summits as supplicants; and by Tokyo III in 1993 the political benefits were wearing thin.

The summits were made more attractive to the Russians from 1994 onwards, by shifting attention from the economic to the political agenda. Whatever their economic troubles, the Russians had a right, as permanent members of the UN Security Council, to be in the political exchanges at the summit. So at Naples the Russians were admitted as full members to the foreign policy discussions, which were moved from the first to the second day to accommodate them. This part became known as the P8, while the economic part was still G7. This move was greatly welcomed by Yeltsin, but it encouraged him to seek access to the economic discussions as well. He pressed to be invited to the entire summit, making the G7 into the G8.

The G7 leaders did not think the Russians could contribute anything to the economic discussions but disliked rebuffing Yeltsin outright.

As a result, each summit from Naples 1994 onwards marked a small advance in the Russian campaign for full summit membership. At Halifax 1995 the G7 leaders accepted the Russian proposal for a special nuclear safety summit in Moscow. This enabled them to involve Yeltsin in another summit-related event, while keeping their economic circle intact. At Lyon 1996, Chernomyrdin took the place of Yeltsin, who was occupied in his re-election campaign. Even so, global issues like the environment were moved from the economic to the political day, to please the Russians.

In 1997 Clinton made Denver the first 'Summit of Eight', because the Russians took part alongside the G7 participants from the outset. The main summit communiqué was issued by the Eight and covered all the global issues and foreign policy topics, as well as some economic subjects, notably Africa. The symbolism for the Russians was strong. The move brought immediate political dividends, as it helped reconcile Russia to NATO enlargement. In substance it was less of a change. The Russians by now took part in the discussion of foreign policy and global issues and were associated with the documents issued. They did not have much to add on any economic subject. With Yeltsin present, the leaders' discussions lost some of the informality they valued so much. When he spoke, he seemed to be addressing them, rather than taking part in a conversation.

Contrary to some fears, the Russian presence throughout did not emasculate the economic part of the Denver summit. The economic G7 remained very much in being, especially at finance minister level. While the foreign ministers met together with their Russian colleague, the G7 finance ministers did not, except over one lunch. The G7 leaders had a short meeting without Yeltsin and issued a substantial document on parts of the economic agenda, notably trade and finance. A Russian journalist spoke ruefully of the 'G8 minus 1'.

Even so, adding the Russians increased the prospect that, over time, the summit would move away from economic to political and 'global' issues. There could be tension in future over what was done with the Russians present and what without them. The participation of the Russians complicated the summit preparations in two ways: some items had to be prepared twice - once without them and once with them; when they were present it became harder to reach consensus, because their economic position was so different from the others. Admitting the Russians to all the summit, not just part of it, also re-opened the whole question whether the summit still had the right membership. As noted in Chapter 6, the argument was growing that the G7 was no longer representative of the range of countries active in the international system. In particular, large, populous countries, like China, India, Mexico and Brazil, deserved more weight as they opened up their large, internal markets. But the G7 resisted further enlargement, for reasons given later in this chapter.[3]

Globalisation and the Review of Institutions

The Naples summit of 1994 launched the summit review of international institutions. Clinton had come to Naples to propose a new programme of trade liberalisation, to follow on from the Uruguay Round. But he had not prepared the ground in advance; and the European Union thought this premature, since the Uruguay Round had been long and painful and was not yet ratified.

The Naples summit agreed instead on a more open-ended institutional review, to focus on:-

> (1) how the global economy of the 21st century will provide sustainable development with good prosperity...
> (2) what institutional changes may be needed to meet those challenges...

The immediate reason for this review was given as the impending 50th anniversaries of the institutions founded at the end of World War II. 'We are conscious' said the leaders 'of our responsibility to renew and revitalise these institutions'.

The summits also recognised, more gradually, the stimulus for the review provided by globalisation. Naples 1994 noted:-

> New forms of international interaction are having enormous effects on the lives of our peoples and leading to the globalisation of our economies.

Halifax 1995 introduced the institutional review by saying:-

> The process of globalization, driven by technological change, has led to increased economic interdependence: this applies to some policy areas seen previously as purely domestic...

The economic communiqué from Lyon 1996 began with a thoughtful preamble on globalisation. This was seen as 'a source of hope for the future'; but it could also 'generate new risks of instability', while 'certain parts of the world could become marginalised'.[4]

The institutional review was set as only one of the tasks for the next year's summit. The Canadians decided to make it the principal objective for Halifax in 1995 and to build the agenda around it. This was a wise decision, but not without dangers. For example:-

- The heads of government had little direct experience of international institutions and did not normally attend their meetings, though their accompanying foreign and finance ministers did.
- The summits had never considered the general issue of the reform of international institutions. The then British Prime Minister, Harold Wilson, had tried to interest the very first summit in this subject, at Rambouillet in 1975. But he had no success and the topic was never revived.[5]
- The summits had, over the years, made many specific recommendations to institutions, notably the IMF, the World Bank and the GATT, and usually looked to established organisations to carry forward the understandings reached at the summit. But partly because of the anti-institutional tradition of the summits, they always kept the other institutions at arm's length and remained detached from them.
- The G7 finance ministers had had an unhappy experience at the Annual Meeting of the IMF/World Bank in Madrid, in September 1994. On that occasion their proposals for a new issue of Special Drawing Rights (SDRs), agreed among themselves with great difficulty, were rejected by the other members and the IMF Managing Director as inadequate.

But there was ready agreement, in the preparations for Halifax, that all this should now change. The G7 members recognised, whether consciously or not, that the end of the Cold War confrontation had transformed the institutions, through world-wide membership and the emergence of new influential actors. They could no longer dictate to the institutions and expect them and their members to follow blindly. But they were still well-placed to take the initiative and influence the institutions profoundly, if they acted with tact and openness to the views of others.

The G7 recognised also that strong and effective international institutions would help them to resolve the tensions of globalisation, between domestic and international pressures. They could use them to counter protectionist and inward-looking tendencies. These were feared both in the United States, especially after the mid-term elections of November 1994 were so unfavourable for the Clinton Administration, and in the European Union, which seemed to the non-Europeans obsessed by its own internal dynamics. But to strengthen the institutions the G7 members not only had to contribute ideas; they also had to provide a good example.

This meant that they should identify themselves with the drawing up of multilateral rules and implement them effectively. They should commit themselves to observe the rules strictly and to cooperate in their enforcement. They should undertake to use multilateral dispute settlement mechanisms to resolve any disputes among themselves, to abide by the judgements and to work to create such mechanisms where they did not yet exist. Such an approach would strengthen the institutions, influence others to keep the rules also and help to restore the reputation of the G7 itself.

The G7 leaders did not attempt to conduct a comprehensive review in a single year - that would overload the agenda again. In their preparatory work the Sherpas surveyed the field, dividing the subject matter by issue rather than by institution, and drew up a programme of action which occupied Halifax 1995, Lyon 1996 and Denver 1997.

Two major issues were identified for immediate treatment:-

- *International financial and development issues,* especially the work of the IMF and the World Bank. Finance became the main theme for Halifax, with technical issues pursued at later summits. Development got more attention at Lyon and Denver.
- *The United Nations family,* especially its economic humanitarian, and other related activities.

Two more were identified and reserved for later treatment:-

- *International crime* was a new threat, which was encouraged by globalisation.[6] Although earlier summits had promoted measures on drug trafficking, money laundering and smuggling of nuclear materials, more international action was needed. But the G7 leaders did not feel sure enough of their ground to make firm recommendations at Halifax. They called for more preparatory work on crime, to enable them to take decisions the following year, and for parallel work on terrorism, though the two were not linked.
- *The global environment,* following up the initiatives launched at the United Nations Conference on the Environment and Development (UNCED) in 1992.

Finally:-

- *International trade* was considered not to need a review, because the conclusion of the Uruguay Round and the creation of the World Trade Organization were so recent. The leaders at Halifax and later summits were content to urge that unfinished business from the

Round be completed and to promote some new items for the WTO's agenda.

International Finance

It was Chrétien's personal decision that Halifax should concentrate on international financial questions. In his long political career, he had attended the first Bonn summit in 1978 as Canada's finance minister. He and his advisers recalled that Giscard's aim, when he launched the first summit in 1975, had been to create a 'viscous' exchange rate system.[7] Chrétien aspired to do something similar in 1995. He found very little support at first, but everything changed when the Mexican financial crisis broke in December 1994.

Back in 1982, Mexico's debt problems had precipitated a crisis in the international banking system. But under President Salinas (in office 1988-94) Mexico had become a star of the open economic system, joining the US and Canada in NAFTA and becoming the first new member of the OECD for twenty years. The election year of 1994 was marked by political unrest, but everyone gave Mexico the benefit of the doubt in economic policies. So the haemorrhage of capital at the end of 1994 and the collapse of the peso were a total surprise. All neighbouring currencies were caught in the turbulence. With Mexico on its doorstep, the United States took the initiative with the IMF in assembling a rescue package. They faced their other partners with new proposals as a *fait accompli*, though it was the largest rescue package on record - $40 billion, including $18 billion in IMF funds. The Europeans signed up reluctantly, believing Mexico should accept stronger conditions from the IMF in return for support on this scale.

All the G7, however, accepted that the IMF was not equipped to prevent speculative crises on this scale or to rescue countries overwhelmed by such huge financial shifts. The Mexican crisis also shifted the normal balance of power within the G7 on monetary questions. The Americans usually lined up with the Germans among the most resistant to change in the IMF and the World Bank; but they could not ignore the consequences of a Mexican collapse and shifted to promoting reform. The issue thus became firmly established on the Halifax agenda. Public interest was further aroused by the collapse of Barings Bank and by the intense speculation against the US dollar in the spring of 1995.

The Halifax conclusions on financial issues were meticulously prepared in advance, so that they occupied about a third of the economic declaration and were supported by a separate background document issued on the summit's authority. The recommendations were endorsed by the leaders essentially without change, but did not go through on the nod. The heads of government had their liveliest discussion on the first day at Halifax on this topic. Chirac, in a striking image, denounced international speculators as the AIDS virus of the world economy.

The summit recommendations reflected the AIDS analogy in that they did not offer a cure but rather concentrated on how countries could avoid becoming exposed to speculative financial crises. In particular:-

- The IMF should have a better early warning system and should conduct stronger surveillance of all member countries' policies. Countries should meet set standards in providing economic and financial data and should be publicly identified when they did so. The IMF's policy advice should be more pointed and it should tell countries frankly when their performance was not good enough.

- A new emergency financing mechanism should provide countries in crisis with faster access to IMF funds, on strict conditions. In support of this, the additional funds available to the IMF under the General Agreement to Borrow (GAB), amounting to 18.5 billion SDRs, should be doubled.

- Since financial crises could now start not with excessive bank debt, as with Mexico in 1982, but in the new integrated capital markets, better cooperation was needed between the authorities supervising both banks and securities markets.

- Procedures should be explored for 'orderly resolution' if financial rescues should fail - i.e. procedures for countries which were comparable to those for insolvency for companies.

These measures amounted to a considerable strengthening of IMF disciplines. They tightened up surveillance of economic and monetary policy for all countries, not just those receiving balance of payments support from the IMF, and set new standards. They shifted the IMF more towards the setting and policing of rules.

The heads of government were careful not to present these ideas for change in the IMF on a take-it or leave-it basis. But they were not acting in a vacuum. The IMF had already begun work on similar lines since the Mexican crisis, into which the G7 proposals would fit easily. Despite the rough treatment given to G7 ideas at Madrid in 1994, the IMF and World Bank staff and the other members were very ready for the G7 leaders to take the initiative, provided they could accommodate the ideas of others too. So the Halifax conclusions initially found wide acceptance. Later summits in this series considered work done on detailed aspects of this programme. Lyon 1996 endorsed a G10 report which concluded that 'insolvency' was not realistic for countries and proposed more modest measures. Both Lyon and Denver 1997 encouraged work being done by G7 finance ministers on financial regulation and supervision. No one at Denver, however, forecast that, within ten days of the summit, another much worse financial crisis would break out. This crisis would preoccupy the two summits of the sixth series held so far (Birmingham 1998 and Cologne 1999) and is examined in Chapters 10 and 11.

International Development

The Halifax recommendations for the World Bank and regional development banks were less radical. The summit communiqué and the supporting background document stressed that the concessional resources of the World Bank and the International Development Association (IDA) should be concentrated on the poorest countries, who had no access to other sources of finance, and on basic social programmes and other poverty-reducing projects, which did not attract private capital. For other aspects of development, the heads of government advocated the promotion of a healthy local private sector and measures to attract foreign private finance. This reflected the declining role of the public sector in G7 countries themselves and the reduced resources available to the state.

As Chrétien chose finance as his major subject for Halifax, so Chirac chose development for Lyon 1996. The longest passages in the summit communiqué concerned development policy and development institutions (including the UN, treated separately below). Chirac invited the heads of the World Bank, IMF, United Nations and WTO to meet the G7 leaders and they issued a joint statement - the first such meeting of its kind.

The most important achievement at Lyon in this field was agreement on the 'Heavily Indebted Poor Countries' (HIPC) initiative. This was an advance in nature as well as in scale over the terms for debt relief agreed at earlier summits in Toronto, London and Naples. The earlier proposals gave poor countries relief on their bilateral debts to governments or government-backed agencies. But they gave no help with their mounting debts to international institutions, notably the IMF and World Bank. The institutions had always refused to allow debt re-scheduling, for fear it would damage their credit rating. But at Lyon they endorsed the idea of new lending on easy terms to help countries repay old debt. The presence at Lyon of Camdessus for the IMF and Wolfensohn for the Bank facilitated agreement. Chapter 11 looks at this subject in more detail.

Denver 1997, at American suggestion, focused on help for Africa. The outcome was on balance a disappointment. It was a welcome innovation for the summits to discuss Africa. But the extensive communiqué paragraphs were an uneasy blend of the US approach, which required all beneficiaries to meet conditions, and the European and Canadian approach, which focused on greatest need. It was hard to find anything specifically African which would not equally apply to other developing countries. There were no precise commitments on new trade access for African countries. A vague undertaking in the communiqué to 'continue to improve, through various means, access to our markets for African exports' was repeated for all least-developed countries in the G7 statement and had no visible effect. The international financial institutions were urged to give more attention to Africa. But there were no promises of additional aid from the summit participants, though the US at least recognised that aid was needed as well as private finance.

The United Nations Family

The institutions of the United Nations family were the only ones which had managed to preserve a world-wide membership throughout the Cold War. But they often survived by dint of strained and laborious compromises between East, West and a group of non-aligned countries discontented with both. These rivalries made efficient organisation and management extremely difficult.

When the Cold War ended, the potential for collective UN action expanded hugely. The Security Council, for example, could usually count on Russian cooperation and at least Chinese acquiescence in international action. But the new demands on the UN outran its capacity. Its organisational structures and methods, eroded by the years of the Cold War, were strained to the limit, while its finances were undermined by persistent arrears from most members states, most conspicuously the United States.[8]

The preparation of UN issues for Halifax was less detailed than for financial reforms. The problems were more diverse and incoherent and concerned a more varied group of institutions. There was uncertainty among the Sherpas on whether proposals from the G7 would be received at all positively by the rest of the UN membership. But at Halifax itself the heads of government concluded that the 50th anniversary of the United Nations provided an ideal chance to start a process of renewal, which would not be repeated. The leaders themselves, including Yeltsin, had the most animated exchange on their second day at Halifax on this subject. They strengthened the text offered by the Sherpas. The result was the most extensive treatment of UN issues ever attempted by a G7 summit, taking up nearly another third of the published declaration.

The general aim of the Halifax recommendations was to give the UN a stronger organisational structure, with less confusion of responsibility; to advocate more systematic management techniques; and to restore the UN's finances. The leaders looked especially at the humanitarian, development, environment and other economic and social work of the UN and its agencies. They recommended, for example:-

- More systematic responses to humanitarian disasters, through better cooperation among UN bodies and the World Bank.
- The UN Economic and Social Council (ECOSOC) should exercise effective policy coordination, notably between the UN itself and the specialised agencies.
- Removing overlap between some institutions, such as the WTO and the UN Conference on Trade and Development (UNCTAD) and considering whether other UN institutions were needed at all.

The summit leaders gave much thought as to how to follow up their ideas for reform, so as to gain the widest possible support from other UN member states and the staffs of UN bodies. They did not want to alienate others or to provoke suspicion of their intentions. So they agreed to work together to promote change in all UN contexts where reform was being considered, building up coalitions of support from all parts of the membership. Major UN events, such as the special anniversary meeting in October 1995, would be occasions to take their ideas forward. Other gatherings outside the UN framework, such as the Commonwealth Heads of Government Meeting and the summit of Asia-Pacific Economic Cooperation (APEC) countries, both due in November 1995, would also be used to promote their ideas, seek reactions and gather wider support.

The Lyon 1996 summit kept up the momentum on this subject. The G7 communiqué contained detailed recommendations for reforming and regrouping the economic work of the UN Secretariat in New York, which were subsequently put into effect. The summit documentation included a meticulous assessment of measures taken and progress achieved in each of the UN organisations targeted at Halifax. Denver made further progress, especially by giving full backing of the G7 and the Russians to the reform proposals of the new UN Secretary-General, Kofi Annan.

Despite this sustained summit attention, UN reform faced many obstacles, as compared with the reform of IMF and IBRD.

- *First,* in the Fund and Bank, senior management accepted the need for change and were happy to work with the G7. At the UN, it was not until the arrival of Annan that there was enough support for the ideas being proposed by the G7 for reshaping the UN institutions and its secretariat.

- *Second,* the persistent US arrears in payments to the UN were a double handicap. They reduced the authority of the G7, while adding to the UN's troubles.
- *Third,* in Fund and Bank the summit worked on policy proposals, with some consequential changes in management and organisation. But with the UN almost all was management and organisation - the policy content was small. Persuading people to make changes was much harder.

When the institutional review ran out of steam after 1997, many of the UN reforms marked time.

International Crime

Halifax did no more on crime than set up a new group of officials to prepare proposals for Lyon 1996, alongside the existing group on terrorism. The crime group (soon to be called the Lyon Group) prepared detailed recommendations for the 1996 summit and generated a higher level of cooperation between interior ministries in the process, building on earlier work on drugs and money-laundering. The Lyon summit endorsed their recommendations. But the leaders themselves - and especially the Americans - were distracted by a terrorist attack on US servicemen in Saudi Arabia. Much of the original crime material was side-tracked to fill out an emergency statement on terrorism.

When the subject came to Denver 1997, the passage prepared for the draft communiqué on international crime looked rather routine, given the expectations created in Lyon. However, the leaders clearly wanted faster progress. The final communiqué passage was therefore expanded and there was more in the foreign ministers' report. But the account of great activity concealed a lack of real movement, which accounted for the leaders' impatience. Different legal approaches, e.g. on extradition, were an obstacle; interior ministries were becoming more outward-looking but not justice ministries; and international institutions were weak. The leaders therefore decided to make this a principal subject for Birmingham in 1998.

The Global Environment

Halifax 1995 gave some attention to the environment, in the context of UN reform. It recommended distinct mandates for the two leading bodies on the environment: the Commission on Sustainable Development (CSD) and the UN Environment Programme (UNEP). The CSD should be the forum for defining and agreeing strategic goals for sustainable development, while UNEP should be the world's environmental conscience.

At Denver, the summit inevitably focused on the environment, given its coincidence with the fifth anniversary of the Rio conference. But it was unable to bridge the differences between the US and Europe on climate change, ahead of the Kyoto conference, or on a forestry convention.

The Europeans were fortified by a collective EC decision to reduce greenhouse gas emissions to 15 per cent below 1990 levels by 2010, following on the commitments made at the 1992 Rio Conference. They wanted their other summit partners to do the same. But the others could not go beyond the principle of quantified targets and reductions by 2010. Similarly, the Europeans and Canadians wanted the summit to call for a forestry convention. But the US and Japan could not agree; and the summit settled for an 'Action Program', to be reviewed the following year. The summit gave an ambiguous response to a call from Kohl for a new environmental institution, to ensure compliance with international commitments, and the idea lost ground. The leaders agreed more easily on measures to strengthen existing institutions, especially UNEP.

Collective Management: Easing the Strain

As noted earlier in this chapter, the G7 leaders moved to admit Russia but resisted all other suggestions for widening their circle. This was because they recognised, at least unconsciously, that they needed more than ever the close links provided by the summit process to defuse disputes among themselves and to counter the strains of globalisation. The present G7 membership provided the best opportunity for exerting reciprocal pressure between the highly developed countries of Europe, North America and Japan, which would be lost if the composition were changed.

The tensions between G7 members already analysed in Chapter 5 persisted into this fifth summit series. Conspicuous examples were:-

- The bitter confrontation between Canada and the European Union over fishing in the Northwest Atlantic. Exasperated by the EU's failure to curb over-fishing by certain European states on the Grand Banks just outside its 200-mile limit, Canada took the law into its own hands and in March 1995 arrested a Spanish trawler in international waters.[9]
- The US, after long and fruitless negotiations with Japan on opening its markets for American cars, threatened to introduce punitive tariffs on luxury cars entering the United States after the end of June 1995.

The tense bilateral exchanges, right up to the deadline, awkwardly straddled the Halifax summit.

- After Cuba shot down an aircraft flown by Cuban exiles based in the United States in February 1996, Congress introduced legislation applying sanctions to any firms, domestic or foreign, which did business with Cuba. Similar legislation followed imposing penalties on firms investing in Iran or Libya. As it was election year, Clinton did not veto either measure. The EU and Canada strongly protested that these Helms-Burton and d'Amato Acts breached international commitments.

These examples illustrated the sort of economic disputes which disturbed the post-Cold War world:-

- *First*, the security restraint no longer applied. It was hard to imagine a major power like Canada forcibly arresting a trawler of another NATO member country while the Cold War was on, even if a small country like Iceland might have done so.
- *Secondly*, the frontier between domestic and external policy was obscured. Canada claimed that foreign over-fishing had destroyed its native Atlantic fishing industry. The American complaints were about the way the internal Japanese market for cars operated, not about any restrictions at the border. The Cuban and other legislation applied US domestic law extraterritorially
- *Thirdly*, the disputes were aggravated by the absence of a multilateral dispute settlement mechanism or the refusal to use one. The Northwest Atlantic Fisheries Organization (NAFO), which regulated fishing in the region, contained no such mechanism to which Canada or the EU could apply. For the cars dispute, Japan and the United States should properly have used the dispute settlement mechanism of the new WTO, but the United States declined to do so. When the EU demanded a WTO panel on the US law on Cuba, the Americans threatened to declare it a matter of national security outside the WTO's jurisdiction.

None of these disputes were put on the agenda for the summits. The G7 summits, with their wide exposure to the media, had become a bad place to resolve acute bilateral disputes where domestic interests were strongly engaged. Summits were much more successful in helping to anticipate or deter such disputes and to reinforce the international machinery for solving them. That was, in fact, the principal achievement of the summits of this series, through the medium of their review of international institutions.

In spite of these disputes, there were signs as the fifth summit series progressed that transatlantic and trilateral tensions were easing. The institutional review provided a fairly uncontroversial context for summit discussions. Open disagreement at the summit, or failures to respect summit commitments (such as over ending the Uruguay Round), became less frequent. (The main exception was the clash over climate change at Denver 1997, where the Europeans had been irritated by US triumphalism.) The EU and US established a new contractual relationship at their Madrid summit of December 1995. A similar link between the EU and Canada followed a year later, delayed by the fall-out from the fisheries crisis.

The three disputes noted were all resolved positively. Canada and the EU agreed to support a new UN Fisheries Convention, which included dispute settlement. The US and Japan struck a bilateral deal on cars, just within the deadline, and made more use of the WTO in future disputes, e.g. over alcoholic drinks and photographic film. Clinton and the European leaders (Blair, as Presidency, and Commission President Jacques Santer) finally reached an agreement over Cuban and other sanctions on the margins of the 1998 Birmingham summit, so that the EU withdrew its case in the WTO. While these disputes were kept out of the G7 summits themselves, the ties among the leaders fostered by the summit process helped to resolve them.

Conclusions

The institutional review was a real innovation for the G7 heads of government. The summit had never tackled this sort of reform, since it started twenty years ago. For the first time, the leaders decided to work not from outside international institutions but from inside them. They placed their review clearly in the context of globalisation.

The Halifax summit picked out the international financial institutions and the activities of the UN family as the first areas for treatment. It was striking that the heads of government did not begin with the easier parts of the system, where only a few adjustments might be needed. They started instead with two aspects of the system which the analysis in Chapter 6 identified as being the most intractable, where there had been only limited advance towards open, rule-based international regimes. This series of summits made most progress with reform of the IMF, World Bank and United Nations system, where they had a well-defined set of institutions to work on. They made less impact on crime and the environment, partly because they started later on these topics but mainly because of institutional inadequacy - a lack of institutions in crime and too many of them in the environment. Naples 1994 launched the institutional review. Halifax 1995 and Lyon 1996 produced substantial achievements. But by Denver 1997 the momentum was largely exhausted and this proved a disappointing summit, notably in the chosen subjects of African development and the global environment. At the same time the progressive admission of the Russians was complicating the conduct and the preparation of the summits. The institutional review had begun the renewal of the summits. But this renewal was far from complete and the summits risked sinking back into frustration. A further impetus was needed. Tony Blair provided this for the 1998 Birmingham summit, which began the sixth and current summit series. This will be examined in Chapter 10.

Notes

1   This chapter is drawn largely from 'The G7 Summit and the Reform of Global Institutions', *Government and Opposition*, vol. 30 no. 4 (Bayne 1995). This article was written after I had attended the Halifax summit as British High Commissioner to Canada (see also Bayne and Putnam 1995, written before the summit). The chapter is supplemented from three short papers written for the University of Toronto G8 Research Group (Bayne 1997a and 1997c), with whom I attended the Denver summit as a correspondent of the LSE Magazine. My sources for Naples and Lyon are less good.

2   The choice of summit sites is a useful indicator of efforts to make the summit more informal, as the meetings have moved away from capital cities. Summits in the US, Italy and Canada were always held away from the capital (the 1981 Ottawa summit mostly took place at Montebello, 40 kilometres away). At first, Britain, Germany and Japan always met in the capital, while French summits were always in or close to Paris. During the 1990s, first Germany moved to Munich, then France to Lyon and then the UK to Birmingham. The Okinawa 2000 summit will complete the process.

3   A recent advocacy of summit enlargement is by Professor Jeffrey Sachs, 'Helping the World's Poor', *The Economist*, 14 August 1999.

4   These quotations from the communiqués issued at Naples 1994 (paras. 2-3), Halifax 1995 (para. 12) and Lyon 1996 (preamble paras. 2-3) are all accessible on the website of the University of Toronto G8 Research Group, www.g7.utoronto.ca.

5   For Wilson's initiative, see Putnam and Bayne 1984, p. 141. His 1976 list included only 38 international bodies concerned with the economic subjects discussed at the summits. The growth of summit activity would have put this figure into several hundreds 20 years later.

6   The late Susan Strange produced a provocative, well-documented analysis of the links between globalisation and crime. See Strange 1995 and 1996.

7   For the ambitious agreements at Bonn I 1978, see Putnam and Bayne 1987, pp. 84-92; for Giscard and a 'viscous' exchange rate system, see p. 39.

8   A critique of the UN's economic programmes in this period is in Arnold 1995.

9   The tension over Atlantic fisheries determined the choice of date for the Halifax summit, held in June 1995. In many ways Canada (and the rest of the G7) would have preferred a July date, as in the six previous years. But in July Spain took over the EU Presidency and would have attended the summit in that capacity.

9 New Attitudes to International Organisations

Most of the international organisations included in the summits' institutional review, described in the previous chapter, were founded just after World War II. Among global organisations, the IMF and World Bank were launched at the Bretton Woods conference in 1944. The United Nations was inaugurated in 1945, with a substantial economic element from the start. The GATT emerged from the Havana Conference of 1948, but was only transformed into the World Trade Organization (WTO) in 1995. The OECD, with limited membership, had its origin, at one remove, in the Marshall Plan which began in 1947, as explained in Chapter 4. As they approached their 50th anniversaries, many of these organisations conducted analyses of their performance, as a guide to what to do in future.[1]

This chapter examines the use which G7 governments make of these international economic organisations. In this it differs from the analyses conducted by many of these institutions as they reached their 50th anniversaries, as well as from the summits' institutional review described in the previous chapter. Those analyses and the summit review focused on the institutions themselves. This chapter focuses instead on the G7 governments, asking what they wanted from the organisations and how they got it.

The chapter mainly concentrates on the two most influential institutions for mature Western economies: the IMF and the WTO, successor to the GATT. The analysis sometimes extends to the World Bank and to the economic arms of the UN, though these are of greater importance for developing countries. A separate section looks briefly at institutions of limited membership - the G7 summit itself, the OECD and the Commonwealth - in relation to the global ones.

The principal thesis advanced here is that, since the end of the Cold War, the policy-making activities of these organisations, and the demands laid upon them, have expanded strongly. That is because their member governments are making more active and deliberate use of the organisations to advance their national objectives, especially in reconciling the tensions between domestic and international politics generated by globalisation. This is particularly true of G7 governments, but it also applies more widely.[2]

Adapting to the End of the Cold War

In the 1940s, when the international organisations were founded, governments wanted to escape from the economic controls imposed by war, following several decades when protectionism was the conventional wisdom. They were seeking to create an open, competitive world economy governed by international rules. But the organisations they created could not escape the impact of the Cold War, which marked their formative years. After the Cold War thawed and melted, over the years 1989-91, there was a gradual transformation of these organisations. As outlined in Chapter 6, the end of the Cold War brought one direct and three indirect changes.

The direct change concerned membership. The UN and its agencies had worldwide coverage from the outset. But the Soviet Union and its allies refused to join the IMF, World Bank or GATT. That encouraged some other countries to stay out, especially of the GATT, which brought no financial advantage. After the Cold War ended, the IMF and World Bank became truly global organisations, with over 180 members, like the UN itself. Membership in the WTO also rose steadily to over 130, with a queue of some thirty more wanting to join including China, Russia, Taiwan and Saudi Arabia. Even the OECD, which had remained stable at 24 members for three decades, added Mexico, the Czech Republic, Hungary, Poland and South Korea.

The three indirect changes were as follows, the first being the most important:-

- *First,* there were now no alternatives to the open, competitive economic system. While it lasted, the centrally-planned approach had offered both a rival economic system and scope for those who favoured a 'third way' between the two, like the New International Economic Order. The Cold War thus masked and distracted from the advance of globalisation, which greatly accelerated since it ended.
- *Second,* the Cold War confrontation of hostile super-powers preoccupied governments worldwide. Security issues took priority over economic ones. Since the Cold War ended, security concerns remained active (for example Yugoslavia and NATO expansion) but economic issues acquired equal weight. In economic disputes governments were not constrained by the need for unity against an external threat.

- *Third,* governments embraced the benefits of globalisation - more growth and investment, more choice and better quality products for their citizens. But they worried about the consequent loss of their own power. Globalisation seemed to make them more vulnerable to external upsets. While it rewarded success, it penalised mistakes. Governments wanted to show their electors that they were still in charge: they were choosing economic policies which took advantage of international trends; they were not simply at the mercy of external pressures.

These changes led G7 governments, as well as others, to reconsider the use they made of these organisations and their attitude to them.

Governments and Organisations

For four decades and more, governments traditionally entrusted policy towards international economic organisations to their permanent officials. Elected ministers gave them relatively little attention. Ministers in the GATT met only five times in the fifteen years from 1980 to 1994. In the IMF ministers had met more regularly each year since the 1970s. But often this meant no more for the minister than a speech, a press conference and some arguing over a text prepared by officials. The prevalence of permanent officials marked the character of the institutions. Instinctively, permanent officials valued continuity. They took the long view. They were endlessly ingenious, in adjustment, extension and adaptation, but they were not innovative. This accounted, for example, for the odd reproductive cycle of international economic institutions. New institutions were very rarely born; old institutions never died. Only one new institution - the European Bank for Reconstruction and Development (EBRD) - was created in direct response to the end of the Cold War. Parliaments likewise paid little attention to the work of international economic institutions - the US Congress being a conspicuous exception - and the same went largely for the media and the private sector.

But as the 1990s proceeded, elected ministers became less prepared to leave it all to their officials and this soon influenced the institutions themselves. In democracies, elected ministers put a premium on change - that was how they got into office. They were thus naturally innovative. They were impatient and wanted to see quick results. They wanted to be closer to the media, to business circles and to other elements in their domestic constituencies. Thus the WTO, in operation since 1995, was a new institution, not just an adaptation of the old GATT. WTO ministers met regularly, at least every second year. Expectations were low before their first such meeting, in Singapore in December 1996. But the ministers gave the WTO a fresh impetus, reflected in new agreements on telecommunications, information technology and financial services concluded in 1997. For the IMF and World Bank, the joint ministerial Development Committee, long neglected, was made into a serious forum for World Bank business. Senior bankers gathered in increasing numbers at the annual conference of the IMF and World Bank, to get access to the world's finance ministers. The Asian financial crisis of 1997 provoked calls for 'new international financial architecture', discussed in the next two chapters. Former ministers were chosen as the heads of the institutions, such as Renato Ruggiero at the WTO and Donald Johnstone at the OECD.

The IMF and the WTO were very different institutions. The IMF, like the World Bank, had an unusual system of voting and representation. Votes and seats were allocated by size of quota. Large countries, like the US and UK, got seats of their own on the Executive Board and ministerial committees, while smaller ones were grouped in constituencies and had to occupy their seat by turns. This system made it harder for small, poor countries to get their voice heard. But it ensured that the IMF and World Bank only took decisions supported by the members who would pay for them. It made for caution - and this caution was reinforced by the conviction that sudden changes would unsettle the financial markets for which the IMF was responsible.

Representatives to the IMF and World Bank came overwhelmingly from finance ministries.[3] Within national governments, finance ministers and their officials often had a hard time. They had to battle with other ministries, who wanted to spend more than they thought wise, and they promoted unpopular policies of restraint and self-denial. But at the IMF they were among friends; and they stoutly protected 'their' organisation against interference by foreign ministries and other outsiders. Even the European Commission made no impact at the IMF - the member states acted for themselves. (This detachment of the EU from the IMF could not persist after eleven member states adopted a single currency in 1999. But the involvement of the 'Eurozone' in the IMF remained controversial.)

The IMF and World Bank were established organisations, with large budgets and plentiful staff. By contrast the WTO, like its predecessor the GATT, looked thin and improvised. The permanent staff was very small and the institution relied heavily on member governments to organise and carry out its activities. But while the IMF was a cautious institution, slow to change, the tradition of the GATT was more dynamic. The GATT made its impact through a series of negotiating rounds, each one ratcheting up the level of openness in the world trading system. The new, strengthened dispute settlement mechanism of the WTO made a considerable impact. But this worked best by encouraging the parties to negotiate a settlement, rather than by imposing judgements and penalties.[4] The GATT bred a race of dedicated trade negotiators, adept at the techniques which enabled deals to be struck. The European Commission negotiated on behalf of the member states of the EU, while they sat silent and were often not even in the room.[5] The old saying was that negotiating in the GATT was like riding a bicycle: you have to keep going; if you stop, you fall off. This concept of movement providing stability was a powerful one in the globalised world of the 1990s.

The economic institutions of the UN were in general much less influential than the IMF or the WTO. Unlike its security role, the economic responsibilities of the UN were only defined vaguely in the Charter, so that its activities were dispersed and lacked focus. The decision-making process, through non-binding resolutions, was unsatisfactory. It created a gap between the decisions adopted and the ability to carry them out, which encouraged procedural manoeuvring and ambiguity. The UN made its greatest impact when it went beyond resolutions to legally binding treaties, as on climate change or the law of the sea. But even in such global issues, where the full participation of all countries was needed, governments seemed to take their UN commitments more lightly than those made to IMF or WTO.[6]

What Governments Want from Global Organisations

In the late 1990s G7 governments - ministers rather than their officials - increasingly looked to the organisations for help with their domestic objectives: to unlock the benefits of globalisation and to avert its dangers. They wanted international economic institutions to do four things: to endorse their current policies (their most important objective); to share their burdens; to extend their reach; and to give good value.

Endorsing current policies

A government wanted to be able to say: 'What we are doing has the total endorsement of the IMF (or the WTO). It is therefore clearly right'. This gave governments an instrument to justify their current policies, which they would use with their critical media; in parliament, to rally supporters and counter the opposition; and to reassure private business opinion and the financial markets. The key feature was that the government's unchanged policies should be blessed by the institutions. Where the institutions required changes in policy, that was less welcome, since the government appeared to be giving in to outside pressures.

At first sight the process looked wholly self-serving. Governments apparently wanted institutions which served as echoes or yes-men, to parrot approval of whatever they did. But it was not as simple as that. Why should governments care about the approval of the institutions? It was because the IMF and the WTO embodied the standards of good behaviour in macro-economic policy and in international trade. They were regarded as such not only by governments but also by private investors and the financial markets. They gave governments 'the seal of good housekeeping'. No government, not even the strongest, wanted to be seen defying these institutions.

This meant governments would take great pains to ensure their policies were such as would earn the institutions' approval. Since the institutions were made up of governments, this might be a wholly circular process, with each scratching the other's back. But this was not the case, because governments were not monolithic.[7] Finance ministries promoted budgetary rigour, to keep inflation down and external accounts in balance. They confronted other ministries, who had ambitious spending plans, which they often claimed would stimulate growth. In this struggle the finance ministry, outnumbered at home, appealed to its own institution, the IMF, to redress the balance. As the guardian of exchange rate stability and the source of help in correcting external imbalances, the IMF was a consistent and powerful advocate of prudent macro-economic policies.

The WTO had a similar function in the confrontation between the advocates of competition and open markets and the partisans of protective measures to favour national champions and preserve jobs. The WTO was the ally of the open market camp, helping to counter the voices favouring protection, which were often the loudest because they had most to lose. It was surprising that GATT negotiations ever succeeded in overcoming this vocal opposition. When they were limited to a single sector, like textiles, it was hard for them to do so. That was why the GATT usually proceeded by large negotiating rounds, each one more ambitious than the last. (The next such Round in the WTO is due to start in 2000.) No country wanted to bear the responsibility for the failure of such a round, which could endanger the entire system.[8]

Thus the institutions were far from being the echo of their member governments. They served instead as a conscience for governments, helping them to take, to implement and to justify difficult and unpopular decisions. Getting international institutions to endorse governments' policies was thus not a soft option. It strongly influenced governments in their choice of policies, steering them towards those which had a stronger international content and enabled them to take advantage of globalisation.

Sharing their Burdens

A government sometimes wanted to defend unchanged economic policies; and sometimes to justify changing them. It might not be helpful domestically if the change appeared to be imposed by an outside institution. But the government could go beyond the institutions themselves, to mobilise the other members to help them with their domestic problems. It helped any one government to show that the IMF was advising prudent but unpopular macro-economic policies not only for them but for other governments too. No country was suffering alone; all were part of an equality of misery, which made the strict measures easier to bear. Sometimes, governments were obliged to adopt new and unpopular policies not of choice but of necessity - for example to regain the confidence of the financial markets or to obtain loans from international sources, including the IMF itself. This applied less directly to G7 governments, since none had had to call on the IMF for funds since the UK and Italy in 1976. In such cases pressure from the international institution could be turned to the government's advantage by using the institution as a scapegoat. The government transferred onto the IMF's shoulders the domestic blame it received for the unwelcome austerity. The IMF - rather than the government - might become the target of hostile demonstrations. But if the IMF medicine worked, the government might later take the credit. This held good even after IMF policies were strongly criticised following the Asian financial crisis - see chapter 11 below.

With the GATT and WTO this process worked rather differently. There was plenty of evidence to show that countries benefit from unilateral removal of trade barriers. It was therefore in their own interest to remove them, rather than to bargain them away. But governments found it very hard to justify domestically giving up a protective measure without getting something in exchange. The GATT's practice of negotiating the removal of trade barriers on a reciprocal, non-discriminatory basis helped to overcome this problem. Governments could justify the removal of their own barriers because this opened the markets of others. No one got something for nothing; but trade restrictions were progressively removed.

Extending their Reach

The first two headings have considered how the institutions helped governments with domestic policy-making. But governments also used them, of course, to achieve external economic objectives, such as obtaining access to markets or getting their debts paid. This was the traditional role for the institutions; they provided a means of concentrating pressure and combining influence. By the mid-1990s governments were using the institutions more purposefully in this context. This was illustrated by the widespread recourse to the new dispute settlement mechanism of the WTO, which soon carried a much heavier case-load than its predecessor in the GATT. In doing this, governments found the institutions had two advantages. They set the standards of good behaviour, which few could ignore. They were also impersonal, so that governments often used the institutions as channels to put across tough and unpalatable messages and were content to shelter behind them. Some governments, especially the United States, were strong enough to pursue their objectives bilaterally if they preferred. But others, even other G7 members, were not. The institutions provided them with a means of keeping a check on the Americans and sometimes on the EU too.

While there were many economic areas where governments welcomed the involvement of the institutions, there were some where they kept the institutions out and settled things on their own or bilaterally. Governments seemed happiest to see international organisations engaged in policy-making in subjects where they were not too deeply involved themselves, either as player or regulator. The evolution of the GATT into the WTO revealed this. The GATT had provided multilateral rules from the outset for trade in manufactures and industrial raw materials, where governments intervened little. As sectors like telecommunications and financial services were deregulated and privatised, trade in services, originally outside GATT, was brought under the new WTO. In contrast, agriculture proved intensely difficult in the Uruguay Round because governments were so deeply involved in supporting it. Air services, where governments intervened heavily, still largely escaped the WTO. This trend was less evident in the IMF. But the IMF too began to give more attention to the supervision of banking and financial markets, as these markets moved out of direct government control and as central banks themselves became more independent.

The general message was clear. Where governments were themselves deeply engaged in support or close regulation, they preferred the institutions to keep their distance. But governments were generally withdrawing from many sectors which they covered previously and giving more scope to the private sector and the market. It follows that more subjects would be regarded as fit for the institutions. All this gave the institutions more work. But it also created a serious problem for them.

Getting Good Value

As the institutions were asked to take on new tasks, they needed to take on more staff and expand their budgets. But the opposite was happening in the national budgets of their member governments. Most of these were reducing their public spending, both to correct their budget deficits and because of the shift of their former responsibilities to the private sector. Governments found they could not justify spending more on the institutions while they were cutting back at home. So they wanted to cut back on the budgets of international institutions too, even as they asked them to do new things. The IMF, the World Bank and other financial institutions were protected against this trend to some degree, since they could earn their own income from their loan operations. This enabled finance ministries to spare 'their' institutions somewhat from the budgetary squeeze felt elsewhere. But the WTO, the OECD and the UN all depended on the subscriptions of their member governments. The WTO, despite the appeals of its Director-General, had to fulfil its wider mandate with the slender resources allocated to the GATT. These financial limits seriously constrained the organisations. The danger was even that the institutions, starved of funds, would see their authority decline, so that they could no longer advance the aims of their member governments.[9]

How Governments Get What They Want

Now that governments had more precise objectives in these organisations, they were no longer content to feed in their wishes and hope for the right answer. As ministers got more involved, they sought actively to steer the organisations so that they were facing in the direction they wanted. This steering process was more complex than it used to be. In the early days of the IMF, and in all the GATT rounds that preceded the Uruguay Round, rich Western countries made all the running, with the developing countries being spectators at best. But since the IMF and WTO became virtually worldwide institutions, there were many more active members who insisted on being involved.

Most of the institutions had provision for taking votes - in the IMF and World Bank by weighted voting, in others usually 'one country, one vote'. But there was a strong preference for taking decisions by consensus, so that all were associated with them. This meant that, in principle, each member had a veto. But there were two powerful constraints on using it. First, a veto could only be used to prevent something; a veto could not achieve an active objective. Members who relied on their veto too much could be accused of frustrating the institution's purpose and weakening its ability to act. Second, a member who vetoed the proposals of others would find its partners disinclined to follow its own favoured ideas. So countries with positive objectives in the institutions would use the veto sparingly. In these conditions, governments - both G7 members and others - used four broad techniques to achieve their chosen objectives in international economic organisations. They were: singleness of purpose; coalition building; manoeuvring for the middle ground; and exploiting the machinery.

Singleness of Purpose

Singleness of purpose simply meant a government must decide what it wanted from the organisation and pursue it consistently. This was obvious enough, but it was not as easy as it sounds. It required all parts of government to accept a single objective, reconciling, for example, the tensions between growth and inflation, between openness and protection. Some governments habitually weakened their position by playing out their domestic disputes in public at international meetings. Others found internal consensus only at the cost of losing direction or flexibility. This was a particular problem in the EU, when the Commission or Presidency had to act for all member states. A successful government would maintain and defend its own unity of purpose while seeking out and exposing the contradictions within other governments holding opposing views.

Coalition Building

Coalition building was a familiar technique, fundamental to success in the organisations. The aim was to build up a group which supported your own position that was sufficiently large and varied to carry the day, with a bandwagon effect sweeping everyone into an eventual consensus. The key to success was to have a broadly based group, reflecting views of all sections of the membership. One such successful coalition was the Cairns Group of agricultural exporters in the Uruguay Round. Launched by Australia, it contained members from all regions. Throughout the negotiations the Cairns Group obliged the US and the EU to address agriculture seriously and work for a solution.

Building coalitions was hard work, especially for a single country. Most other countries would want to trade their support against something and a single country risked having to compromise too far. It therefore helped to have a circle of natural allies, who would share the work of coalition building without being 'paid' for it. The UK, for example, was well placed with regard to natural allies in the global institutions. It could for example call on the G7 countries collectively, as a small but highly influential group, or on the Commonwealth, a source of allies with a wide geographical spread. (The role of these two bodies is discussed further later in this chapter.)

The EU could also provide the UK with natural allies. This worked well in UN contexts, where the European Presidency spoke for all. It was less effective in the IMF, where the member states spoke for themselves. In the GATT and WTO handling the EU was highly complex. The Northern Europeans - Germany, the Netherlands and the Nordic countries - were the UK's natural allies; the Mediterranean members, including France, were not. Success for the UK in the Uruguay Round thus meant steering the EU into a liberal position without provoking a veto from France or others. But without this collective pressure on the EU members, it is unlikely that the Round would ever have reached a successful conclusion.

Manoeuvring for the Middle Ground

Most collective decisions in the institutions were compromises, which found the middle ground between extremes. For a government to get what it wanted from an international economic institution, the art was to contrive that the middle ground satisfied its national objectives. This was an advanced and risky technique. If pursued without singleness of purpose, governments would just be carried by the tide and would be criticised for this at home. It worked best when there were some governments that wanted to go further than you did, so that those who wanted to go less far could be brought to a mid-point that met your needs. If yours was the extreme position, you would need a very strong coalition to carry the day and not have to settle for something less than your objective. One expedient was to bid for something initially well beyond your requirements, in the hope of dragging others to a point acceptable to you. This was a strategy regularly adopted by the US, but it was hard for less powerful countries to carry it off.

Some examples may illustrate this technique. In the IMF the extremes were often occupied by the developing countries, as the most demanding, and by Germany and Japan, as the most cautious. The US might be at one extreme or the other: highly cautious over quota increases and SDR allocations, most forward over commercial bank debt relief and the rescue of countries in financial difficulty, like Mexico. The UK was more often inside the extremes and thus better able to get what it wanted.

At the start of the Uruguay Round the United States was the most ambitious, the developing countries were the most reserved. As the round progressed, positions shifted. On agriculture, the EU and Japan were the most reluctant. In several other areas the United States, initially so ambitious, became inflexible. Countries like Britain, which had wide, but not unlimited ambitions, built varying coalitions to achieve satisfactory deals. Britain sometimes used EU solidarity to bring others along, sometimes worked from within to get the EU itself to move.

Exploiting the Machinery

Exploiting the machinery was a less precise technique. It required a government to be expert in the workings of each institution and in the mentality of its members, so as to take advantage of them. For example, the institutions did most of their work in English. This gave an advantage to the British and other participants fluent in English, who were often in demand to draft texts or to chair committees. Governments that were committed multilateralists, who paid their subscriptions on time and who took the trouble to cultivate the institution's staff were all more likely to get what they wanted because the institution started by being well-disposed towards them.

Institutions of Limited Membership

Policy-making in global economic organisations was thus becoming more important for member governments as a way of achieving national objectives. But it was an erratic and cumbersome business to get good decisions out of these huge organisations, with up to 180 members. To improve the speed and quality of policy-making for the whole organisation, countries naturally combined in steering or pressure groups - an extension of the technique of coalition building. In particular, institutions of limited membership, originally created for quite other purposes, were adapted to promote policy-making in the global organisations. This section looks at three of these: the G7/G8 summit, the OECD, and the economic side of the British Commonwealth.

The G7 Summit

As earlier chapters of this book have explained, the G7 summit was founded in response to the collapse of the fixed exchange rate regime, the first oil crisis and the ensuing recession. It was intended to resolve differences among its members, so that together they could provide leadership to the economic system. The summits were also used to give mutual encouragement among their members when taking difficult economic decisions. British Prime Minister Thatcher thought it worth leaving the 1983 election campaign to attend the Williamsburg summit, because it would 'lend international endorsement to the sort of policies we were pursuing'.[10] The summit was not meant to be linked to wider institutions, but to remain detached from them. Early summits naturally addressed issues being handled by the wider institutions: the IMF exchange rate regime in 1975 and the Tokyo Round of GATT negotiations up to 1978. But the idea was that anything agreed at the summit would be taken over by the wider institutions without change and without argument.

Something of this approach persisted right up to the end of the Uruguay Round in 1993. But by that time there were signs of open revolt in the global organisations at being dictated to by the G7, visible for example at the 1994 Annual Meeting of the IMF and World Bank in Madrid. From then on, as described in the previous chapter, the G7 summit introduced a fundamental change in its attitude to global organisations. The G7 members realised that they could no longer dictate to the institutions and expect their decisions to be followed blindly. But they were still well placed to take the initiative and to influence the institutions profoundly, provided they acted with tact and openness to the views of others. From the 1995 Halifax summit onwards, the G7 concentrated on its institutional review, making recommendations for reform of the IMF and World Bank and a wide range of United Nations activities. In all this the G7 members were careful to operate tactfully and persuasively, building wide coalitions of support within the relevant organisations. Their efforts were generally well received and had a positive impact on established institutions.

The OECD

The OECD, as described in Chapter 4, was founded in 1961 as the successor to the Organisation for European Economic Cooperation (OEEC), which coordinated the economic policies of the recipients of Marshall Aid and helped to restore the post-war European economy. The OECD maintained the tradition of close policy exchange and peer review among the industrial democracies. It had a mandate which went much wider than IMF or WTO, embracing all economic and many social policies. In the 1990s it encouraged the development of market economies in the former communist countries of Europe and admitted three of them to membership.

The OECD attracted the support and interest of a very wide range of government departments in the member countries, who valued the analytical work produced by its expert staff. But without the negotiating pressure generated by the WTO or the strong sponsorship which finance ministries gave to the IMF, the OECD's impact was more diffuse than either. Member governments valued it as a source of good ideas which they could later claim to have thought of themselves. The OECD increasingly came to serve as a source of ideas for its members in wider international organisations also, especially the GATT and now the WTO. With its large staff of economists and analysts, it was better equipped to do this than the WTO itself, which had to concentrate on the negotiating process. Many of the ideas which resolved the difficulties in the Uruguay Round originated in the OECD, especially in the contentious field of agriculture.

The OECD was also used as a testing-ground for commitments intended for wider international adoption. This proved much more controversial. In 1995 OECD members began negotiating a Multilateral Agreement on Investment (MAI), which would set non-discriminatory rules in this field and reduce the barriers faced by investors. The intention was that this should also be open to OECD non-members who wished to join, and it should provide a stimulus to a wider agreement on investment in the WTO. From the outset, however, it was uncertain whether it would advance this purpose. Some developing countries were critical of the OECD process, regarding it as a way of dictating to the rest of the WTO members and presenting them with a *fait accompli.* Subsequently the MAI attracted strong criticism from OECD member governments, especially France, and from NGOs. The negotiations were abandoned in 1998.

The Commonwealth

The Commonwealth grew out of the former British Empire. It had both political and economic aspects and for many years the former took priority. South Africa was a cause of division in the Commonwealth throughout the 1980s. But the ending of the apartheid regime, as well as the end of the Cold War, liberated the Commonwealth and gave it a new lease of life. The economic services the Commonwealth offered to its members were modest in scale and there had not been a tradition for Commonwealth members to adopt agreed positions to promote initiatives in global organisations. But that changed with the 1990s and the Commonwealth became a leader in ideas for debt relief offered to the poorer debtors.

As noted in Chapter 5, Commonwealth finance ministers, meeting in Trinidad in 1990, endorsed a British proposal for debt reduction to help poor countries meeting IMF targets. This scheme, called 'Trinidad terms', was an improvement on the 'Toronto terms' agreed by the 1988 G7 Summit. 'Trinidad terms' became 'London terms' through adoption at the 1991 summit and subsequently by the IMF. These initiatives provided major relief on debt owed to governments. But many poor countries owed most of their debt to the institutions, especially the IMF and World Bank themselves, on which no relief was available. So Commonwealth finance ministers in 1994 recommended a further method of reducing institutional debt for poor countries with a long record of IMF compliance. This again was adopted, as the Heavily Indebted Poor Countries (HIPC) initiative, first by the Lyon G7 summit (see Chapter 8 above) and then by the IMF and World Bank, at their Annual Meeting in 1996. The Commonwealth ministers kept up the pressure for action with the 'Mauritius Mandate' agreed in September 1997 - more details are in Chapters 10-11. In October 1997 the Commonwealth Heads of Government Meeting in Edinburgh, issued an economic declaration which envisaged a stronger joint role for the members in global organisations like the IMF and WTO. It did not go so far as to endorse the call for a new comprehensive Round in the WTO, but it moved in that direction.[11]

The Commonwealth lacked the weight of the G7 or the intellectual apparatus of the OECD. But in promoting objectives in international economic organisations it had the advantage of including countries of all sizes, all regions and all levels of development. In that sense it was a very effective coalition. But the diversity of its fifty-three members could also be a weakness in the search for a common approach and 'singleness of purpose'. At Edinburgh, for example, India's difficulties with the WTO prevented the heads of government from taking a more forward line on a new Round.

Conclusions

This analysis has examined how G7 (and other) governments made use of international economic institutions, including those reviewed by the summits of 1994 to 1997. It has sought to demonstrate that, since the end of the Cold War, the policy-making role of the organisations has expanded. Member governments perceived the value of these organisations in advancing domestic as well as external objectives and demanded more from them. As governments' direct control over economic activities shrank, through privatisation and deregulation, they were content to see more issues subject to international rules. In trade matters at least, governments were prepared to submit to international dispute settlement through the WTO. Institutions of restricted membership, like the G7 summit, the OECD and the Commonwealth, were being adapted so that they could contribute to better policy-making in the global organisations.

The autonomy of the organisations did not increase as a result of this; on balance, it decreased. Governments were less passive towards the organisations than they had been. They wanted to steer them in directions which served their own national objectives. Ministers were exerting closer supervision over what the organisations did. In particular, while asking the organisations to do more, governments became very restrictive in supplying any extra finance and slow in paying their subscriptions.

This was not necessarily a stable state, as the system had not yet absorbed all the consequences of ending the Cold War. Governments might in future agree that their interests would be well served by giving the organisations not only more to do, but also more autonomy in doing it. Or they might decide that their objectives were better achieved by downgrading the organisations and doing more unilaterally or through regional groupings. But neither of these trends was gathering strength at the end of the 1990s. Instead the institutions themselves were subject to new demands, almost as soon as the summits' institutional review had run its course.

The Asian financial crisis of late 1997, which in 1998 spread to other countries like Russia and Brazil, imposed intense strain on the IMF and World Bank. It led to calls for 'new international financial architecture', which featured prominently at the G8 summits of Birmingham (1998) and Cologne (1999) - see Chapters 10-11 below. Meanwhile the WTO became more firmly established and prepared to launch a new negotiating round in 2000. But trade as a subject was neglected by the summits, which allowed some disputes to fester between the US and EU, to the point at which they threatened the achievements of the WTO.

In both areas - finance and trade - G7 governments made more use of the global institutions than before. But at the same time they resisted any transfer of autonomy. In consequence, the greater intensity of activity did not always lead to wider agreement. In some ways it became harder to settle even simple matters, like the choice of a new Director-General of the WTO to succeed Ruggiero in 1999. The demands made on the summits to resolve disputes among the G7 and to provide wider leadership remained as great as ever.

Notes

1   For the main reviews of the organisations, see: for IMF and World Bank, James 1996 and Kenen 1994; for WTO, Croome 1995; for UN, Arnold 1995, Roberts and Kingsbury 1993 and Urquhart and Childers 1990-94; for OECD, Sullivan 1997.

2   This chapter is drawn from 'International Economic Organisations: More Policy Making, Less Autonomy' in Bob Reinalda and Bertjan Verbeek, eds., *Autonomous Policy Making by International Organisations*, (Bayne 1998a). This in turn was a version of 'What Governments Want from International Economic Institutions and How they Get It', *Government and Opposition*, vol. 32 no. 2, pp. 361-379 (Bayne 1997b).

3   Central banks are also represented at the IMF, though in a supporting rather than a leading role. Some Northern European countries, including the UK, involve their development ministries in their World Bank delegation.

4   This view is not held universally. Professor Jackson, for example (see Jackson 1998, chapter 4), would prefer to see the WTO adopt more judicial procedures at the expense of negotiation. But that would increase the risk, already considerable, that a major WTO member would reject a panel judgement.

5   The rule applies strictly for negotiations on trade in goods, where Article 113 (now renumbered 133) of the European Union Treaty applies. It is less clear for services, where the negotiations also cover investment; in practice the member states allow the Commission to remain the chief negotiator, but take more of a part themselves.

6   For example, the Denver 1997 summit, held five years after UNCED in June 1992, showed that the record of meeting commitments made there had been disappointing. Although all EU countries had undertaken to stabilise their emissions of greenhouse gases at 1990 levels by 2000, only Germany and the UK were likely to meet the target. See *Financial Times*, 9 and 27 January, 3 March 1997). On UN economic programmes generally, see Arnold 1995; on environmental commitments and summit compliance, see Kokotsis 1999.

7   This is an example of the 'two-level games' first analysed by Professor Robert Putnam in his influential article 'Diplomacy and Domestic Politics: The Logic of Two-Level Games' (Putnam 1988). See also Evans, Jacobson and Putnam 1993.

8   Single sector negotiations can succeed, as shown by the conclusion of WTO agreements on telecommunications, information technology and financial services during 1997 (*Financial Times*, 17 February, 27 March and 15 December 1997). But the risk of failure is greater, as shown by the earlier abortive negotiations on telecommunications and financial services.

9   The UN's chronic financial problems were the first preoccupation of Kofi Annan, when he took office in 1997 as the new UN Secretary-General. Arriving at the OECD the year before, Donald Johnstone was obliged to bring in budget cuts of 10 per cent. Neither institution could contemplate a programme such as was proposed by James Wolfensohn at the World Bank, which initially proposed spending $250 million on restructuring, since cut back by about a half. See *Financial Times*, 9 January and 18 March 1997 (UN); 27 November 1996 and 21 February 1997 (OECD); 20 February and 14 March 1997 (World Bank).

10 Her decision is recorded in Thatcher 1993, p. 290. She did the same in 1987 to go to the Venice summit - ibid., pp. 586-7.

11 The texts of the Edinburgh economic declaration and the 'Mauritius Mandate' are published in *The Round Table*, no. 345, January 1998, pp. 87-95. See also Jenkins 1997 and Bayne 1997d.

10 The Reform of the Summit Itself: The Sixth Series, 1998-?

By the Denver summit of 1997, it was clear that the institutional review launched in 1994 was running out of steam. Although the British had been among the strongest advocates of the institutional review, Tony Blair, as host to the 1998 summit, could see that new impetus was needed. He decided to focus the Birmingham summit - the first to meet in the UK outside London - on the renewal of the summit process itself. Birmingham 1998 was thus a highly innovative summit in organisation and procedure. It was the first summit where leaders met alone, without their ministers, fulfilling the aspiration of the founders Giscard and Schmidt, which had never been achieved before. It was the first G8 summit, with the Russians as full members; this completed a process of assimilation, which began in earnest at Naples 1994 and in fact went back to Paris 1989, when Gorbachev first wrote to the G7 seeking entry. Birmingham therefore marked the beginning of a new summit series, which was still running at the time of writing.[1]

Political Leadership: The New Summit Format

The political context for Birmingham 1998 and Cologne 1999 served to encourage harmony among the participants. The imbalance between Europe and the United States observed at Denver in 1997 tended to correct itself over the next two years. Though the US economy remained very buoyant, Clinton lost ground politically. Persistent sexual scandals led to his impeachment early in 1999, though he was acquitted. Uncertainty about Congressional support made him unable to obtain 'fast-track' authority for trade negotiations and delayed the release of new money for the IMF. The European economies began to recover. The new European currency - the euro - was successfully launched in eleven EU countries on 1 January 1999 and this gave a political boost to the Europeans, even though the value of the euro against the dollar was weaker than they had hoped. The Japanese leaders present - Hashimoto in 1998, Keizo Obuchi in 1999 - were hampered by the persistent sluggishness of Japan's economy.

151

But Hashimoto was lucky that Birmingham had to focus on Asian problems, like India and Indonesia, where Japan had something to contribute; and Obuchi was helped at Cologne by unexpected good news about Japan's economic performance in early 1999. The leader in greatest difficulty was Yeltsin, who was fighting against economic collapse, political disorder and his own failing health. Shortly before Birmingham he dismissed his long-serving prime minister, Victor Chernomyrdin, and had worked through three more prime ministers by Cologne.[2]

The previous summit series had been marked by a shift away from the political right as Clinton and Chrétien in North America were followed by Blair in Britain and Jospin in France. This leftward trend was now pursued even more strongly in Europe, with Gerhard Schroeder as Chancellor in Germany and Massimo D'Alema as Italian Prime Minister. The G7 governments, taken together, were closer to the centre-left than at any time in the summit's history, completely reversing the trend to the right seen in the third and fourth summit series of the 1980s and early 1990s.[3] This reflected a move by governments in most G7 countries to capture the middle ground rather than a shift right across the ideological spectrum. But it made the leaders on balance more interventionist and concerned with social issues and thus ready for innovation at the summit.

Heads-Only Summits and Their Consequences

Six years before, in 1992, Blair's predecessor John Major had tried to get his colleagues to agree to reshape the summit. His aims, noted earlier in Chapter 5, had been:-

- More informal discussions, among leaders alone;
- Lighter preparations and a shorter agenda;
- Shorter and simpler summit documents.

Only limited progress had been made in this direction during the fifth summit series, as Chapter 8 recorded.

Blair at Birmingham achieved almost all these objectives:-

- Heads of government came to Birmingham without supporting ministers. They met for a full day 'in retreat' at a country house, far from the media and all but a few members of their delegations.[4]
- The summit had a limited agenda of three items, two of which - employment and crime - were publicly identified in advance.

- The Birmingham economic communiqué was only ten pages long, together with a G7 document of four pages and a foreign policy statement of three pages. This was less than half the length of the Denver summit documentation.

The Germans adopted the new format without hesitation for the Cologne summit of June 1999, and the Japanese undertook to maintain it for the Okinawa summit due in July 2000.

This did not mean G7 and G8 activity was reduced or simplified; quite the opposite. Birmingham was preceded by more intense preparations than ever, in the Sherpa network, in specialist groups and in other ministerial meetings. Employment was prepared by a meeting of employment and finance ministers in London in February; crime by interior ministers in Washington in December 1997. Environment ministers met in Leeds Castle, England, in April and energy ministers in Moscow in March. A major innovation was the series of meetings of foreign and finance ministers in London on 8-9 May 1998, a week before the summit, to prepare some items for Birmingham and dispose of others which did not need the leaders' attention.

These ministers met in four combinations and issued documents totalling over 40 pages. The G7 finance ministers did the groundwork for the summit on the world economy, the new financial architecture and financial crime. A short meeting of G8 finance ministers issued national employment plans. The G8 joint foreign and finance ministers disposed of development (leaving debt relief for the poorest for the summit) and electronic commerce. The G8 foreign ministers dealt with the environment, issuing a separate paper on forests but reserving climate change for the leaders. They also disposed of UN issues, nuclear safety and non-proliferation, land-mines, human rights, terrorism and 17 regional issues, only two of which (Kosovo and Middle East) were picked up again by the leaders.

The British preparations were purposeful and well organised. By limiting the main summit agenda to three items and settling two of these well in advance, they prevented extra subjects from cluttering up the list. The financial crisis which broke out in Asia a few weeks after the Denver summit determined the choice of the third item, to which the British hosts successfully attached the problem of debt relief for low-income countries, which they had promoted at earlier summits. On the political side, two sudden crises which had blown up in the week before Birmingham - Indonesia and Indian nuclear tests - were naturally added to the agenda.

At Birmingham, the leaders could thus have an extended discussion of a few selected items. They appreciated this freedom and got through their agenda faster than expected, leaving time for bilaterals and other contacts. This format, however, inevitably focused attention on the leaders themselves and their personal contribution to the outcome. This was of varied quality. There was substantial discussion of crime and debt, which led to some advances. But other items, like employability and financial architecture, were treated more summarily. On these the main contribution of the leaders was to add their authority and their impetus to the work being done at lower levels.

The preparations before Cologne were rather more hasty and improvised. Nothing was done before the German elections, which brought in the new government headed by Chancellor Schroeder. Even then some confusion prevailed, because of tension between Schroeder and his first finance minister, Oskar Lafontaine. But as the summit approached, a pattern emerged, partly under the pressure of continuing financial upheaval and the crisis in Kosovo.

In the twelve months following Birmingham there was intensive work in the G7 finance ministers on financial architecture (see Chapter 11 below), while the G8 foreign ministers held important meetings in summer 1998 on South Asian nuclear tests and in spring 1999 on Kosovo. As the summit approached, G8 labour ministers met in Washington and G8 environment ministers in Schwerin, Germany. The pre-summit ministerial meetings were simpler than before Birmingham but less integrated. G8 foreign ministers met near Cologne on 8-10 June. They issued a six page document on both global and regional issues, but their most important achievement was to agree, together with regional states, on proposals for Kosovo and a Stability Pact for South Eastern Europe (20 pages together). G7 finance ministers met separately, without Russia, on 11-12 June in Frankfurt. They agreed documents on debt relief and on new financial architecture (24 pages), though these were not issued publicly until the summit a week later.

The Cologne summit itself focused on debt relief for the poorest, where the G7 leaders were personally engaged, including Schroeder himself; and on Kosovo, where Yeltsin's involvement was vital. Despite the intensive preparations on financial architecture, once again the leaders largely endorsed what their finance ministers had done and added little themselves. Schroeder was not able to organise a 'retreat', as Blair had; and, for all their good intentions, the length of summit documents began creeping up again. The main communiqué and foreign policy statement were no longer than at Birmingham, but the G7 document was twice as long, and there was an additional 'Charter on Life-Long Learning'.

G7 and G8

Denver 1997 was the 'Summit of the Eight'; Birmingham was the first G8 summit. One immediate consequence was Yeltsin's conclusion that Russia was now eligible to host a future summit. At Birmingham, he bid to do this in 2000, taking over Japan's turn in that year. Hashimoto refused this, but Yeltsin pressed his point, saying that he wanted to host a summit no later than 2000, when his presidential term expired. Birmingham broke up with the matter unresolved and by Cologne a year later Yeltsin seemed to have forgotten about it. At both summits the G7 leaders held a meeting without Yeltsin and issued a statement on issues where Russia had nothing to contribute.

Blair chose subjects for Birmingham which were intended to encourage Russian integration into the G8. They made real contributions to the discussions on crime and employability and even on debt, as they were now in the Paris Club. But this process did not get far. During the preparations there were occasions when the Russians tried to water down economic commitments which the other seven could accept, though this did not visibly weaken the summit documents. As in the past, Yeltsin sought to make Russia more involved in the G8 by proposing future meetings to be held in Moscow, on crime and on the 'millennium bug'.

After Birmingham, events conspired to frustrate the integration of Russia into the economic work of the summit, while reinforcing the political value of the G8. Even at Birmingham the work on financial architecture had been done by the G7. Russia's financial collapse in August 1998 showed it was part of the problem affecting the world financial system and could hardly contribute to its solution. The conclusions on debt relief for poor countries at Birmingham formed part of the G8 communiqué and thus appeared to involve the Russians. A year later the 'Cologne Debt Initiative' was briefly 'welcomed' in the G8 communiqué, but the initiative itself was spelt out in the G7 leaders' statement and the related document from G7 finance ministers. So both the main economic results from Cologne came from the G7 only and the Russians had nothing to contribute.

The main foreign policy issues at Birmingham - India and Indonesia - were suitable enough for G8 treatment but did not give salience to Russia. At Cologne, however, the key issues on Kosovo could not be resolved without Russian involvement - indeed some of them were of Russia's making. The outcome of Cologne demonstrated the potential value of the G8 grouping, both at foreign minister and head of government level.

Globalisation and the Summit Agenda

The choice of themes for Birmingham identified this as the first summit which would address directly popular anxieties about globalisation: about loss of jobs and job security; about international crime; about panic and instability in the financial markets; and about the world's poorest countries falling further behind.   Birmingham therefore concentrated on employability, crime, new financial architecture and debt relief for poor countries.

Cologne continued the explicit focus on the strains generated by globalisation. It carried forward the work on financial architecture and debt, with especially important results on debt relief; these two aspects of globalisation are examined in more detail in the next chapter. The Cologne summit expanded the G8's range on the other issues. It added education and social protection to employment and coupled conflict prevention to crime as aspects of international public order.   In the process some traditional summit subjects, such as trade and the environment, got pushed to the edge of the agenda.

G7 Economic Subjects

New Financial Architecture

It was not part of the original British plan to have this on the agenda at Birmingham. But the financial crisis which started in July 1997 and led to the collapse of Thailand, Korea and Indonesia demanded the attention of the leaders. After the initial rescue operations orchestrated by the IMF and the World Bank, the G7 finance ministers had been active in early 1998 devising measures to deter future crises and deal with them if they came.

At Birmingham the crisis seemed under control.   The leaders endorsed the detailed report of their finance ministers on proposed reforms of the IMF, World Bank and other institutions. These focused on getting better economic data; on closer and more transparent policy surveillance; and on better standards and more cooperation in financial supervision. This was all solid, sensible work, which revealed close advance consultation with the Fund and Bank. The strong endorsement from the summit was intended to ensure that steady progress continued over the months ahead.

The lull in the crisis, however, was deceptive.[5] In August Russia, having used up an IMF drawing in a few weeks, was obliged to abandon the defence of the rouble and defaulted on government debt.   In early October financial collapse threatened Brazil and a major American hedge fund, Long-Term Credit Management, needed a massive rescue. Blair prepared to call together the G7 leaders for an emergency summit - the first of its kind.

At this point the tide turned. During October the IMF put together a substantial package for Brazil; and the G7 finance ministers agreed on a strategy for reform, helped by a new informal 'Group of 22' called together by the Americans and including many Asian and other developing countries affected by the crisis. The G7 leaders issued a written declaration on 30 October 1998 endorsing their ministers' work, without needing to meet.

Over the next nine months leading to Cologne there was intensive work by the G7 finance ministers across a wide front. A new Financial Stability Forum was created, bringing together regulators of financial markets. There were proposals to strengthen or replace the IMF's Interim Committee and arguments about the future of the Group of 22. The IMF was encouraged to develop and apply new standards of economic data required from all its members and new codes of practice in monetary and fiscal policy. The G7 debated how to reduce the risks to the system from offshore financial centres and highly-leveraged institutions and how to get the private sector to play a more helpful role in financial rescues.

The Cologne summit endorsed a lengthy report from the finance ministers on these and other topics, discussed further in Chapter 11. But, as at Birmingham, the leaders did no more than give their authority to what their ministers had prepared. They did not act to resolve some of the outstanding differences among the G7, for example on how to involve the private sector. They were in no mood for radical action and seemed to have concluded, once again, that the immediate crisis was over and the urgency of the reforms had receded.

Debt and Development

The British had always wanted Birmingham to focus on debt relief for low-income countries. It was a topic which attracted much public interest. While the leaders met 'in retreat', Birmingham was the scene of a massive demonstration, when 50,000 people walked round the conference site urging complete debt forgiveness for poor countries by 2000.[6]

The summit did make some advances in this subject. It endorsed the aim of having all eligible countries engaged in the Heavily Indebted Poor Countries (HIPC) initiative (agreed at the Lyon summit of 1996) by the year 2000. When countries had the necessary track record in IMF-approved policies, they should get the relief they need for 'a lasting exit' from their debt problems. Interim debt relief should be available to them if needed; and accelerated measures were offered to African countries emerging from conflict. Birmingham was intended to accelerate the HIPC process, which was flagging. But there was still plenty of scope for foot-dragging. The Germans remained unenthusiastic about the whole process - this emerged clearly from briefings by Kohl and his officials. The issue of IMF gold sales (left open at Lyon back in 1996) was still unresolved, so that the financing of the HIPC process remained uncertain. The sums available for low-income countries, whether in debt relief or from other sources, looked meagre when compared with the huge rescue packages assembled for Thailand, Korea and Indonesia. The organisers of the big demonstration were very disappointed.

This picture was transformed when the German government changed. Early in 1999 Schroeder announced his intention to make debt-relief a centre-piece of the Cologne summit led by a much more generous German approach.[7] This gave new encouragement to the charities and other NGOs involved, who organised another massive demonstration in Cologne and handed over a petition to Schroeder. In the summit preparations every G7 member advanced proposals for improving the HIPC initiative, with the German plans now being the most generous after the British.

The G7's 'Cologne Debt Initiative' recommended to the IMF, World Bank and Paris Club major improvements to the design and financing of the HIPC programme. Debt relief should release resources for health, education and other social needs. The relief provided should reduce eligible countries' debt to no more than 150 per cent of exports (instead of 200-250 per cent hitherto) and should become available after three years of observing IMF discipline instead of six. Relief on government debt covered by the Paris Club should go up from 80 per cent to 90 per cent or even more, while any remaining aid debt should be forgiven altogether. Sales of 10 million ounces of IMF gold were recommended, while the G7 would consider further bilateral contributions 'in good faith'.

In total these reforms would reduce the debts of eligible countries by more than half - from $130 billion to something over $60 billion. They went a long way towards the demands of the major charities behind the public campaign, though they were clearly short of complete cancellation. The major test would come with the financing, on which the G7 commitment was weakest. But if fully implemented, the Cologne Debt Initiative will rank as a major summit achievement. The details are analysed in Chapter 11 in a general account of debt relief initiatives.

Both the Birmingham and Cologne summits briefly addressed other measures intended to benefit poor countries. At Birmingham the leaders endorsed the OECD's 21st Century Strategy for economic and social development; they promised work on untying of aid; they supported the WHO's campaign against malaria and other campaigns against AIDS; and they offered some trade and investment measures for least-developed countries. All these were welcome confirmations of support, at summit level, of international work in hand. But they fell short of the expectations raised at Denver, especially on help for Africa. Cologne recognised the importance of having developing countries benefit from the new round of WTO negotiations. The G8 communiqué contained a commitment to increase the volume of official aid - the first such commitment from the summit for many years. But the prospects of getting aid untied seemed to be pushed off into the future. The Americans' difficulties in getting aid funds out of Congress remained a persistent constraint.

G8 Economic and Global Issues

Employability

Detailed preparations before Birmingham on the theme of 'employability and inclusion' involved the preparation of employment plans by each country. These were endorsed by G8 finance ministers when they met a week before the summit.[8] When the leaders themselves turned to this topic, the discussion was harmonious, with none of the transatlantic clashes of earlier years, but it was brief and general. The communiqué endorsed the substantial work accomplished by employment and finance ministers during the year, but added nothing new. The main achievement of the summit in this field was to give impetus to work at lower levels, in an atmosphere of greater readiness to learn from the experience of others.

G8 employment ministers met again before Cologne; but at the summit itself the leaders decided to widen the basis of their discussion to focus on education, especially lifelong learning. This was identified as a major contribution to employability and to a harmonious society in conditions of globalisation. The summit adopted a separate 'Cologne Charter on Lifelong Learning' and agreed on specific projects on educational exchanges among the G8, on raising education standards and on using technology for distance learning. Cologne also focused on the need for social safety nets to protect those left behind by globalisation, to 'give globalisation a human face'. The communiqué urged international institutions like the IMF, the World Bank and the ILO to give attention to this topic, recognising implicitly the damage done to Asian countries in the recent financial crisis from the lack of social protection.

International Crime and Public Order

The G8 leaders had their longest discussion at Birmingham on international crime, beginning with a briefing from the head of the UK National Crime Squad, supported by videos. They responded well to this original approach and agreed without difficulty on a series of points focusing on hi-tech crime, money-laundering and other financial crime, trafficking in persons and the illegal manufacture and smuggling of firearms. They undertook to support current UN work on drugs and on drawing up a convention on transnational organised crime. They agreed to hold a G8 ministerial meeting on crime in Moscow in 1999.

This was the first time the leaders had a well-prepared discussion on this theme. It could be what Birmingham 1998 is best remembered for. Cooperation among the G8 was already quite far advanced. But even here, it was clear that cooperation between law-enforcement agencies had gone further than judicial cooperation; it was easier to catch the criminals than to bring them to justice. In the wider UN context there was still a long way to go before the G8 leaders could think they were winning the war against international crime.

In the run-up to Cologne the crisis in Kosovo shifted attention away from the dangers of crime in undermining society to the corrosive effect of civil conflict. Cologne began to formulate an approach to 'human security' and crisis prevention which addressed the root causes of conflict and threats to human rights; these included crime, drug trafficking and terrorism. This approach enabled the G8 to bring together these different aspects of international public order. The G8 ministerial meeting on crime, to be held later in 1999, was expected to produce recommendations for the 2000 summit in Okinawa.

Trade

At both Birmingham and Cologne there were short exchanges only on trade, looking forward to the next series of WTO negotiations, due to begin in 2000. At Birmingham the Europeans argued the case for a comprehensive 'Millennium Round', but they did not convince the US. A year later, at Cologne, Clinton would go no further than 'broad-based and ambitious negotiations .... achieving substantial and manageable results'. Though Cologne focused on making the WTO more responsive both to 'civil society' and to developing countries, there was no attempt to define the content of a new round or even to resolve the deadlock over the new Director-General of the WTO.

On both occasions, the opportunity was wasted for a serious discussion on trade and investment and the protectionist pressures unleashed by globalisation. Clinton's failure to get fast-track authority put him in a weak position. The presence of the Russians, who were not even members of the WTO, also inhibited discussion. If the summit should lose the capacity to innovate or to reach conclusions on international trade matters, that would make it harder to get good results from the WTO negotiations once they began.

Environment

The British had allowed plenty of time for this topic at Birmingham, expecting a difficult exchange on climate change as at Denver in 1997. But no one was in the mood for that; and agreement was easily reached on exhortations to all to sign the Kyoto Protocol within the next year; to bring in the necessary domestic measures to meet their commitments; and to work together with developing countries. At Cologne too, environmental topics got little attention - except for the new and controversial issue of food safety and genetic modification. There was a prospect of open disagreement between Europeans and North Americans on the treatment of genetically modified organisms (GMOs), on which Chirac proposed a new international institution. The matter was defused by passing it to the OECD, with a promise of a further exchange at Okinawa in 2000.

G8 Foreign Policy Issues

Indian Nuclear Tests

Birmingham was an unusual summit in that foreign policy discussions were dominated by two Asian issues - the turmoil in Indonesia and India's nuclear tests shortly before the summit. The Indonesian crisis was soon resolved by President Suharto's departure, but the tension in South Asia worsened when Pakistan also conducted nuclear tests a few weeks later.

The Indian nuclear tests had taken all G8 countries by surprise and their reactions diverged. US legislation obliged Clinton to introduce economic sanctions. Japan did the same, because of its horror of nuclear war - and this made Clinton and Hashimoto allies. Canada was also in this camp. But the Europeans traditionally disliked sanctions; Blair wanted to try persuasion first; and Chirac could hardly punish India for doing what France itself had done in 1995. The leaders did not allow these differences to turn into the sort of dispute they had had over sanctions in the past.

Clinton made no real effort to get the Europeans to impose sanctions. Instead the leaders focused on what should happen next and - after condemning the Indian tests - put all their weight behind getting India to sign up to the Comprehensive Test Ban Treaty and the Non-Proliferation Treaty. The leaders also urged restraint on Pakistan, though without success.

The G8 foreign ministers followed up Birmingham promptly, meeting in June with other countries that had renounced nuclear weapons to put pressure on India and Pakistan to do likewise. Sustained diplomatic activity over the next year, especially by the Americans, seemed to be having its effect, with both countries inching towards accepting the treaty commitments. Shortly before Cologne, all this was set back by the ill-advised incursion into Kashmir from Pakistan. But the G8 leaders gave this little attention, being wholly preoccupied with Kosovo.

Kosovo and the Balkans

The G8 leaders had already used the Birmingham summit to give a warning to Yugoslav President Slobodan Milosevic - Kosovo being one of only six foreign policy issues discussed at head of government level. In the year to Cologne the internal repression by the Belgrade Serbs in Kosovo got much worse and Milosevic proved wholly obstinate. On 24 March 1999, NATO began a bombing campaign aimed at crippling Serbian military capacity and obliging Milosevic to admit a NATO-led peace-keeping force to Kosovo and accept a political settlement.

The immediate consequences were shocking for NATO. The Serbs increased their violence to the point where hundreds of thousands of refugees fled from Kosovo, in pitiful conditions. The Russian government, from Yeltsin downwards, denounced NATO's action and threatened to intervene in support of Milosevic. It was the worst dispute between Russia and NATO since the Cold War ended.

In this dangerous situation, the G8 framework proved its worth. The Germans called a G8 foreign ministers meeting in Bonn in early May. This meeting agreed principles for a peace settlement in Kosovo, fully endorsed by the Russians and very close to NATO's original objective. Yeltsin nominated ex-prime minister Chernomyrdin as his personal emissary, working together with the EU's representative, President Marti Ahtisaari of Finland. NATO continued and intensified its bombing campaign, which gradually wore down Milosevic's resistance. In early June he accepted the peace plan presented to him by Chernomyrdin and Ahtisaari, requiring the withdrawal of all Serbian troops from Kosovo, the return of the refugees and the introduction of an international force composed of contingents from NATO forces and Russia.

When G8 foreign ministers met on 8-10 June outside Cologne, they were able to tie up all the details on Kosovo - as they thought. They agreed on terms for a UN Security Council resolution, adopted unanimously apart from a Chinese abstention, which gave the Kosovo operation the United Nations cover it had not had before. They also moved to address the wider problems of the Balkan region, which had been profoundly shaken by the conflict in Kosovo and the huge flows of refugees. The G8 joined with eight regional governments, the other EU member states, Turkey and many international institutions to draw up a Stability Pact for South Eastern Europe, to reinforce peace and stimulate economic recovery.

Despite all this progress, the position of Russia and of Yeltsin himself remained ambivalent. The Kosovo settlement was very unpopular in Russia and there was always a fear that Yeltsin would disown Chernomyrdin. The peace-keeping arrangements within Kosovo also angered the Russians. Kosovo was divided into five sectors under the responsibility of the US, Britain, France, Germany and Italy - five of the G8 countries. The Russian military wanted a sector of their own. NATO resisted this, fearing that it would become a safe haven in Kosovo for the Serbian troops, which were meant to withdraw totally. On 12 June, less than a week before the summit, a contingent of 200 Russian troops stationed in Bosnia drove across Serbia and into Kosovo to occupy Pristina airport, before any NATO forces were ready to move. This was in flat defiance of the security arrangements worked out in NATO and even took Ivanov, the Russian foreign minister by surprise. But it had the backing of Yeltsin himself.

Intensive negotiations followed in Helsinki between the Russians and Americans to resolve exactly what Russian troops would do in Kosovo. These reached a compromise. But everything depended on how Yeltsin would behave when he met the other G8 leaders in Cologne. This would be his first international visit since he nearly collapsed at the funeral of King Hussein of Jordan in April. He was only coming for the last day of the summit, on 20 June, leaving his new prime minister, Stepashin, to cover the first two days. Would he have more surprises in store?

Russia and the G8

"I am among my friends now" said Yeltsin, as soon as he met the other heads of government.[9] That set the tone for the meeting he attended, lasting only one hour. Yeltsin endorsed all that Stepashin had agreed to earlier, as well as the other arrangements for Kosovo made at Helsinki and elsewhere.

Thus the Cologne summit proved extremely well-timed. It enabled the G8 leaders to give their authority to all the agreements made at lower levels on Kosovo and the Balkans. Schroeder announced a further summit meeting for the G8 with their partners in the new Stability Pact, which took place on 30 July. Cologne provided the occasion for bringing Russia back into close cooperation with the leading NATO powers, after the dangerous confrontation over Kosovo. It also illustrated very well the dynamics of G8 summitry.

Full G8 membership meant a lot to Yeltsin. He had worked for it for seven years, well before any of the present Western leaders took office. It showed him operating on equal terms with Clinton and other Western heads of government, maintaining Russia's power and influence despite its economic troubles. It was unlikely that Yeltsin would abandon this privileged position because of Kosovo, but the summit was needed so that Yeltsin could be seen in company with his peers. Just as calling Denver 'the Summit of the Eight' helped to reconcile Yeltsin to NATO enlargement, so the timing of Cologne helped to reconcile Yeltsin to cooperating with the West over the disciplining of Serbia.

If Yeltsin was committed to the G8, so were the G7 members committed to Russia. Ever since they invited Gorbachev to London in 1991, they had accepted a responsibility to help Russia economically and to prevent it collapsing into chaos, however misguided Russian policies might be. Fundamental economic mismanagement led to Russia's default on its debt in August 1998 and little had been done since then to correct what was wrong. Even so, the G7 had encouraged the IMF and World Bank to reach new agreements with Russia to provide more financing. At Cologne they promised relief on Russia's outstanding debts if these agreements were implemented. They even suggested possible relief on debts taken over by Russia from the former Soviet Union if the economic reforms went far enough, though here the Germans were expected to drive a hard bargain.[10] Beyond this, the G7 leaders promised more intensive technical help to reform the Russian economy, making their Sherpas directly responsible. To satisfy Yeltsin, these commitments appeared in the main G8 communiqué, not in a separate statement on Russia. In substance, however, they recalled the undertakings made by the G7 to Yeltsin - and even to Gorbachev - in the early 1990s, when the attempts to reform Russia's economy were only just beginning.

Cologne was presumably Yeltsin's last G8 summit, as the Okinawa summit in July 2000 would take place after his term as Russian President expired. While Yeltsin was unpredictable in many ways, his attachment to the summit was constant and he persisted in his goal of making Russia a full member. The G7 leaders would have to come to terms with Yeltsin's successor. They would have to convince the new Russian President of the merits of G8 summit membership and of the obligations it carried. As before, they would seek to use this to support democracy and sound economic management in Russia and to encourage responsible Russian foreign policy. At the same time they would need to preserve their ability to act as G7 in those areas where Russia could not contribute. This would be a major task for Okinawa.

Conclusions: The Renewal of the Summit

Birmingham 1998 and Cologne 1999 provide evidence that a fundamental renewal of the summits was taking place. The main pointers to change were the following:-

- These two summits were each hosted by leaders of new left-leaning governments returning to power after more than 15 years in opposition. That made both Blair and Schroeder ready to innovate, in both summit format and summit agenda.
- The new format of heads-only summit gave the leaders a new freedom to set their agenda and organise their time. The price was a separate but ever-growing G7/G8 bureaucracy at lower levels.
- Birmingham and Cologne focused explicitly on globalisation and especially on how to help those who were put at risk by it. The agenda shifted towards social issues, like employability, and to the problems of developing countries. The two-year focus on debt-relief for the poorest brought a real advance.
- These were G8 summits, with Russia present from the start. The G8 format paid political dividends in bringing a settlement to Kosovo and averting a dangerous clash with Russia - Cologne was fortunately timed for that. But it also obliged the G7 to keep Russia afloat until it could fully join the world economy - which is still a long way off.
- Because of Russia's weakness, the main economic work of the summit was done by the G7 and will be for many years. The outcome on debt relief depended on the personal involvement of heads of government. On financial architecture the leaders simply endorsed their finance ministers' work. Both Birmingham and Cologne happened when the crisis seemed to be over, so that the leaders lacked the incentive to resolve differences among the G7.
- G8 work on social issues like employment, education and crime was useful in binding in the Russians, though because policies were slow-

acting it was hard to show results. But where, as in trade, the main differences arose between Europe and the United States, the presence of Russia could inhibit progress.

- For the first time, the summits showed themselves responsive to pressure from public opinion, especially in the sustained campaign for debt relief. But they seemed inclined to give legitimacy to the views of 'civil society' without being sure who they represented.

These changes were, on balance, encouraging to the G8 leaders, who saw results from their own efforts. They also reflected further improvements in collective management among the G8 powers, which will be discussed further in Chapter 12. The attitude of the media to the summits, however, still remained ambivalent and their coverage of summit results was generally superficial and incomplete. In part this was due to the nature of summit documents. Even though both the British and Germans kept the main G8 communiqué to ten pages or less, this was still too long for full quotation. At Cologne a long G7 statement and the Charter on Lifelong Learning added to the weight of paper.

In 2000 the summit will be in Okinawa, the first time the Japanese have held a summit outside Tokyo. Unlike the British, but like the Germans, the Japanese have not selected their agenda in advance. They will have to handle Clinton in his closing months and presumably a successor to Yeltsin. In the Japanese political system the head of government has less authority than in Europe or North America. Even so, the procedures developed before Birmingham and Cologne should give plenty of guidance to the Japanese on how to organise an effective summit in the new style.

Notes

1   This chapter is partly drawn from two notes prepared for the University of Toronto G8 Research Group (Bayne 1998b), with whom I attended the Birmingham summit, again as the LSE Magazine's correspondent. I have less direct sources for Cologne.
2   Yeltsin's prime minister was Sergei Kiriyenko at the time of Birmingham in May 1998. Yevgeny Primakov took over in August 1998, after the Russian default. He was replaced by Sergei Stepashin shortly before Cologne. Stepashin in turn was succeeded by Vladimir Putin in August 1999.
3   By 1999 virtually all the EU member states had left-leaning governments, with Spain the only major exception.
4   In organising a 'retreat' for G7 leaders, Blair was following a well-established practice at Commonwealth Heads of Government Meetings (CHOGM). See Bayne 1998c for a comparison of the Birmingham summit and the Edinburgh CHOGM of October 1997, both chaired by Blair.

5   A paper given by Dr DeAnne Julius at a conference just before Birmingham raised the prospect that the financial crisis was far from over; see Julius 1998.

6   The Jubilee 2000 campaign was largely orchestrated by the British charity Christian Aid, which had done serious analytical work on poor countries' debt problems. See Lockwood, Donlan, Joyner and Simms 1998 and Chapter 11 below.

7   Schroeder announced this policy change in an article in *Financial Times*, 21 January 1999.

8   These employment plans developed the type of job-creating measures examined at an LSE conference organised by Professor Richard Layard shortly before Birmingham. See CEP 1998.

9   Yeltsin's remark was widely reported by the media, e.g. *The Times*, 21 June 1999.

10   These G7 promises soon led to results. Despite a very shaky record in economic management since the default of August 1998, the IMF was prepared to agree a standby credit for Russia of $4.5 billion in July 1999. In August the Paris Club accepted to roll over outstanding Russian debt, though they would not agree to debt reduction. For a critical comment, see Martin Wolf in *Financial Times*, 11 August 1999.

11 Globalisation: Financial Architecture and Debt Relief

The 1990s were the decade of globalisation. While the Cold War lasted, the internationalisation of economic activity affected many countries, but not all. After the communist empire collapsed, as argued in Chapter 5, this trend crossed the whole world. After initial problems of adjustment, rather like the disruption caused by the thaw after a long winter, the benefits of globalisation seemed well established by the mid-1990s. The Uruguay Round was concluded and ratified and its agreements were being put into effect. Wider areas of trade, like services and agriculture, were being brought under international rules and the WTO's dispute settlement mechanism was being used to good effect. The Mexican financial crisis had been serious, but it was quickly brought under control and the IMF and World Bank were strengthened to deal with future upsets. Economic growth picked up everywhere, even in Africa, so that in May 1997 the IMF brought out one of its most optimistic forecasts.[1] Meanwhile, globalisation had accelerated. In the five years 1991-1996, world output grew by about a quarter; world trade by about a half; world direct investment flows doubled; and world portfolio investment flows tripled.

The financial crisis of 1997 came as a rude shock to this progress. The upheavals could be directly attributed to the speed and freedom of capital flows brought about by globalisation. The financial crisis sharpened concern about other risks and dangers of globalisation. Up till then, the G7 summits had been content with occasional references, apart from the thoughtful preamble to the communiqué from Lyon 1996. The G8 summits of the sixth series - Birmingham 1998 and Cologne 1999 - made globalisation their central theme.

This chapter looks first at these summits' treatment of globalisation in general. It then focuses on the international response to the two financial dangers associated with globalisation: contagious speculative panic and the chronic indebtedness of low-income countries. It argues that the G7 at both summit and finance minister level contributed to the collective management of both problems, as always seeking to reconcile domestic and international politics. In debt relief for the poorest, the heads of government responded to humanitarian pressure and became personally committed. They themselves made things happen and engaged their reputations. But in new international financial architecture, the leaders were content largely to endorse the work of their finance ministers. As the immediate crisis passed, they seemed to lose momentum, without being entirely confident that the new measures would deter future crises.

Globalisation and the Summits

One might have expected the economically powerful members of the G7 (if not Russia) to take an optimistic, self-confident line on globalisation, praising it as the source of their prosperity. But Birmingham did not do that. Consciously or not, the G8 had picked out four issues which most reflected popular fears about globalisation. These were: employability and the risk of job loss; trans-border crime, especially drug-smuggling and financial crime; international financial reform, after the panic of the Asian crisis; and debt relief for low-income countries at risk of falling deeper into poverty. The references to globalisation were therefore integrated into the summit documents, as they treated the different issues. For example, on jobs the leaders said:-

> The challenge is how to reap the benefits of rapid technological change and economic globalisation whilst ensuring that all our citizens share in these benefits.....

On crime:-

> Globalisation has been accompanied by a dramatic increase in transnational crime..... Such crimes pose..... a global threat which can undermine the democratic and economic basis of societies.

On financial crisis:-

> Globalisation has the power to bring immense economic benefits..... But the Asian financial crisis has revealed that there are potential weaknesses and vulnerabilities in the global financial system.

On world poverty:-

> One of the most difficult challenges the world faces [is]: to enable the poorer developing countries..... to benefit from the opportunities offered by globalisation.[2]

In these passages the G7 and G8 leaders, while recognising the advances and opportunities created by globalisation, expressed their anxiety about its risks and dangers, especially for poor countries and less privileged members of society. At Birmingham, Blair got his colleagues to agree that globalisation, while beneficial and inevitable, was not an undiluted good and needed to be managed accordingly.[3]

At Cologne a year later Schroeder led his colleagues further down the same track. The preamble to the 1999 G8 communiqué summarised the message delivered the year before. In those areas, like employment and development, where the link with globalisation was already established at Birmingham, the message was taken as read. At Cologne several new topics, like social protection and conflict prevention, were put into the context of globalisation. On social protection the leaders said:-

> As the process of globalisation has gained momentum..... rapid change and integration has left some individuals and groups feeling unable to keep up..... We therefore need to ... give globalisation a 'human face'.....

On conflict prevention:-

> In many countries, violent conflicts and civil wars continue to be an obstacle to making good use of the opportunities of globalisation.[4]

Some of the themes of globalisation treated by these summits mainly concerned the impact of international factors on domestic policy and how national governments should react; for example employment, education and crime prevention. Others concerned the structure and management of the global economic system. This chapter deals with the two most important issues in this second category: new international financial architecture and debt relief for low-income countries. While Chapter 7 looked at the GATT and the WTO, concerned with world trade, this chapter examines the global financial institutions, the IMF and the World Bank, together with the part played in debt relief by a plurilateral organisation, the Commonwealth.[5]

New International Financial Architecture

From Mexico to Asia

The Asian financial crisis (as it was called at first) began on 3 July 1997 when the Thai authorities were no longer able to defend the parity of the baht against the dollar. The crisis spread rapidly to the other currencies of the region. Thailand, Korea and Indonesia all negotiated programmes to gain drawings from the IMF which, by the time of the Annual Meeting of the IMF and World Bank in September, seemed to have restored stability. But the markets were not satisfied. Further capital outflows and plunges in exchange rates led to another round of IMF rescue packages, associated with debt reschedulings. By early 1998 a total of $115 billion had been committed for the three countries together.[6] All of them, together with most of their neighbours, faced deep and prolonged recession, aggravated by the chronic weakness of Japan's economy.

This crisis was never meant to happen. It did not really begin in 1997. It was a revival, in a more acute form, of the troubles which overwhelmed Mexico at the turn of 1994 and 1995. Like the upheavals of 1997, the Mexican crisis was marked by the collapse of exchange rates, the haemorrhage of volatile capital and rapid contagion both around the region and further afield. It had been checked by an exceptional IMF programme, mobilising the record level of $40 billion, early in 1995. The 1995 Halifax summit was largely concerned with reforms to the IMF and World Bank provoked by the experience of Mexico, as Chapter 8 recorded.

Halifax had agreed a four-point plan, which was rapidly adopted by the IMF and World Bank. The four elements were:-

- Stronger IMF surveillance for all countries, based on better data.
- A new emergency financing mechanism, backed by extra funds.
- Better cooperation between regulators and supervisors of banks, securities markets and other financial institutions.
- Exploring procedures for 'orderly resolution' for countries, akin to insolvency for commercial firms.

At Halifax Chirac had called international speculators the AIDS virus of the world economy. The Halifax measures were intended to deter further outbreaks of the disease.[7] Instead they only provided a period of remission, before the crisis broke out worse than before. Why did this happen?

The answer is that the implementation of the Halifax programme was tardy and incomplete. To take the four elements in reverse order:-

- The G10 looked at the idea of 'orderly resolution' for countries. They declared it impractical, but offered only modest alternatives.
- G7 finance ministers did serious technical work on regulation and supervision, reporting to Lyon 1996 and Denver 1997. But progress was slow, because of underlying differences of approach.

- The necessary extra funds for the new mechanism were committed far too slowly. The essential American share was not voted by Congress until October 1998.
- That left stricter surveillance as the only defence. This on its own was not enough, as countries in difficulty had every incentive to conceal unwelcome data.

As a result, the work on reform had to start again.

The Initial Reforms

There was one crucial difference between the 1997 Asian crisis and the earlier Mexican one. The Mexican upheaval happened because of mistakes by the government, which ran up a huge budget deficit financed by short-term borrowing. The three Asian countries were running prudent fiscal and monetary policies. Their main mistake, in hindsight, was to fix their national currencies to the US dollar. This encouraged irresponsible financial behaviour by both local borrowers and Western lenders, which turned to disaster when the dollar ended its long period of weakness and began to strengthen. The extravagance of the private financial sector was encouraged by weak and sometimes corrupt systems of financial supervision, nicknamed 'crony capitalism'. So this was a crisis caused by the private sector.

This had two important consequences:-

- The IMF recovery programmes were widely criticised. The IMF applied its usual medicine of fiscal and monetary tightening to restore stability, at an inevitable cost to economic activity. Many observers, including the World Bank, argued that this was the wrong way to curb a crisis provoked by the private sector. The IMF defended itself, but confidence in it was shaken.[8]
- Governments generally felt that the private financial sector, especially Western lenders, had got off too lightly. Funds provided by the IMF or G7 governments were used to pay off debts to Western private creditors, who were largely the cause of the crisis, while citizens of the borrowing country suffered severe hardship. The G7 looked for ways of 'bailing in' the private creditors to future rescue operations, rather than bailing them out.

The G7 finance ministers worked up a package of reforms in the first half of 1998, which was brought together for the leaders at Birmingham. By then the crisis atmosphere had eased, especially as growth in the United

States and even in Europe resumed, apparently unaffected by the crisis in Asia. The Birmingham summit endorsed proposals under four headings, two of which picked up elements of the 1995 Halifax programme:-

- *Increasing Transparency* This went beyond better economic data and stricter surveillance to advocate more openness both in national fiscal and monetary policy-making, based on new IMF codes of good practice, and in the IMF's own activities.
- *Strengthening Financial Systems* This intensified the work done since Halifax on better financial regulation. It recommended 'a system of multilateral surveillance of national financial supervisory and regulatory systems'. But the summit did not agree on how this should be organised.
- *Helping Countries Prepare for Global Capital Flows* This was intended to prevent other countries making the same mistakes as the three Asians in encouraging irresponsible capital flows. But the summit did not agree on whether capital controls were acceptable or not.
- *Ensuring the Private Sector Takes Responsibility* The aim was to develop a framework for associating private lenders with the resolution of financial crises.

There were no proposals on further financing and only a few hints of future institutional change. It was intended that this programme would be completed at the IMF/World Bank meeting in October 1998. But it was sharply overtaken by events.

The Crisis Deepens

The rouble had survived the initial Asian crisis and at the time of the Birmingham summit in May 1998 Russia did not look under threat. In July Russia negotiated a loan of $11 billion from the IMF against a new reform programme, expecting total finance of $20 billion from Japan, the World Bank and other sources. Russia at once received its first IMF drawing of $4.8 billion. But the markets sensed that this was not enough to fill the widening gap in Russia's public debt. The whole amount was exhausted in a single month of massive capital outflows. Russia appealed for more: but the G7 decided it would not 'bail out' Western private lenders to Moscow any more. So in mid-August Russia ceased to defend the rouble and defaulted on its government debt.

Many Western lenders suffered major losses in the Russian 'meltdown' and one was hit fatally. On the eve of the IMF/World Bank

Annual Meeting the highly-leveraged American hedge fund Long-Term Capital Management revealed that it was insolvent. The Federal Reserve mounted a desperate rescue operation, financed by participating banks, which averted collapse. But it looked for the first time as if the financial crisis had the power to unsettle even the United States. Simultaneously the Brazilian economy came under attack, with capital flight in advance of the presidential elections. Brazil appealed to the IMF, which assembled a $40 billion support package. But there was no participation from the private sector.

The Proposals for Cologne

At the IMF meeting in early October the G7 finance ministers agreed on the scale of the problems but could not agree on the solutions. By the end of the month, however, they were ready to announce the outline of a new programme of reforms. These were partly drawn from reports by the G22, an informal group called together by the US and involving Asian and other developing countries affected by the crisis. This programme was further elaborated at G7 meetings in February and April 1999 and at the IMF/World Bank spring meetings. It formed the basis of what the G7 heads of government endorsed at Cologne. Meanwhile the crisis atmosphere receded again. The loosening of monetary policy by the Federal Reserve and other G7 central banks in October restored confidence to the markets. The Brazilian package, after a shaky start, proved effective; Russia's crisis at least grew no worse; and no other country suffered a haemorrhage of capital. The leaders met in Cologne in June 1999, almost two years after the Asian crisis began, with a sense that calm had returned.

The Cologne programme had six components, each more elaborate than the earlier proposals:-

- *Strengthening the Institutions* The main innovation was the Financial Stability forum, to provide multilateral surveillance of financial regulators - see below. There was a modest strengthening of the IMF's Interim Committee, which should become permanent *de jure* rather than *de facto*. An 'informal mechanism among systemically important countries' was proposed. This built on the G22, which had been created by the US in 1998 but had not become permanent. The Europeans protested against its strong Pacific bias and insisted on widening the circle in 1999. The composition of the new body was not resolved at Cologne.
- *Transparency and Best Practice* Cologne endorsed all the transparency measures proposed at Birmingham, including codes of

best practice, many of which had been brought into effect in the IMF and World Bank. The G7 called for more transparency in the private sector too.

- *Financial Regulation in Industrial Countries* The new Financial Stability Forum (which first met in April 1999) brought together the G7, the Fund and Bank and the international groupings of regulators for banks, insurance and securities; it would be open to other countries too. It began by focusing on three issues which contributed to the crisis: risk assessment for banks; highly leveraged institutions, like hedge funds; and offshore financial centres.

- *Financial Systems in Emerging Markets* This expanded the advice from Birmingham on handling capital flows, admitting the possibility of measures to control inflows. It added some recommendations on exchange rate policy, discouraging countries from defending fixed rates at all costs.

- *Crisis Prevention and Involving the Private Sector* The key innovation was the new Contingent Credit Line, agreed at the IMF in April 1999, and intended to protect countries following sound policies from the contagion of financial instability. This was strongly promoted by the United States, especially after Congress had finally released the US contribution to the financing agreed back at Halifax in 1995. But some believed that any country drawing on it would automatically become a target for speculation. The provisions for involving the private sector were now much more detailed, as a result of the lessons learned from Russia and Brazil. But the rules were so elaborate it was unclear they could ever be applied.

- *Social Policies to Protect the Poor* This was a belated recognition by the G7 of the social damage done by financial crises. The proposals were mainly focused on the World Bank and the UN, including principles of good practice in social policy.

All these proposals were intended for endorsement and completion at the 1999 Annual Meeting of the IMF and World Bank in September 1999. Some additional progress was made then, for example in agreeing the composition of a new 'Group of 20', the successor to the G22. But the involvement of private lenders in financial rescue operations remained controversial; and there was no strong sense of momentum behind the reform proposals.[9]

Assessment of the New Financial Architecture

Free movement of capital is one of the dominant features of globalisation. Much of this capital has been used to underpin rapid growth, especially in the countries of East Asia. But this growth in the volume and speed of capital movements has not been constrained by any structure of rules and has far outstripped the capacity of governments to control it. Even by Halifax in 1995 a single day's transactions in the foreign exchange market was equal to twice the total reserves held by the G7 countries. So the financial upheaval which began in Asia in 1997 soon spiralled out of control and affected even healthy economies by contagion. This appeared to be one of the greatest dangers of globalisation: a volatile and unpredictable financial system, where money moved abruptly and on impulse and penalised countries whose economic policies were sound as well as those which were imprudent.

The response to the crisis by the G7 and the international financial institutions was extensive and detailed, but not radical. Far-reaching ideas like creating a World Financial Authority or giving the IMF enough resources to be a world 'lender of last resort' were not pursued. Instead the G7 preferred to recommend a very large number of adjustments to the existing machinery. This did not really produce new architecture, but rather repairs and modifications to the current building.

There was a conscious attempt to introduce more rules and respect for rules into the international financial system. This was seen in the pursuit of transparency, especially in the codes of good practice for fiscal and monetary policy. It was also seen in the surveillance of national regulators by the new Financial Stability Forum, which at once turned its attention to two areas where the rules were weakest - offshore financial centres and highly-leveraged institutions. But while the IMF and other bodies could create rules, it was not clear how these could be enforced against those who chose to defy them.

The moves to improve financial regulation and supervision were welcome. But the new international arrangements were very weak when compared with what each country could do nationally. There was no lender of last resort or international financial regulator. International discipline would depend on national authorities working together and there was persistent difficulty in agreeing on standards. Countries were happy to observe international standards only as long as they did not differ from their national ones.

In exchange rate regimes the G7 made no attempt to tighten the rules. The difficulties of defending any form of fixed parity made the G7 reluctant to advocate anything except floating rates. This looked like an admission of defeat. As a result, countries were turning to other measures to obtain the benefits of exchange rate stability: eleven member states of the EU had adopted a single currency, while countries like Argentina were considering adopting the US dollar as their national currency.

The new reforms provided some sources of extra finance. The 'New Arrangements to Borrow' agreed at Halifax were finally in force and the IMF had agreed on its Contingent Credit Line. But the troubles of the past two years had drained the resources of the IMF and World Bank to dangerously low levels.

The financial crisis raised new questions about the competence of the IMF and the World Bank and about their respective roles in a world dominated by private capital flows. Some critics argued for merging them or even for replacing them altogether. The G7 reforms gave both Fund and Bank many more things to do and some additional resources. But their institutional structure remained largely untouched.

Almost all the new proposals intended by the G7 for wider adoption were intended to discourage the outbreak of future crises. But behind all this activity, there was a sense that future crises were inevitable. The G7 did not seem confident that their measures would work; rather they seemed resigned to recurrent financial crises as the price to be paid for the benefits of dynamic, globalised capital markets.

Both the Uruguay Round, which created the World Trade Organization (see Chapter 7), and the reforms of the international financial system since the Mexican crisis were responses to globalisation, to maximise its benefits and guard against its dangers. There was, however, a clear contrast between them. The Uruguay Round was comprehensive, in that it brought virtually all trade under international disciplines. It was radical, in that it created a new institution, the WTO, and a much stronger dispute settlement mechanism. The new financial reforms, though extensive, were cautious and piecemeal. In some areas, like exchange rates, there were still no agreed disciplines and in others it was unclear if the rules would prevail against the volatility of the markets. Institutional change was limited, with no reshaping of the Fund or the Bank. The G7, including the summits, were far more active in finance than they had been in trade. But after five years of financial reforms, from Halifax to Cologne, the advance of rule-based systems still seemed inadequate to counter financial instability or deter future crises.

Debt Relief for Low-Income Countries

From Toronto Terms to Naples Terms

The financial upheavals were a crisis which mainly affected those who had benefitted from globalisation. But the G7 were also concerned by the problems of those countries which had not benefitted. Globalisation tended to polarise the performance of economies, both developed and developing. The successful did even better. The unsuccessful fell even further behind.[10]

Regional performances diverged, though in every region there were exceptions to the trend. In general, the countries of East Asia benefitted most from globalisation up to 1997, using it as the means of overhauling the mature economies of the West. The countries of sub-Saharan Africa did least well. Many African countries were worse off by the mid-1990s than they had been 10 or 20 years before. The region as a whole was trailing, though performance had picked up since 1995. Many developing countries had made great strides by outward-looking policies, expanding the share of trade in national income. But for low-income countries as a group trade had not increased as a proportion of GDP and for some 40 countries it had fallen in the past 10 years. In consequence, low-income countries were taking a dwindling share of world trade and losing out in globalisation.[11]

The main initiative taken by the summits to help these countries was by the relief of their debts. The impetus in most cases came from the UK and Canada, who used their membership in both the G7 and the Commonwealth to advance their proposals.[12] In the G7 they sought support from major creditors, while in the Commonwealth they mobilised backing from developing countries, before proposals were put to the IMF, the World Bank and the Paris Club. The first moves came from the Toronto G7 summit of 1988 and were taken up and applied by the IMF. These proposals - called Toronto terms - provided that the major creditor governments, meeting in the Paris Club, would grant relief equal to one-third of their debts to low income countries eligible for rescheduling, subject to these countries following economic programmes agreed with the IMF.[13]

This got the process started; but Toronto terms soon proved inadequate. The next initiative came from Commonwealth finance ministers meeting in Trinidad in 1990, where then British finance minister, John Major, proposed that relief go up to half of the eligible debt owed to the Paris Club. This took advantage of the acceptance of 'debt reduction' in the 1989 Brady Plan for middle-income debtors, i.e. that debts need not be repaid in full. This was endorsed at London III in 1991 and the degree of debt relief was raised to two-thirds of eligible debt by Naples 1994; what began as Trinidad terms became Naples terms.

The Heavily Indebted Poor Countries (HIPC) Programme

Naples terms would still not suffice for many poor countries. They only covered their debts to governments, not the large proportion owed to the IMF and World Bank themselves. These institutions had never allowed relief on their loans, fearing that their high credit rating would suffer. When Commonwealth finance ministers met at Valletta in 1994, just after the Naples summit, British finance minister Kenneth Clarke proposed a further set of measures to help poor debtor countries observing IMF discipline: all aid loans to be converted to grants; relief on debt owed to the Paris Club raised to 80 per cent; and special loans on softer terms from the IMF and World Bank to offset earlier lending, with rates subsidised through the sale of IMF gold. His Commonwealth colleagues backed these proposals. They were largely endorsed (though not IMF gold sales) by the 1996 Lyon summit, where the heads of the IMF and World Bank joined the leaders. The entire IMF and World Bank then adopted them as the Heavily Indebted Poor Countries (HIPC) initiative.

The benefits of the HIPC programme looked substantial. The aim was to reduce each country's debt to a sustainable level, which it could service without compromising its development goals. The Heavily Indebted Poor Countries were defined as those countries eligible for soft loans from the World Bank's International Development Association (IDA) whose external debts were more than twice their annual export earnings. Forty-one countries met these criteria, most being in Africa. Ten of them were Commonwealth members.

The conditions of the HIPC programme were demanding. Each eligible country must meet the targets of an IMF reform programme for three consecutive years. This should lead to a 'decision point', after which a debt relief programme could be drawn up and agreed by the IMF, World Bank, Paris Club and other creditors. The agreed relief took effect from 'completion point', reached within three years of the decision point, while IMF discipline continued. Among the G7, Britain, France and Canada urged that the process move through as fast as the rules allow. But Germany and Japan had reservations about the impact of the HIPC programme on IMF and World Bank policy and especially resisted selling IMF gold to finance it. The Americans insisted on strict respect for IMF conditions. So these three tended to slow things down.

Birmingham and the HIPC Programme

Between the Lyon and Birmingham summits, the progress made in launching the HIPC process was slow and varied widely between the 41 eligible countries. By May 1998 only eight countries had made reasonable progress. One country alone, Uganda, had reached completion point. Five others, including Mozambique, had passed decision point and should reach completion between late 1998 and early 2001; so had two more who only needed relief from the Paris Club, not the Fund and Bank. All the other eligible countries were further behind and 13 had yet to start the process at all. Many in this last group were victims of civil conflict, like Angola and Rwanda.

At the Commonwealth finance ministers meeting in September 1997, British finance minister Gordon Brown launched another initiative, called the 'Mauritius Mandate', aimed at using the deadline of 2000 as pressure for faster progress. This called for all HIPC countries to have embarked on the process of sustainable exit from their debt problems by the year 2000; and to have firm decisions on debt relief for at least three-quarters of them by the same date.

Major British-based NGOs concerned with development were also expressing concern at the slow progress. They focused on the human deprivation which the debt burden caused for countries like Uganda and Mozambique, which had to spend more on debt service than on health or primary education. A large group of charities and NGOs, led by Christian Aid, launched the Jubilee 2000 campaign. This focused on the public slogan 'Break the Chains of Debt' which implied full debt relief for poor countries by 2000. It was reinforced by more detailed proposals to speed up the HIPC process, widen its eligibility, increase the relief given and give special treatment to countries suffering civil conflict.[14] At Birmingham, Jubilee 2000 organised a mass demonstration - a human chain of 50,000 people six miles long to encircle the Birmingham convention centre, where the G8 formal meetings were held.

Blair's objective at Birmingham was simple: to get the G8 to endorse as much as possible of the 'Mauritius Mandate'. A clear G8 endorsement would help to move matters forward in the IMF, World Bank and Paris Club. It might also have been received positively by the Jubilee 2000 campaign. In the event, the commitments made in the G8 communiqué were dismissed with deep disappointment by the demonstrators. Blair accepted that the summit did not go as far as they wanted. But he defended the outcome; the G8 had made progress and the agreement was a step forward.

At Birmingham the G8 endorsed the target of getting all countries into the system by 2000. But there was no commitment to having debt packages agreed for 75 per cent of them by that date. There was a less precise undertaking 'to ensure that when they qualify countries get the relief they need', with the additional prospect of 'interim relief measures where necessary'. The G8 introduced a new concept of helping 'poor post-conflict countries' to get emergency debt relief. The G8 were thus more precise about what they expected the debtor countries to do but vaguer and more conditional on what they would do themselves. There was still scope for the sceptics to keep slowing the process down. But equally, there were openings for further pressure to move things forward.

The Cologne Debt Initiative

The charities and other NGOs did not give up after the disappointing results of Birmingham. They continued to press for more rapid and radical debt relief. They argued that, even after Birmingham, the HIPC programme moved as slowly as before. When countries fulfilled all their obligations to the IMF, the amount of debt relief received was negligible. Mozambique would receive relief of only $10 million on a total debt of $120 million. The NGOs picked up the G8 commitment at Birmingham to the OECD targets for reducing poverty in developing countries and insisted that poor countries could never reach these targets unless they could shift more resources from debt repayment into education and health. They planned another massive demonstration for the Cologne summit, backed by a petition with two million signatures.[15]

A fundamental change in the German position gave strong encouragement to the NGOs. In January 1999 Chancellor Schroeder announced his intention to make debt relief for the poorest a central issue for the Cologne summit. He called for deeper and faster debt relief, for the complete forgiveness of aid debt and for more generous financing, hinting at German agreement to IMF gold sales. Schroeder's announcement stimulated all the other G7 countries to put in their own proposals for improving the HIPC programme and other approaches to debt relief. The British and Canadian ideas were the most forthcoming, building on the work they had done in the Commonwealth. But the German proposals were equally generous, as Schroeder and the federal chancellery overcame the doubts of the finance ministry, who had been the most reluctant hitherto. The Americans were prepared to relax their insistence on long periods of observing IMF programmes. The greatest hesitation came from

France and Japan: the French still had a high level of aid debt; the Japanese had problems with the concept of debt forgiveness in government finance.

The Cologne Debt Initiative, as finally agreed, was set out in the G7 statement by the leaders and a supporting report by G7 finance ministers. The Cologne agreement preserved the basic approach to debt relief in the HIPC programme but recommended a complete overhaul of the terms and conditions. There were five main elements:-

- *Poverty Reduction* The funds saved through debt relief must be channelled into basic social programmes, such as health and education. The G7 asked the World Bank and IMF to ensure that this happened. These provisions met criticism of debt relief from two opposite directions. The charities had argued that debt repayments were preventing poor countries from spending enough on education, health and other development programmes. Opponents of debt relief, however, argued that the money saved was often diverted into unproductive uses, such as buying military equipment.

- *Faster Debt Relief* Under the HIPC programme debtor countries had to observe three years of IMF discipline to 'decision point' and another three before 'completion point' when relief actually started. Cologne maintained the two stages, but allowed for relief to start much quicker after 'decision point', i.e. after three years, not six. The leaders added a provision, not in the finance ministers report, aiming to get three-quarters of eligible countries to their decision point by 2000. This key provision of the 'Mauritius Mandate', denied at Birmingham, was endorsed at the Cologne summit.

- *Deeper Debt Relief* The HIPC programme aimed to reduce poor countries' debt to 'sustainable levels', defined at 200-250 per cent of exports. But this ratio had proved too high. Cologne lowered it to 150 per cent. For debts owed to national governments covered by the Paris Club, the proportion of relief was raised from 80 per cent to 90 per cent and even more if needed. All aid debts not already converted to grants should be forgiven.

- *Total Value of Debt Relief* The G7 estimated that these measures would more than double the debt relief available under the HIPC programme, from $12.5 billion to $27 billion in 'net present value' terms and $50 billion in nominal terms. A further $20 billion (nominal) would come from forgiving aid debt. The G7 calculated that this would reduce by more than half the stock of $230 billion debt owed by HIPC countries and not already covered by debt relief schemes.

- *Financing* Much of the sluggishness in the HIPC programme was due to the reluctance of G7 members to find the necessary finance for it. Wolfensohn, the World Bank President, had warned earlier in 1999 that the programme risked collapse without adequate funds to enable the Fund and the Bank to offset their earlier loans to debtor countries. Cologne recognised that more finance would be needed, including contributions from G7 members, but the provisions here were less precise than elsewhere. It was finally agreed that the IMF should use the interest on the proceeds from selling 10 million ounces of its gold. However, there were fears this would depress the world gold price - already hit by sales from the Bank of England - and several HIPC countries were gold exporters. On bilateral contributions, especially to the World Bank, the G7 would only 'consider [them] in good faith', while calling for 'appropriate burden-sharing', reflecting the uneven distribution among the G7 of aid debt yet to be forgiven.

The Cologne Debt Initiative was a major advance. It revealed the limits of what had actually been achieved at Birmingham. But the exchanges at Birmingham were necessary to open up discussion of the subject and reveal the strength of public concern. Without Birmingham, Cologne would not have gone so far. Even Cologne did not satisfy those Jubilee campaigners who wanted forgiveness of all debt.[16] But the G7 judged this would do more harm than good; since it would make it impossible for poor countries to raise loan finance in any form in future.

The Cologne Debt Initiative, like the financial architecture proposals, required endorsement from the entire membership of the IMF and World Bank. This endorsement was given at the Annual Meeting in September 1999. Further progress was made then in mobilising the necessary finance: the IMF decided to revalue its gold internally, rather than selling it; and G7 members and others pledged bilateral contributions totalling $2.5 billion to the World Bank's trust fund.[17] This was a good start. But the Cologne Debt Initiative would be judged for its sustained performance, on several criteria: on speeding up the HIPC process, to meet the deadline of 75 per cent of eligible countries at decision point by 2000; on generating enough finance to meet this demanding target; and on delivering extensive savings in debt repayments, which could be used for health and education programmes.

If the Cologne Debt Initiative was fully implemented and its targets were met, both in 2000 and thereafter, that could finally take the specific item of debt relief for low-income countries off the summits' agenda. But that would not exhaust the G7's responsibility towards poor developing countries. These countries would still be poor after their debts were forgiven. They had not hitherto benefitted from globalisation. Most of them had instead fallen further behind. There were signs of a quickening interest among the G7 in the problems of poor countries, going back at least to Lyon 1996. The Cologne summit showed this in its treatment of trade, social protection and conflict prevention. In these areas the G7 leaders needed to go beyond statements of intent and actually make things happen, as they had done over debt.

Conclusions: The Summits and Global Finance

The pressures of globalisation obliged the G7 leaders at Birmingham 1998 and Cologne 1999 to give priority to the international financial system and to the reform of the IMF and the World Bank. On both debt relief and new financial architecture they produced extensive results. But the results produced, and the summits' contribution to them, were not of equal value.

In the recurrent treatment of debt relief for poor countries, from 1988 onwards, the G7 summits made a major contribution to helping these countries. This was about the only summit initiative focused on the poorest countries. It was open to some severe criticisms; but it was clear that if the heads of government themselves had not pushed for action on debt relief for the poorest, nothing would have happened at all. The G7 leaders were not content with a single initiative, but kept coming back to try and correct its defects. Furthermore, these measures to help the poorest were not provoked by any systemic crisis or major threats to the G7's economic interests. They contained a clear ethical motivation.

The HIPC programme, which they announced proudly at Lyon in 1996, turned out much slower and less generous than it sounded. While the relief was meant to render their debts 'sustainable', when it finally arrived it made little difference. The amounts available looked meagre alongside the funds mobilised for just three Asian countries in crisis. The G7 were reluctant to finance the HIPC programme on a sufficient scale. The British and German campaigns before Birmingham and Cologne brought the G7 to recognise these defects. From now on there is some prospect that the HIPC programme should work as it was intended.

With debt relief for low-income countries, the G7 summit made things happen. It was their intervention that counted, not their finance or other ministers. In consequence, the reputation of the summit became closely linked with the success of debt relief. If the Cologne Debt Initiative should be fully implemented and bring real relief to poor countries, the summit's stock would rise. If not, public confidence in the summit and its ability to respond to the dangers of globalisation would fall sharply.

In their treatment of financial architecture the summits were also returning to a subject they had addressed recently, at Halifax in 1995. In this topic they were responding to systemic crises and direct threats to their economic interests. They sought to restore calm, to prevent a recurrence and to provide for better crisis management in future. By an accident of timing, both the Birmingham and Cologne summits were held when the financial crisis was in abeyance. The idea of an unprecedented special G7 summit was mooted in October 1998, when the crisis was at its height, but this proved unnecessary.

The summits in both 1998 and 1999 provided occasions for the G7 finance ministers to pull together their work in progress and submit it to the heads of government for them to give it their authority. The approach of a summit encouraged the finance ministers to settle outstanding differences among themselves (as evidently happened in October 1998) and to isolate those that remain to be resolved at the higher level. To serve this purpose the summit discussions needed to be carefully prepared and in this respect the finance ministers did their work well.

The G7 leaders provided their ministers with the authority they needed and this had great value. Beyond this, however, they appeared to make no personal contribution. There was no sign that they resolved any outstanding differences, in the absence of crisis pressures obliging them to do so. On debt relief the leaders were innovative; on financial architecture they remained cautious. Earlier summits had provided examples of resolution of differences by the leaders; Rambouillet 1975 legitimised floating and Paris 1989 accepted the debt reduction of the Brady Plan - in each case bringing agreement where there was division before. Birmingham and Cologne, however, left many matters unresolved: the future of the IMF Interim Committee; the composition of an 'informal group of systemically important countries'; the enforcement of new rules on transparency and financial regulation; proper regimes for capital flows and exchange rates; and methods for involving the private sector in financial rescues. In all this the G7 leaders seemed to betray a lack of confidence that they could construct a new system robust enough to deter financial crises in future. They recognised the forces of globalisation in this area but were not sure they could control them.

Notes

1   The IMF's *World Economic Outlook* for May 1997 (IMF 1997), pp. 1-14, perceived no dangerous tensions in the world economy, with inflation subdued everywhere and financial markets calm.

2   The quotations are from paras. 6, 13 and 18-19 of the G8 communiqué and para. 6 of the G7 statement. Texts available on www.g7.utoronto.ca.

3   Blair had taken a similar line at the Edinburgh Commonwealth Heads of Government Meeting in October 1997; see Maud 1998 and Bayne 1998c.

4   The quotations are from paras. 19 and 39 of the G8 communiqué. For text, see www.g7.utoronto.ca.

5   This chapter is drawn in part from 'Globalization and the Commonwealth', *The Round Table*, no. 344, pp. 473-484 (Bayne 1997d) and 'Britain, the G8 and the Commonwealth', *The Round Table*, no. 348, pp. 445-457 (Bayne 1998c).

6   For a joint account of the IMF and World Bank response to the Asian crisis, prepared before Birmingham, see Camdessus and Wolfensohn 1998.

7   A volume of papers, edited by Professor Peter Kenen and introduced by Lawrence Summers (then Deputy Secretary of the Treasury), reviewed in October 1996 the progress made in IMF reform since Halifax (Kenen 1996). Most contributors were satisfied with the progress and did not anticipate future crises like the Mexican one.

8   For example, Stanley Fischer, IMF Deputy Managing Director, replied in *Financial Times*, 17 December 1997 to criticisms by Martin Wolf and Professor Jeffrey Sachs in *Financial Times*, 9 and 11 December 1997. See also the exchange in *Foreign Affairs*, Feldstein 1998 and Fischer 1998.

9   The members of the new G20 are: Argentina, Australia, Brazil, Canada, China, France, Germany, India, Italy, Japan, Mexico, Russia, Saudi Arabia, South Africa, South Korea, Turkey, UK, US, the EC and the IMF/IBRD. It thus includes all the G8 summit participants; Canada holds the chair. See *Financial Times*, 27 September and *Guardian*, 28 September 1999. Private creditors were angered by the IMF's apparent acquiescence in Ecuador's default on its 'Brady bonds', issued on the settlement of its last debt crisis.

10 An IMF analysis of globalisation concluded: 'A key lesson seems to be that the pressures of globalization, especially in the last decade or so, have served to accentuate the benefits of good policies and the costs of bad policies' (IMF 1997, p. 72).

11 The relationship of trade to GNP in low-income countries is analysed in World Bank 1997, pp. 292-295 and Table 6.1.

12 France was also active in the early initiatives, as Jacques Attali's account of the Toronto 1988 summit reveals; see Attali 1995, entries for 1-2 June 1988.

13 An instructive account by a UK participant of the development of debt relief for the poorest from the Lawson proposals of 1987 is in Evans 1999.

14 The Jubilee 2000 campaign identified Germany as the main obstacle. Christian Aid supplied postcards, complete with German text urging greater generosity, for its supporters to send to the finance ministry, to Kohl, and to Schroeder as opposition leader. Over 15,000 postcards were sent, but probably irritated the Kohl government at the time.

15 For a pre-Cologne critique of the HIPC programme, see *Financial Times*, 12 June 1999.

16 A target figure of $165 billion in debt reduction had earlier been suggested by Christian Aid (Lockwood and others 1998, p. 32), though for a larger group of 52 countries. The charity argued that the extent of relief should vary according to capacity to pay without comprising basic development programmes.

17 Some of the financial pledges, including that from the US, were dependent on legislative approval. The revaluation of the IMF's gold reserves would liberate additional funds without requiring actual sales which might depress the market. See *Financial Times*, 27 and 28 September 1999.

Conclusion

12 The World Catches Up With the Summits

I have been researching and writing about the summits for 16 years, more than half their lifetime. Vicariously - if not in reality - I accompanied the leaders as they scaled all the summits from 1975 to 1999. The experience was itself rather like climbing a mountain. The higher one went, the further one could see, so that the view appeared quite different from a new angle. In particular, what looked like isolated peaks from lower down revealed themselves as all part of the same range.

What conclusions can be drawn, then, from looking back over the complete chain of summits to date, from Rambouillet 1975 to Cologne 1999? This chapter of conclusions follows the threefold analytical framework used throughout this book.[1] It concentrates on the more recent summits, from 1988 onwards, classified into the fourth, fifth and sixth summit series. The main theses argued in this chapter are:-

- *Collective Management* By the mid-1980s, the summits' performance was in decline. Progress in cooperation was only made when the US took the initiative, which happened rarely. But during the 1990s both trends were reversed. The level of cooperation achieved at the summits rose steadily. A true pattern of collective management began to emerge, with the Europeans originating cooperative actions at least as often as the US. There were various reasons for this: the stimulus of the Cold War's ending; more solidarity in Europe; political shifts in G7 countries; a better understanding of the demands and dangers of globalisation. There were also negative, inward-looking trends on both sides of the Atlantic, as well as in Japan.
- *Reconciling the Tensions of Globalisation* The summits were created to settle problems which had baffled solution at lower levels and where only the heads of government could resolve the tensions between domestic and international pressures. Each summit was presented as a new event, confronting fresh challenges and marking new achievements. Each summit host tried to build up this impression of innovation and originality. This approach, however,

191

could only be sustained with difficulty, even in conditions of interdependence limited to industrial democracies. The advance of globalisation, removing barriers to trade, investment and financial flows, expanded the range of potential conflict between domestic and international demands. The summits were obliged to keep coming back to problems and to treat them iteratively. This practice of iteration at the summits, rather than their individual outcomes, became fundamental to the summit process and the progress achieved.[2] This is illustrated by reviewing the themes treated at Birmingham and Cologne. These reflected contemporary anxieties about globalisation, but had much deeper roots.

- *Political Leadership* The practice of iteration had institutional consequences for the summit. The summit apparatus grew inexorably, at both ministerial and official level. Attempts by the leaders to prune this growth made little progress: like the monstrous hydra killed by Hercules, every time one head was cut off two new ones grew up in its place. The dilemma was only resolved by cutting the summit loose from the G7/G8 apparatus and allowing the heads of government to meet on their own, with a limited agenda. But they could only do this because a wide variety of ministerial and official groups had met beforehand, to dispose of those issues that did not need to go to the leaders and to refine those that did. Because the G7 and G8 ministers concerned now had their own established groups (which could involve other countries), they were content that heads of government should meet on their own.

The new summit format gives the leaders more freedom than before to choose what they will do. The final section of this chapter looks briefly to the future. It argues that the leaders at the summit need not focus so much on government action, as hitherto, but should look wider. In future the summits ought to involve the private sector more and use the new communications technologies to make the case for the benefits of globalisation.

Collective Management: Slowly Improving Performance

Grading the Summits

The record of the summits up to 1986 in achieving cooperation among the participants was summarised in Table 11.1 of *Hanging Together* (Putnam and Bayne 1987). This table showed wide variations in performance from one year to the next. The long-term trend, however, was of declining cooperation. Early summits, especially Rambouillet 1975 and Bonn I 1978, scored the highest marks. The summits of the 1980s were less productive of cooperation and some of them, like Versailles 1982 and Bonn II 1985, actually made matters worse in some respects.

A new table of summit achievements in cooperation, up to and including Cologne 1999, is given in Table 12.1 of this book. This is essentially the same as the table published on page 68 of Peter Hajnal's book the *G7/G8 System* (Hajnal 1999, Table 7.1), the second volume in this G8 and Global Governance series. The table in this book, like Hajnal's, incorporates the early markings given in *Hanging Together*. There are some differences, however, which need explanation.

In *Hanging Together* cooperation was limited to agreement on policy issues. The present table has extended cooperation to include agreement on durable institutional innovations. This leads to upward adjustment of the marks for Ottawa 1981, which started the Quad of trade ministers, and for Tokyo II 1986, which launched the G7 finance ministers. Later summits also get marks for institutional advances, like absorbing the Russians into the G7 process.

As before, some summits made matters worse in certain areas, offsetting the progress made elsewhere. So Houston 1990 is marked low on 'trade - no net advance'; the revival of difficulties over agriculture, which frustrated the Uruguay Round, cancelled out the progress made with other parts of the trade agenda. For some later summits, from Lyon 1996 onwards, the areas of cooperation identified differ from those given in Hajnal's table. Lyon itself has been marked down, as it does not appear as productive as Halifax 1995, Birmingham 1998 or Cologne 1999.

The table illustrates, in summary form, the revival of summit performance, as described in earlier chapters of this book, from the low point of the mid-1980s. The summits of the 1990s show, on average, a clear improvement in cooperation over those of the 1980s, even though they do not equal the achievements from the 1970s. A more detailed analysis, by summit series, confirms this improvement.

The summits of the fourth series, 1989-1993, were stimulated by the end of the Cold War to cooperate better, though the tensions and difficulties of this period are shown by wider variations in the marks. The fifth summit series, 1994-1997, which concentrated attention on the institutional review, yielded a richer cooperative harvest than the fourth, with somewhat greater consistency. But the low mark for Denver 1997 shows that the impetus for renewal was running out. The two summits of the sixth series so far, 1998-1999, receive high marks for innovation and cooperative achievement. If this performance was sustained, the renewal of the summits under their new format would equal the cooperation achieved in the first heroic age of summitry. But this cannot be taken for granted. Two summits are a small sample and later events may undermine the good marks given to Birmingham and Cologne.[3]

Beyond Hegemony

The record of summitry up to 1986, as examined in *Hanging Together*, suggested that American leadership was a necessary, though not sufficient condition for cooperation at the summits. When the US asserted strong leadership, together with at least one other G7 member, cooperation was likely. When the US tried to lead alone, the results were disappointing. When the Americans did not give a lead, the summits were inconsequential.

The 12 summits from 1988 onwards show a different pattern, moving away from the condition of 'subjective' American hegemony to more genuine collection management. During this period cooperation was certainly stimulated by American initiative. But it was just as likely to derive from European initiative, with European G7 members taking the lead collectively or even singly. There were some examples of successful Canadian initiatives, though very few from Japan. The pattern is best illustrated by looking at the summits series by series, from the fourth series onwards.

The Fourth Series, 1989-1993 During the five years of the fourth series, as noted in Chapter 5, cooperation at the summit focused on trade, debt, the environment, drugs, helping Eastern Europe and helping Russia. There were also efforts to slim down the summit format.

- On *trade*, the initiative for the Uruguay Round had come from the US, backed by Japan. While the Round lasted, up to Tokyo III 1993, the US could be considered the driving force, with two renewals of fast-track negotiating authority. Within the trade agenda, however, G7 members had different priorities: the US pressed on agriculture; the EU wanted better dispute settlement; Canada first promoted the idea of a WTO.

- On *debt*, the US promoted debt reduction for middle-income countries through the Brady Plan, endorsed at Paris 1989. But later summits turned to debt relief for poor countries, with London III 1991 taking forward work begun at Toronto 1988. Here Britain, France and Canada were the leaders and the US was reluctant.

Table 12.1:   Achievements of the G7/G8 Summits, 1975-1999

Year	Summit	Grade	Achievements
First Series			
1975	Rambouillet	A-	Monetary reform
1976	San Juan, Puerto Rico	D	Nothing significant
1977	London I	B-	Trade, growth, nuclear power
1978	Bonn I	A	Growth, energy, trade
Second Series			
1979	Tokyo I	B+	Energy
1980	Venice I	C+	Afghanistan, energy
1981	Ottawa	C	Trade ministers' quadrilateral
1982	Versailles	C	East-West trade, surveillance
Third Series			
1983	Williamsburg	B	Euromissiles
1984	London II	C-	Debt
1985	Bonn II	E	Nothing significant
1986	Tokyo II	B+	Terrorism, surveillance, G7 finance ministers
1987	Venice II	D	Nothing significant
1988	Toronto	C-	Debt relief for the poorest
Fourth Series			
1989	Paris	B+	Helping Eastern Europe, environment, debt
1990	Houston	D	Trade - no net advance
1991	London III	B-	Helping USSR
1992	Munich	D	Nothing significant
1993	Tokyo III	C+	Trade
Fifth Series			
1994	Naples	C	Russia into P8
1995	Halifax	B+	Institutional review, IMF and UN reform
1996	Lyon	B	Debt, development
1997	Denver	C-	Russian participation, Africa
Sixth Series			
1998	Birmingham	B+	New format, crime, debt, finance
1999	Cologne	B+	Debt, Kosovo, finance

- On the *environment* the initiative came from Europe, especially Germany and France. Specific contributions originated from Japan (energy) and Canada (oceans). The US was again reluctant, but this did not prevent some good cooperation focused on UNCED in 1992. (Such cooperation, however, eluded the later Denver 1997 summit.)
- On *drugs* the initiative seemed genuinely shared. The Europeans backed American concern about cocaine in the Western hemisphere, while the US supported European action against heroin from the East. The Financial Action Task Force (FATF), the most durable summit decision, was launched by France.
- *Helping Eastern Europe* was also a shared initiative. Paris 1989 took up the subject as a result of Bush's visit to Warsaw and Budapest, but he proposed that the European Commission take the lead in coordination. [4]
- On *helping Russia*, however, the initiative clearly came from Europe. Germany and France led the formation of a European position which they pressed on a reluctant US at Houston 1990. Britain proposed inviting the Russians to meet the G7 at London III 1991. American initiative in this area only began with Clinton, before Tokyo 1993.

Reforming the summit format was pressed hardest by Britain, but made only limited progress.

The Fifth Series, 1994-1997 The main areas of cooperation in the four years of the fifth series, as recorded in Chapter 8, were: the institutional review; international finance; development and debt; UN reform; and international crime. The Russians moved from half members to full members of the summit process.

- The *institutional review* was first proposed by the Europeans, to counter a new American trade initiative at Naples 1994. The Europeans, with Canada, provided the main impetus. The Americans took a full part in individual topics, but allowed the review to peter out at Denver 1997.
- *International finance* became the prime subject for Halifax 1995 because of the Mexican crisis six months earlier. The Americans had put together the Mexican rescue with the IMF in a way which angered the Europeans. In contrast, Halifax allowed everyone to contribute and produced good cooperation, even if implementation fell short.
- On *development*, the summits continued to work on debt relief for poor countries, with the UK leading. The US became more cooperative; Germany and Japan were the obstacles to progress.

France stimulated a general development focus at Lyon 1996, but the focus on Africa proposed by the US for Denver 1997 fell short, because the Americans themselves could not offer enough.[5]

- The pressure for *UN Reform* came from Europe, mainly from Britain and France. The US was inhibited by the non-payment of its UN subscription.
- *Crime*, like drugs, was an issue of shared concern. The US linked this with terrorism at Lyon 1996, because it was the victim of a recent terrorist attack.

The move to admit Russia to the G7's political exchanges at Naples 1994 was jointly encouraged by the US and Europe, with Japan being the most reserved. The US made Denver 1997 'the Summit of the Eight' in order to reconcile Russia to the enlargement of NATO.

The Sixth Series, 1998-1999 The two summits so far of the sixth series inaugurated a new format, with leaders meeting alone. The main areas of cooperation, as given in Chapter 10, were: financial architecture; debt; crime and internal disorder; and Kosovo. Jobs and trade also received attention.

- The *new format*, confirming the summit as G8, was a British initiative, with Blair picking up on Major's earlier efforts. The hesitation about leaders meeting without their ministers had come mainly from Germany and Japan. They acquiesced when the US came out in support.
- On *new financial architecture* the Americans were the most active, promoting a new IMF facility and calling together a new 'Group of 22'. All other G7 members contributed their ideas too. But the EU was inhibited from joint action, because the UK was not in the euro-zone and the European Central Bank had no responsibility for what happened outside Europe.
- On *debt relief* for poor countries the lead came as always from the UK. A decisive advance was possible at Cologne 1999 because Germany reversed its earlier opposition.
- *Crime and internal disorder* remained a common concern. Europeans like Germany and Italy widened the agenda because of their worries about the impact of Kosovo.
- On *Kosovo* the Americans focused on security concerns, while the Europeans concentrated on post-war reconstruction in the Balkans. For the first time, cooperation on a policy issue depended on Russia.
- *Jobs* came onto the Birmingham 1998 agenda because of the UK, backed by the US, but with ready acceptance from the rest of the G8.

- *Trade*, as noted, had been driven by the US up to 1994. But by Birmingham and Cologne the Europeans had taken over the lead. They called for a new comprehensive WTO round, starting in 2000, and had Japan's support. But the more limited US aims inhibited cooperation, in a way which may be ominous for the future.

This detailed examination shows a wide variety of stimuli to cooperation. There are clear examples, particularly in international finance, where the Americans took the lead and the Europeans followed. There are just as many examples of European initiative. In these cases sometimes the Americans remained reluctant, as with the environment; sometimes they became cooperative followers, as with debt relief for poor countries. Over time, roles could be reversed. In dealing with the Russians, the early initiatives came from the Europeans, but the lead later passed to the US. In international trade liberalisation the Americans began as the leaders, but the Europeans became the prime movers as US support weakened. Finally, on a growing number of issues there appeared to a be a genuine collective effort and a sharing of burdens, as over drugs, crime and Kosovo.

The Americans sometimes inhibited cooperation by pressing too hard, rather than seeking alliances. Among the Europeans, France, Germany and Italy normally sought to build up a European consensus before seeking US backing. Britain sometimes did the same, but at other times lined up support from the US or Canada (through the Commonwealth) before its European partners. Canada, like Britain, sometimes looked for US support first, sometimes European. Japan seemed largely passive throughout.

Explaining the Improvement

The summits from 1988 onwards thus produced a certain revival of cooperation, in conditions that did not just rely on American hegemony. What were the reasons which produced this double movement towards better performance and real collective management?

The first reason, in terms of time, was the stimulus provided by the end of the Cold War. All the G7 participants recognised that this was a historic change, which required a collective response from the West. This gave the G7 the incentive to provide leadership in mobilising help first from Eastern Europe and then for Russia - even though it proved harder than expected to agree among themselves and to implement effective programmes of assistance.

Second, from 1988 onwards, the Europeans proved more successful than before in producing joint initiatives for the summit, for example on the global environment and helping the Russians. The Europeans did not always act together; the UK often preferred to seek support for its initiatives in North America before it turned to Europe. But there were none of the open disagreements within Europe that had surfaced at earlier summits, for example at Bonn II in 1985.

Third, during this period there were a number of changes among the summit leaders that encouraged more cooperation. In four of the G7 members - US, Canada, UK, Germany - political parties returned to power after long periods in opposition. In each case the new government was somewhat to the left of its predecessor - and the same trend emerged in Italy. These developments made most of the G7 leaders more disposed to embrace change and new ideas and more prepared to intervene, rather than leaving everything to the market. In Japan, however, political instability combined with economic stagnation had the opposite effect.

The fourth reason is more subjective. But one can argue that, as the 1990s progressed, the G7/G8 leaders came to understand better the demands and dangers of the post-Cold War world of globalisation. At first they were inclined to think a new era had dawned, when cooperation would be easy. They gradually realised that globalisation, for all its benefits, had its darker side. The population in their countries was uneasy and looked for reassurance, while the poorest members of the world community were falling further behind. The G7/G8 leaders concluded that the tensions of globalisation required more sustained attention, with iterative treatment of intractable issues. The consequences of this are examined in the next two sections of this chapter.

Despite these positive trends, collective management at the summit remained very imperfect. The obstacles to cooperation were formidable and in some respects they were growing. In the United States the euphoria generated by the collapse of communism was replaced by a movement towards isolation and protectionism. With Soviet power destroyed, why did the US have to be so active internationally? When these trends appeared in Congress, the Administration could not always prevail against them. So US cooperation was frustrated by the lack of fast-track negotiating authority or the refusal of Congress to vote the necessary funds. Across the Atlantic, the demands of building and enlarging the European Union often made the Europeans give priority to their internal objectives over wider international initiatives. This was most evident in monetary issues. While the successful launching of the euro boosted European morale, it left responsibility even more divided on international monetary and financial policy.

With these inward-looking trends at work in the major G8 participants, collective management at the summits could not be taken for granted.   It would require sustained effort both inside and outside government to sustain the momentum towards closer cooperation.

Reconciling the Tensions of Globalisation: Continuity and Iteration at the Summits

Summits were originally intended, especially by Giscard and his European colleagues, to be single free-standing events. The leaders would gather to address a set of problems that had defied solution at lower levels. Their leadership qualities would enable them to reach solutions: leadership as heads of government, with supreme responsibility; and leadership as representing the most powerful economies, whose joint decisions would be accepted by others. Having reached their conclusions, the leaders would disperse, to be called together when another set of intractable problems required their attention.

Of course, the summits very soon became an annual series. This was because the Europeans went along with the parallel American concept of the summit giving regular and systematic impulses to other international bodies. It did not mean the heads of government had changed their view about their own leadership qualities. To this day the leaders expect to reach agreements or achieve results that have eluded their ministers at lower levels. Why else should they meet at all?

One abiding vision of the summit, which remained prevalent in the late 1990s, was that the summits should make their unique contribution each year by providing leadership and agreed decisions, and then hand on their recommendations to be pursued by their cabinet colleagues or the competent international institutions. With this model the leaders only intervened at the point where they were needed. Preparations would be organised by a light, unbureaucratic structure of personal representatives. This vision still exercises a strong attraction, not least on the leaders themselves.[6]

There were times, especially in the early years, when the summits did operate like this; when issues came to the summit for one or two years and were then entrusted to wider international bodies and did not recur at the summit level. The international monetary system was the central theme for Rambouillet 1975, but it did not come back to the summit again for many years thereafter. Energy issues, central in 1979 and 1980, have not required the same attention since. In more recent years, the summit concentrated on mobilising help for Central European countries in 1989 and 1990, but then switched its attention to Russia.

These were, however, isolated episodes in summit history. The usual pattern was of continuity and iteration. The summits came back and back to the same issues, seldom being able to clear them off their agenda altogether. One can identify four reasons why this happened: perseverance with difficult problems; dealing with new and unexpected issues; institutional inadequacy; and the consequences of globalisation.

Perseverance with Difficult Problems

A few issues became recurrent features on the summit agenda because they were thought to deserve the attention of the leaders every year. Macro-economic policy coordination was such an issue in the early years, although it was then largely delegated to finance ministers. International trade issues always concerned the leaders in some form. While trade negotiations were in progress, as with the Tokyo Round in 1975-79 or the Uruguay Round in 1986-93, the summit encouraged them to reach a successful conclusion. In between global rounds, the summit sought to prevent protectionist trends from regaining ground.

More importantly, many issues kept coming back to the summit because the leaders failed to reach the right solution on their first attempt. The problems that came to the summit were inherently very difficult. If they had been easy, they would have been solved at lower levels. It should be no surprise, and no reproach to the summits, if they did not get them right the first time. But the leaders did not give up and declare it all too difficult. They kept at it, returning again and again to intractable issues until they agreed on an effective and acceptable outcome. It is to the credit of the leaders, and of the summit as an institution, that they persisted, despite the public criticism provoked by their lack of initial success.

This persistence was a dominant feature of summit history. There were many examples of it. It happened with both the Tokyo and the Uruguay Rounds of trade negotiations. The summits set deadlines for their completion, but then failed to honour these commitments because of disagreements among G7 members. But despite this, and in the face of much criticism, the leaders persevered and did finally succeed in bringing the two trade rounds to their desired conclusion in 1979 and 1993. The summits' dealings with Russia showed a similar sequence. They devoted three years, from 1991 to 1993, to different methods of providing help to the Russian economy; and another five years, from 1994 to 1998, to resolving the exact relationship of Russia with the summit. This process ended with the official conversion of the summit from G7 to G8 in 1998. Other examples are examined below.

New and Unexpected Issues

Summits aimed to be innovative. They identified new issues of concern to the world community and stimulated new forms of international action. However, it took time to change people's thinking and develop new policies. For example, the summits from 1989 to 1991 stimulated innovative thinking on global environmental issues in the run-up to the Rio Environment Conference, breaking new ground. During the same period they acted as pioneers in the international treatment of terrorism and drug smuggling, addressing new issues each year.

The summits had a good record in crisis management, once the crisis had broken. But they were no better than anyone else at forecasting crises. They did not foresee the end of the Cold War or the Iraqi invasion of Kuwait. Their record at predicting financial upheavals was especially poor. The summits did not anticipate the turmoil in Latin America in 1982, in Mexico in 1994 or in East Asia in 1997. When the leaders were taken by surprise in this way they had to come back to the issues in question, as they did with debt and financial instability.

Institutional Inadequacy

The recurrence of issues at the summit was affected by the quality and the range of the international institutions to which the leaders could pass on issues for further treatment. Recommendations on trade and financial issues could be passed on readily to the GATT or WTO, to the IMF or World Bank. But in other areas the institutions were fragmented, as with the global environment, or largely unsatisfactory, as with international crime. So the summits had to return to these issues themselves and sometimes create their own apparatus for follow-up in order to maintain any progress.

The Consequence of Globalisation

Globalisation became a major theme for the summits, as argued in earlier chapters. It was also a direct cause of iteration. Globalisation progressively limited the policy instruments in the hands of G7 and G8 governments, particularly instruments of short-term impact. Monetary policy was largely in the hands of independent central banks. Fiscal policy was set in a long-term context and was rarely used for immediate macro-economic impact. Many policy levers formerly in the hands of government had moved to the private sector.

Most of the economic levers still available to governments were not quick-acting. They only made an impact over time. This meant that issues needed several years of summit treatment before any change was visible. The summits at Naples in 1994 and Lyon in 1996 already focused on employment issues. But because the improvement in employment levels was slow to appear, the subject came back onto the agenda in Birmingham in 1998 and Cologne in 1999.

Some Conclusions on Iteration

From this analysis some preliminary conclusions can be drawn. The summits did not achieve results by flashes of prescient, inspirational decision-making, sparked by the personal chemistry between the leaders. There were a few instances of this, but they were very rare. Nor did the summits often achieve, at the first attempt, a definitive settlement of issues which could then be handed on to other institutions. Nearly always their achievement came from dogged persistence, a sort of 'worrying away' at the issues until they had reached a solution.

One operational consequence of this recurrent treatment of issues at the summit was constant pressure on the agenda. More and more issues demanded treatment by the leaders, but few could be put away as definitely solved. Overloading, which had always threatened the summits, came to a head in the early 1990s. From 1992 onwards British Prime Minister Major stimulated a sustained effort to organise the leaders' time better and to allow them more spontaneous debate, rather than being swamped by paper. This eventually led to the summit in 1998 taking place, for the first time ever, among leaders only without supporting ministers. This format was repeated at Cologne in 1999 and is now accepted practice.

But this apparent lightening was deceptive. The foreign and finance ministers were still meeting, though separately, a week before the summit and producing extensive documentation on issues which did not need the personal attention of the leaders. The number of issues tackled by the G7 and G8 did not diminish and the G7 and G8 apparatus continued to proliferate. The next section of this chapter will return to the institutional consequences of this. The remainder of this section looks at iteration in current practice.

Iteration at Birmingham and Cologne: The Four Horsemen of Globalisation

The Birmingham summit was the first to be consecrated wholly to the fears and anxieties generated by globalisation. Earlier summits of the 1990s, from Naples 1994 onwards, recognised globalisation as a powerful, all-embracing force, with benefits as well as dangers. Recognition of this force provided the context for the leaders' decisions. The first response of the leaders to globalisation was to conduct a review of international institutions, to see if they could stand up to the new pressures put upon them and to propose reforms to make them more effective.

This process occupied the summit from Naples 1994 to Denver 1997, after which it ran out of steam. The leaders at Birmingham addressed popular anxieties about globalisation directly. They chose an agenda of four issues related to globalisation that worried their electorates deeply. These were: job loss; crime and internal disorder; financial panic; and world poverty. They returned to the same basic agenda at Cologne, extending it in the light of recent experience, especially in Kosovo.

As argued in earlier chapters, globalisation presented G8 governments with a dilemma. They knew the removal of barriers to economic activity, together with access to new technology, was the cause of their growing prosperity. Governments acted upon this conviction, by getting out of the way of economic competition, renouncing various powers and transferring large portions of former government business to the private sector. But globalisation disturbed the very people upon whom the power of democratic governments depended. The people felt vulnerable to external pressures over which they had no control. They worried that their jobs were threatened, that crime was rising, that financial markets behaved irrationally and that the poorest were neglected both at home and in the world at large. They expected their governments to do something about these worries. Governments in turn wanted to respond. But even where they had the power, they often could not protect their people from the risks of globalisation without forfeiting its benefits.

That is why the advance of globalisation brought certain issues back to public consciousness and back onto the summit agenda. All the themes chosen for Birmingham in 1998 went right back to the origins of the G7 and had recurred at the summit over the years. However, globalisation added a new dimension to each of them. The analysis that follows concentrates on the persistence of these problems and the sustained determination of the summits to tackle them, rather than on the solutions which emerged. All were likely to need sustained iterative treatment, with more attention at future summits.

The First Horseman: Job Loss

Cologne was the fourth summit in six years to address unemployment, responding to popular anxieties about globalisation. Each was prepared by a meeting of employment (and sometimes finance) ministers early in the year. Birmingham focused on 'employability'. Cologne added education and social protection. In these areas, the G8 governments hoped to develop 'best practice' among themselves and to learn from each others' experience, good or bad.[7]

Detailed discussions of employment-promoting measures only began at Naples 1994 for the G7/G8. Education also had not been discussed before, except informally at Toronto 1988. In a different form, however, employment and jobs had been on the summit agenda from the very start. The early summits concentrated on two arguments: whether macro-economic policy should tolerate inflation to sustain jobs; and whether trade protection was justified to preserve jobs. The first argument was soon settled. The declaration from London I in 1977 said bluntly: 'Inflation does not reduce unemployment; on the contrary, it is one of its major causes'.

In the second argument, those advocating trade protection to save jobs were kept in check, but only with a struggle. In 1975-79 and again in 1986-93, the summits gave iterative treatment to the GATT multilateral trade negotiations. They insisted on a successful outcome - even when they could not deliver - because this was the best way of keeping protectionist pressures in check at home. In the interval between the two GATT rounds protectionist ideas made dangerous advances in the United States. This prompted US Treasury Secretary Baker's initiative for the 1985 Plaza Agreement, so that a lower dollar would restore the competitive position of US industry.

After the Uruguay Round the advance of globalisation again revived political arguments in favour of protectionism. The Birmingham and Cologne summits gave their blessing to new WTO negotiations due to begin in 2000. But the summits were not used to resolve trade issues which divided the G7. This was a lost opportunity.

Trade, employment and protectionism were always fundamental issues for the G8. The summits gave the leaders a platform to promote the case for free trade and open markets. They could do this better when they were actively working together to improve employment conditions by other measures. But they would still need to argue vigorously for trade liberalisation, against new forms of protectionism. So trade would certainly return to the summit.

The Second Horseman: Crime and Internal Disorder

Birmingham was the first summit where crime was chosen as a principal theme. This subject did not, however, appear suddenly. Before Halifax 1995, crime was identified as a theme for the review of global institutions and serious work began in the preparations for Lyon 1996. In all the G8 countries there was a growing fear of violent crime and fraud. Globalisation fed this fear. The speed of communications and the openness of borders and markets, which enhanced life for the honest citizen, made conditions easier for the criminal too. In some countries, organised crime could even undermine the fabric of the state; Russia was especially vulnerable. The traumatic experience of Kosovo made the Cologne summit link crime and other threats to 'human security' with conflict prevention.

International public order issues of this kind were the first non-economic issues to be taken up at the summits. German Chancellor Schmidt stimulated a spontaneous discussion on hijacking at Bonn I in 1978. Terrorism and hostage-taking preoccupied the summits of the early 1980s and were the major political issue for Tokyo II 1986. Drugs likewise first came onto the G7 agenda spontaneously, being raised by Reagan and Thatcher at Bonn II 1985. Later summits went deeply into illicit drug smuggling and set up the Financial Action Task Force (FATF) to check the laundering of drug money.

The end of the Cold War had a perverse effect on this subject. More open frontiers made it easier to move illicit drugs from centres of production in Asia to consumers in Europe. New fears arose of the smuggling of nuclear material from abandoned Russian stockpiles. Globalisation kept adding new crimes to the international agenda, such as hi-tech crime and the smuggling of people and firearms.[8]

One major problem with crime was the fragmentation and inadequacy of international institutions in this field. The United Nations could draw up international conventions containing strong commitments, but it had no power to ensure compliance. Similarly, in conflict prevention the UN's capacity had fallen short of its aspirations. The Cologne G8 communiqué outlined a programme both to attack the sources of conflict and to strengthen the UN's capacity to prevent crises. But this work was only just beginning.

The Third Horseman: Financial Panic

Birmingham and Cologne were both obliged to consider the impact of the financial crisis of 1997-98. As argued in Chapter 11, this was not part of the original plan. In 1995, in the light of the Mexican crisis, the Halifax summit had recommended a substantial reform programme which was adopted by the Fund and the Bank collectively. No one expected another financial panic would follow so soon.

This issue too went back to the dawn of summitry. Giscard convened the very first summit in 1975 to put some 'viscosity' into the world financial system. In fact, he had to acquiesce at Rambouillet to a regime of generalised floating, to be endorsed by the IMF. G7 currencies continued to fluctuate against each other, while private bank lending 'recycled' the surpluses of the oil producers. At Versailles 1982 the leaders agreed on a system of mutual surveillance of economic policies, which became a standing activity of the G7 finance ministers. But only a few weeks later Mexico, Brazil and Argentina threatened to default on the debts which they had accumulated by recycling. These were new financial issues for the summit agenda. The debt problems were finally resolved by writing down the debts below their nominal value under the 'Brady Plan', that was endorsed at the Paris Arch summit of 1989.

In the 1990s the financial markets were again transformed. The crises which affected Mexico in 1994 and the three Asian countries in 1997 were harder to predict, spread much further and faster, and required an urgent and massive mobilisation of resources to bring them under control. Birmingham and Cologne therefore confronted the danger that financial instability, encouraged by globalisation, might destroy the international system. The leaders endorsed their finance ministers' work on a 'new international financial architecture' for submission to the IMF and World Bank. But even with these improved precautions, outbreaks of financial panic must be expected to recur. The huge amounts of money circulating in the system, combined with the herd instinct of the markets, far exceeded the capacity of monetary authorities to control them. So it was all too likely that financial panic and financial reform would come back to the G8 agenda again - and the leaders seemed to expect it.

The Fourth Horseman: World Poverty

World poverty might be less serious than financial instability for the economic system. But it was worse in human terms and revealed the risks of globalisation for the poorest. With some notable exceptions, low-income countries, especially in Africa, fell even further behind as a result of globalisation, while the middle-income countries closed the gap on the mature economies.

From the start, the summit agenda had included relations with developing countries, but without making any impact on the problems of the poorest for many years. The first serious contribution came with the

1988 Toronto summit, which endorsed proposals for debt relief for low-income countries, known as 'Toronto terms'. Then the process of iteration began. Toronto terms were improved at London III 1991 and again at Naples 1994. They were expanded into the Heavily-Indebted Poor Countries (HIPC) programme, advocated by Lyon 1996 and supported by the Fund and Bank. But the conditions of access were tough and implementation was very slow; deserving poor countries suffered while waiting.

At Birmingham Blair pushed for measures to speed up implementation of the HIPC programme, setting 2000 as a deadline. Progress was disappointing, largely because of German resistance. Before Cologne Germany completely reversed its position. So the Cologne Debt Initiative cut in half the duration of the HIPC process and doubled the amount of debt relief on offer. If it was fully implemented, the poorest countries would be able to divert debt repayments to necessary social programmes like health and education. This was the outcome of iterative treatment at six summits, from Toronto onwards.

But debt was not the only problem affecting low-income countries. Recent summits had given more attention than their predecessors to issues concerning the poorest. Lyon 1996 looked at development institutions; Denver 1997 focused on Africa. But the results were disappointing. Summit declarations had much good advice and exhortation, but few precise commitments. Promises on trade access for the poorest countries had not yet been kept. Many G7 governments that had squeezed public spending were reluctant to increase aid programmes.[9] The G8 still had a responsibility towards low-income countries, to make them gainers and not losers from globalisation.

Political Leadership: The World Catches up with the Summits

When the summits began in the 1970s they had three distinctive features as an institution; dominance, rarity and bureaucratic independence. All three have eroded over time.

Dominance

In the 1970s, the seven participating countries, plus the Commission and Presidency to represent the rest of the European Community, were the dominant powers in the international economic system. Whatever they could agree among themselves was likely to be accepted by others.

By the end of the 1990s, the G7/G8 members no longer dominated the world economically as they used to do. Many developing countries had become active players and influenced international decisions. Some were very large and populous countries, such as Brazil, China, India, Indonesia and Mexico. They were opening their big internal markets to foreign competition and becoming more internationally minded. Others were smaller economies that had grown rich from outward-looking policies and become trading powers and financial centres, such as Hong Kong (China), Korea, Malaysia and Singapore. Despite the setback for some of these from the Asian financial crisis, the G8 had to pay more attention to their views and deal with them more tactfully and persuasively than in the past.

This dispersion of power in the world economic system was a consequence of globalisation. This had enabled developing countries to compete effectively with the mature economies of the West, to narrow the gap in living standards and to become independent centres of power. This was the positive face of globalisation, to set against the worry that the poorest developing countries were falling further behind.

Rarity

In the 1970s the G7 was among the very few groups meeting regularly at head of state and government level. The only established cycle was the Commonwealth Heads of Government Meetings, held every two years. The European Council, also founded by Giscard, was just beginning. The North Atlantic Treaty Organisation (NATO) also met at summit level, but irregularly.

Since then, and especially in the 1990s, international summit meetings proliferated. NATO came to hold a summit almost every year. The European Council not only had its regular cycle, twice a year, but held special meetings as well, either on its own or with others. The UN had periodic summits on special issues: environment, population or social affairs. Regional and trans-regional bodies also began to meet at summit level: the Organisation of American States (OAS) for the Western Hemisphere; Asia-Pacific Economic Cooperation (APEC) for the Asia-Pacific; and the Organisation for Security and Cooperation in Europe (OSCE). Well-connected heads of state and government were always meeting their peers.

This proliferation of summits was both a tribute to the G7's pioneering role and another consequence of globalisation. As external factors intruded more deeply into domestic policy-making, leaders no longer relied on sending their foreign secretaries or other specialist ministers to international meetings. They had to take a hand themselves.

Bureaucratic Independence

The G7 summit began as a free-standing entity at head of state and government level. Other summits - the Commonwealth, NATO, and the European Council - were each the apex of an established organisation. The G7 summit had its preparatory network formed of the personal representatives of the leaders, the 'Sherpas'. But the G7 did not exist at lower levels.

As the preceding point showed, other institutions, both global and regional, began by meeting at ministerial and official level and later completed their structures by adding a layer of heads of state and government. The G7 summit went through this process in reverse. For the first decade and more there was strong resistance from the leaders, especially from Giscard and Mitterrand, to extending the G7 apparatus downwards. While Carter favoured a sort of summit bureaucracy, this was reversed when Reagan came to power. Specialist G7 groups were set up on occasion, but most had a limited life and were wound up once they had finished their work.

This resistance to bureaucracy started to erode in the 1980s, with the emergence of G7 ministerial groups. The earliest of these established a degree of independence from the summits. This applied to the Quadrilateral or 'Quad' composed of trade ministers from the US, EU, Japan and Canada. Its origins went back to Ottawa 1981. It acted as a pressure group in the WTO and its summit origins were forgotten. The G7 finance ministers emerged publicly at Tokyo 1986. The G7 soon replaced the secretive G5, whose origins predated the summit itself. The G7 finance ministers met as part of the summit framework, but they followed their own cycle for the rest of the year, always coming together on the margins of the IMF/IBRD spring and autumn meetings. Both trade and finance ministers had their apparatus of official deputies. G7 foreign ministers also met annually in September on the margin of the UN General Assembly, to review the post-summit foreign policy agenda.

These groups were followed in the 1990s by a network of G7/G8 meetings tied more closely to the summit cycle. Environment ministers began meeting every year a few weeks before the summit. Employment ministers, sometimes with finance and other ministers, had met four times by mid-1999 to prepare for summits. Future meetings seemed likely. Interior ministers met twice on terrorism and crime; another crime ministerial was due later in 1999. A distinct series of meetings, on various subjects, were designed to embed the Russians in the G8 process, such as the 1996 nuclear summit and the 1998 energy ministerial, both held in

Moscow. There was a full sequence of such specialist ministerial meetings in the six months before Birmingham and again before Cologne.

Unlike the Quad and the G7 finance ministers, which fitted neatly alongside the WTO and the IMF/IBRD, these newer groups did not correspond to a single global institution. All of them also had their own supporting apparatus of officials. Alongside them, the preparation of the summit itself generated another hierarchy of specialist groups of officials, on both economic and political subjects, preparing reports and papers for the Sherpas or for the leaders themselves.[10]

This expanding summit apparatus was not just the usual bureaucratic spread; the leaders could have kept that in check. The most powerful influence on this proliferation was the iterative way the summits now worked. The summits grappled with difficult and unfamiliar issues. They often needed several attempts before arriving at the correct solution. They handled subjects for which there were no satisfactory global institutions. In these conditions, it became natural to create G7 or G8 groups to work on the issues between summits, to prepare future decisions and to keep track of problems, even when they had been handed on to wider institutions. These subsidiary groups, at ministerial or official level, gradually acquired a life of their own.[11]

The G8 summit still had no headquarters, no written procedures and no secretariat. But in other respects it had become much less distinctive and much more like other institutions. The EU, NATO, APEC and the rest completed their pyramids from the bottom upwards, finally adding an apex of heads of state and government. The G8 summit grew its own pyramid from the top downwards, in a haphazard but all-embracing way. As a result, the summit apparatus reached the limit at which it could be managed by the host country for the summit in each year. The Sherpas and their closest collaborators were caught between the demands of the leaders for less paper and more time to talk among themselves; and the plethora of specialist advice and recommendations coming up from the host of other ministerial and official groups.

Detaching the Summit from Its Apparatus

There were two possible ways to escape from this pressure. The first was to create a separate summit secretariat. This had been advocated by outsiders almost since the summits began. But it never had any appeal to the G7 and G8 governments. The second solution was the one adopted. It was to push more subjects downwards and outwards in the G8 hierarchy.

The consequence was that more G8 activity became detached from the summit itself. The decisions of subordinate G8 groups would not have the authority of the summits themselves; but they would carry weight because they were agreed by this influential group of countries. This already happened with the 'Quad' of trade ministers and with the G7 finance ministers. Other G7 and G8 groups were likely to break their links with the summit and establish an independent existence. Some would start with the G7 or G8 members as their nucleus but be expanded to include other countries, like the new Group of 20 created at the IMF/IBRD.[12]

The decision to hold the 1998 summit among leaders only, for the first time ever, should be seen in the light of this bureaucratic evolution. As long as the G7 summit was the source of decision-making on all subjects, foreign and finance ministers were not prepared to see the heads of government settling things on their own. This was felt most strongly in countries ruled by political coalitions, notably Germany, Italy and Japan. It also applied in the United States, where - unlike other G7 countries - the President usually came to his high office without any previous ministerial experience. France, Britain and Canada had no such inhibitions about the leaders meeting on their own. But this group was a minority in the G7. Earlier attempts to promote a heads-only summit, notably by Canada before Halifax 1995, did not succeed. But events moved on after Halifax. At Lyon 1996 and Denver 1997 the leaders and their ministers were all there, but mainly met separately. It was thus less of a step to separate the meetings of the leaders and ministers in time as well as space. The same was happening to the preparatory process. Up to the early 1990s, Sherpas usually met flanked by their foreign and finance ministry sous-Sherpas. Now the sous-Sherpas had their own networks of meetings.

Thus the heads-only summits held at Birmingham and Cologne in 1998 and 1999 did not mean the summit process was getting simpler. It was instead getting both more complex and more dispersed. The heads could meet on their own because established G7 or G8 machinery now existed for treating subjects at a lower level. It was thus easier to select a few issues which would go to the leaders themselves. This separate G7/G8 machinery was not the intention of the summit's founders, Giscard and Schmidt. The process could generate its own dangers: of G8 bureaucracy growing unchecked without the discipline of summit relevance; or increased resistance from non-G8 countries to the spread of G8 groups unrelated to the summit. It was a natural reaction to the pressures of globalisation. But it made the summit more like an ordinary institution. After 25 years, the world had caught up with the summits.

Looking to the Future: Beyond Government

The analysis in this concluding chapter is not intended to belittle the summits or their achievements. It is intended to strip away some of the myths which surround this annual meeting of the worlds' most influential economic leaders - myths which the leaders themselves sometimes encouraged. It aims to show how the summits actually achieved their results.

The leaders made their contribution not by flashes of personal inspiration at a given moment, but by sustained, iterative treatment of difficult issues. It often took several attempts to find acceptable solutions. Few problems could be settled definitively; they were prone to recur in a different form. In developing this iterative approach, the G8 summits gradually became less distinctive than they were. They were not single peaks, but part of the mountain range which made up the international economic system.

The need for repeated treatment of problems tended to choke up the summits' agenda. In the conditions of globalisation, when more and more international issues intruded on domestic policy and bid for the attention of the leaders, this congestion was inevitable. The solution adopted was to extend the lower-level G8 apparatus, in a way which made it easier for the leaders themselves to delegate. They could thus meet on their own for the first time at Birmingham in 1998, where they concentrated on the anxieties felt by their peoples about aspects of globalisation. The response to globalisation had thus become a central focus for the summit.

Meeting on their own gives the leaders a new freedom to shape their own methods of work. How can they best use this freedom to advance their objectives in the future?

One approach would be to look beyond the activities of government. So far the G7/G8 summit has been a wholly governmental process. It involves national governments, the European Commission and inter-governmental bodies such as the IMF, the WTO and the United Nations. But most of this process of governmental action can now be left largely to their ministers, meeting separately from the summits. The heads of government can use their democratic legitimacy to look wider than government. They need to do so, both to reap the greatest benefits from globalisation and to overcome the resistance to it. To achieve this, the summits should develop better links both with private business and with popular opinion, including a response to civil society.

The Private Business Community

To maximise the benefits from globalisation, the leaders need better links to the private business community. Most of the advantages of globalisation derive from the enterprise and innovation of the private sector. It is private industry, for example, which is bringing together new technology and business methods to develop electronic commerce. The latest summits have begun to recognise the contribution of the private sector. At Cologne the G7 leaders invited the private sector to take part in financing debt relief and sought to involve them in 'forestalling and managing' financial crises. But private business will not respond well to exhortation just to put up more money. The leaders need to engage them more directly.

There are some contacts with private business already built into the summit process.[13] But these are rather mechanical and bureaucratic and do not fit well with the 'heads-only' summit format. The heads of government need the opportunity for personal contact with business leaders who have responsibilities and influence comparable with their own. These are the people whose input the heads of government need most, so as to understand better how business is driving globalisation and how new technologies are changing the world. The heads of government should not of course follow blindly whatever advice the business leaders give them. But the quality of summit decisions would be improved and there would be opportunities to get government and business to work together.

The mechanics of such public/private contacts at the summit would not be easy to organise. The leaders would want to confer with a group no larger than their own, to preserve informality. But the group should not just be drawn from the largest multinational companies, since that would increase the suspicion that globalisation only benefits the rich and powerful. It should reflect a wide range of active international business, both large and small. There should be no standing members of any business group, but the composition should vary each year, according to the summit's agenda.

One approach would be to give the initiative for organising the business contacts to the host country for the year, who would propose the topics for discussion and the composition of the group. A second approach would be for each of the heads of government to choose a 'business Sherpa' from their private sector, charged with preparing the business element of the summit. That would recall the very earliest days of the summits, when the Sherpas themselves sometimes came from outside government.

Popular Opinion and Civil Society

To overcome the resistance to globalisation, the G8 leaders need to confront the network of NGOs known as 'civil society'. Here again the summits are beginning to recognise their influence; the Cologne documents recommended that the WTO should be more open to civil society, while the Fund and Bank should consult civil society over debt relief and poverty reduction. But there is a danger that the G8 leaders accord legitimacy to 'civil society' on its own terms and do not differentiate between its component groups. Some of these are constructive and well-informed, like the charities working for more generous debt relief. The summit should treat these groups seriously. But others are destructive and anarchistic, like the violent groups which smashed up buildings in the City of London on the day of the Cologne summit.

Many of the NGOs that make up civil society are hostile to globalisation. They regard it as a sort of Frankenstein's monster which has to be destroyed. Many of their campaigns are aimed at frustrating the sort of cooperation which is sought through the summits. NGOs launched a bitter campaign against the Multilateral Agreement on Investment (MAI) being negotiated in the OECD. Emboldened by the collapse of the MAI negotiations, they turned their attention to the WTO, with violent demonstrations linked to the ministerial meetings in Geneva in 1998 and Seattle in 1999.

The anxieties felt by these members of civil society are real. But their claims and conspiracy theories are misleading or without foundation. The G8 should therefore become the public advocates of the benefits of globalisation. They should use their annual summit to spread this message, to overcome popular anxieties and to counter the misleading claims of non-representative NGOs. They should make all the resources of the new communications technology work for them. It is ironical that groups who want to reverse current trends of progress should be so much more adept at using the internet to frustrate the objectives of elected governments.

A G8 pro-globalisation campaign, to argue convincingly for its benefits and to inform and educate the public, would require a new information policy from the summits. The effectiveness of the summits in spreading their message has been going downhill for many years. As compared with organisations like the WTO or IMF, the summits are secretive and opaque. Their agreed message is only conveyed by the summit communiqué and related documents. These are necessary for fixing what has been agreed between the G8 members. But despite the recent success in cutting them back, they are still too long and boring to interest most of the media. At the early summits the leaders used to brief the press together. Now they all brief nationally, a process which draws attention to the differences between the G8 members rather than to what they have agreed in common.

In the 21st century the preparation and public deployment of a common pro-globalisation message should be a major task for the summits. The leaders should do more in public together and less separately. They should use all the latest techniques available from film, television and the internet to make contact with their populations, to revive their interest in summitry and to capture their attention.

During their first 25 years, the G7/G8 summits have seen the world move from interdependence to globalisation. They have helped to shape that process, through instances of collective management. They have sought to reconcile the tensions between domestic and international politics. As globalisation widened the scope of these tensions, the leaders have successfully delegated much of this activity. With the new freedom that comes from meeting on their own, the leaders should re-assert their political leadership by looking beyond the horizons of governmental action. They should draw more widely on the expertise of private business and become public advocates of globalisation, so that the people listen to them rather than to civil society. Without such advocacy, the leaders may look down from the summit on a landscape clouded with doubt and uncertainty.

Notes

1   This chapter is drawn from 'Continuity and Leadership in an Age of Globalization', in M.J. Hodges, J.J. Kirton and J.P. Daniels (eds.), *The G8's Role in the New Millennium*, Ashgate, the G8 and Global Governance series, Aldershot (Bayne 1999), expanded and updated to cover the Cologne summit. Several of the notes below link this chapter to other contributions in that volume.
2   This analysis is distinct from the study of summit compliance, on which see Kokotsis and Daniels 1999 and Kokotsis 1999. This chapter provides some reasons why summit compliance is less than optimal and explains what the summits try to do about it.
3   It would be a mistake to build too precise an analysis on the marks given to individual summits. But, with that caveat, rough calculations show the summits of the first series scoring an average mark of B. The second series scores C+. The third series falls to C. The fourth series recovers to C+ and the fifth goes up to B-. So far the sixth series averages B+, but it is not clear if this can be sustained.
4   With durable cooperation on debt, environment, money-laundering and helping Eastern Europe, there may be a case for upgrading Paris 1989 to A-, the same mark as Rambouillet 1975. Similarly, the innovations of the institutional review and exchanges on employment may argue for giving higher marks to Naples 1994, though the substantive work on institutions only came with Halifax 1995.

5   Unusually, cooperation on Africa failed because the initiator could not deliver, rather than from resistance by other G7 members. The logic of Putnam's two-level games should have encouraged Clinton to make European achievements the spur to more action by the US. But American triumphalism at Denver made this impossible.

6   This view was eloquently put by the late Dr Michael Hodges, in Hodges 1994 and 1999. For a head of government's view, see Major 1999, pp. 524-528.

7   These issues were reviewed in the conference recorded in CEP 1998, held at the LSE ten days before the Birmingham summit. As Graham Ingham noted in the introduction: 'We cannot claim that the conference provided an agenda which the G8 leaders followed. But it did provide an agenda for the longer term'. See also Layard 1999.

8   For the impact of globalisation on financial crime, see Staple 1999.

9   The British government broke this trend in 1998, by announcing a major increase in official aid funds over the next three years. This would take it from 0.26 per cent of GDP in 1998 to 0.3 per cent in 2001; see *Financial Times*, 15 July 1998. This move encouraged the UK to press for commitments on aid volume at Cologne.

10   For a more detailed account of the G7/G8 apparatus, see Hajnal 1999, pp. 35-44 and especially Table 4.1

11   The impact of the G7/G8 apparatus as a system of world governance has been well analysed by Professor John Kirton, notably in Kirton 1995 and 1999. Baker 1996, pp. 7-8, makes a fair point that Putnam and Bayne 1997 broke off just as the G7 was starting to expand away from the summit.

12   Another example was the special meeting of the G8 foreign ministers on 12 June 1998 to discuss the Indian and Pakistani nuclear tests. They asked Argentina, Brazil, South Africa and Ukraine to join them, as countries which had renounced their capacity to make or deploy nuclear weapons; see *Financial Times*, 13 June 1998. G8 foreign ministers' meetings of this type have developed since the summits adopted the heads-only format.

13   Business groups like the International Chamber of Commerce regularly sent their recommendations to the G7 leaders before each summit. The host head of government received delegations from both the Business and Industry Advisory Committee and the Trade Union Advisory Committee of the OECD.

Bibliography

Note A much fuller summit bibliography is available in Peter I. Hajnal, *The G7/G8 System: Evolution, Role and Documentation*, Ashgate, G8 and Global Governance Series, 1999.

Arnold, T. (1995), *Reforming the UN: Its Economic Role*, Royal Institute of International Affairs, Discussion Paper No. 57, London.
Artis, M. and Ostry, S. (1986), *International Economic Policy Coordination*, Routledge and Kegan Paul for Royal Institute for International Affairs, London.
Attali, J. (1995), *Verbatim III*, Fayard, Paris.
Baker, A. (1996), *The Historical Development of the G-7: An Incoherent and Disjointed Response to Global Interdependence?*, G7RU Working Paper No. 2, School of Public Policy, Economics and Law, University of Ulster, Jordanstown.
Bayne, N. (1984), 'Western Economic Summits: Can They Do Better?', *The World Today*, vol. 40, no. 1, pp. 4-11.
Bayne, N. (1987), 'Making Sense of Western Economic Policies: the Role of the OECD', *The World Today*, vol. 43, no. 1, pp. 4-11.
Bayne, N. (1991), 'In the Balance; the Uruguay Round of International Trade Negotiations', *Government and Opposition*, vol. 26, no. 3, pp. 302-315.
Bayne, N. (1992), 'The Course of Summitry', *The World Today*, vol. 48, no. 2, pp. 27-29.
Bayne, N. (1994), 'International Economic Relations after the Cold War', *Government and Opposition*, vol. 30, no. 4, pp. 492-509.
Bayne, N. (1995), 'The G7 Summit and the Reform of Global Institutions', *Government and Opposition*, vol. 30, no. 4, pp. 492-509.
Bayne, N. (1997a), 'Changing Patterns at the G7 Summit', *G7 Governance*, no. 1, www.library.utoronto.ca/www/g7/governance/g7gove1.htm.
Bayne, N. (1997b), 'What Governments Want from International Institutions and How They Get It', *Government and Opposition*, vol. 32, no. 2, pp. 361-379.
Bayne, N. (1997c), 'History of the G7 Summit: the Importance of American Leadership' and 'Impressions of the Denver Summit'. The first paper is available on www.library.utoronto.ca/www/g7/annual/bayneg8.htm; the second on www.library.utoronto.ca/www/g7/evaluations/forepol.htm.
Bayne, N. (1997d), 'Globalisation and the Commonwealth', *The Round Table*, no. 344, pp. 473-484.

Bayne, N. (1998a), 'International Economic Organizations: More Policy Making, Less Autonomy', in B. Reinalda and B. Verbeek, (eds.), *Autonomous Policy Making by International Organizations*, Routledge, London and New York, pp. 196-210.

Bayne, N. (1998b), 'The Background to Birmingham' and 'First Impressions of the Birmingham Summit'. Both papers are available on www.g7.utoronto.ca, as documents 108 and 245-250 relating to the Birmingham 1998 summit.

Bayne, N. (1998c), 'Britain, the G8 and the Commonwealth: Lessons of the Birmingham Summit', *The Round Table*, no. 348, pp. 445-457.

Bayne, N. (1999), 'Continuity and Leadership in an Age of Globalization', in M. J. Hodges, J. J. Kirton and J. P. Daniels (eds.), *The G8's Role in the New Millennium*, Ashgate, Aldershot, pp. 21-43.

Bayne, N. and Putnam, R. D. (1995), 'Introduction: The G7 Summit Comes of Age', in S. Ostry and G. R. Winham (eds.), *The Halifax G7 Summit: Issues on the Table*, Centre for Policy Studies, Dalhousie University, Halifax.

Bergsten, C. F. and Henning, C. R. (1996), *Global Economic Leadership and the Group of Seven*, Institute for International Economics, Washington.

Cable, V. and Henderson, P. D. (eds.) (1994), *Trade Blocs? The Future of Regional Integration*, Royal Institute for International Affairs, London.

Camdessus, M. and Wolfensohn, J. D. (1998), 'The Bretton Woods Institutions: Responding to the Asian Financial Crisis', in M. Fraser (ed.), *The G8 and the World Economy*, Strategems Publishing Ltd., London, pp. 6-8.

Camps, M. (1975), *First World Relationships: the Role of the OECD*, Atlantic Institute for International Affairs, Paris.

Camps, M. and Gwin, C. (1981), *Collective Management: the Reform of Global Economic Organizations*, McGraw-Hill, New York.

Centre for Economic Performance (CEP) (1998), *Employability and Exclusion: What Governments Can Do*, Papers from a Conference held on 6 May 1998 by the Centre for Economic Performance and the London School of Economics, London.

Croome, J. (1995), *Reshaping the World Trading System: A History of the Uruguay Round*, World Trade Organization, Geneva.

De Menil, G. and Solomon, A. (1983), *Economic Summitry*, Council on Foreign Relations, New York.

Dobson, W. (1991), *Economic Policy Coordination: Requiem or Prologue?* Institute for International Economics, Washington.

Drake, W. and Nicolaidis, K. (1992), 'Ideas, Interests and Institutionalisation: 'Trade in Services' and the Uruguay Round', *International Organization*, vol. 46, no. 1, pp. 37-100.

Evans, H. P. (1999), 'Debt Relief for the Poorest Countries: Why Did It Take So Long?', *Development Policy Review*, vol. 17, no. 3, pp. 267-279, Overseas Development Institute, London.

Evans, P. B., Jacobson, H. K. and Putnam, R. D. (eds.) (1993), *Double-Edged Diplomacy: International Bargaining and Domestic Politics*, University of California Press, Berkeley.

Feldstein, M. (1998), 'Refocusing the IMF', *Foreign Affairs,* vol. 77, no. 2, pp. 20-33.

Fischer, S. (1998), 'In Defense of the IMF', *Foreign Affairs,* vol. 77, no. 4, pp. 103-106.

Franks, O. (1978), 'Lessons of the Marshall Plan Experience', in *From Marshall Plan to Global Interdependence,* OECD, Paris.

Funabashi, Y. (1988), *Managing the Dollar: from the Plaza to the Louvre,* Institute for International Economics, Washington.

Granville, B. (1995), *The Success of Russian Economic Reforms,* Royal Institute for International Affairs, London.

Granville, B. (1999), 'Time for a Rescue', *The World Today,* vol. 55, no. 7, pp. 7-9.

Hajnal, P. I. (1999), *The G7/G8 System: Evolution, Role and Documentation,* Ashgate, Aldershot.

Henderson, P. D. (1993), 'International Economic Cooperation Revisited', *Government and Opposition,* vol. 28, no. 1, pp. 11-35.

Hodges, M. J. (1994), 'More Efficiency, Less Dignity: British Perspectives on the Future Role and Working of the G-7', *The International Spectator,* vol. xxix, no. 2, pp. 141-159.

Hodges, M. J. (1999), 'The G8 and the New Political Economy', in M. J. Hodges, J. J. Kirton and J. P. Daniels (eds.), *The G8's Role in the New Millennium,* Ashgate, Aldershot, pp. 69-73.

Hodges, M. J., Kirton, J. J. and Daniels, J. P. (eds.) (1999) *The G8's Role in the New Millennium,* Ashgate, Aldershot.

Hoekman, B. (1995), *Tentative First Steps: An Assessment of the Uruguay Round Agreement on Services,* Discussion Paper no. 1150, Centre for Economic Policy Research, London.

International Monetary Fund (IMF) (1997), *World Economic Outlook, May 1997,* IMF, Washington.

Jackson, J. H. (1990), *Restructuring the GATT System,* Royal Institute of International Affairs, London.

Jackson, J. H. (1994), 'Managing the Trading System: The WTO and the Post Uruguay Round GATT Agenda' in P. B. Kenen (ed.), *Managing the World Economy: 50 Years After Bretton Woods,* Institute for International Economics, Washington.

Jackson, J. H. (1998), *The World Trade Organization: Constitution and Jurisprudence,* Royal Institute of International Affairs, London.

James, H. (1996), *International Monetary Cooperation Since Bretton Woods,* International Monetary Fund, Washington.

Jenkins, R. (1997), *Reassessing the Commonwealth,* Royal Institute of International Affairs, Discussion Paper no. 72, London.

Julius, D. (1990), *Global Companies and Public Policy,* Royal Institute for International Affairs, London.

Julius, D. (1998), 'Trade and Investment in the Light of the Asian Crisis', *Bank of England Quarterly Bulletin,* vol. 38, no. 3, pp. 280-282.

Kenen, P. B. (ed.) (1994), *Managing the World Economy: Fifty Years After Bretton Woods*, Institute for International Economics, Washington.

Kenen, P. B. (ed.) (1996), *From Halifax to Lyon: What Has been Done About Crisis Management?* Essays in International Finance no. 200, Princeton University, Princeton.

Kirton, J. J. (1995), 'The Diplomacy of Concert: Canada, the G7 and the Halifax Summit', *Canadian Foreign Policy*, vol. III, no. 1, pp. 63-80.

Kirton, J. J. (1999), 'Explaining G8 Effectiveness' in M. J. Hodges, J. J. Kirton and J. P. Daniels (eds.), *The G8's Role in the New Millennium*, Ashgate, Aldershot, pp. 75-91.

Kokotsis, E. (1999), *Keeping International Commitments: Compliance, Credibility and the G7, 1988-1995*, Garland Publishing, Levittown.

Kokotsis, E. and Daniels, P. D. (1999), 'G8 Summits and Compliance' in M. J. Hodges, J. J. Kirton and J. P. Daniels (eds.), *The G8's Role in the New Millennium*, Ashgate, Aldershot, pp. 75-91.

Layard, R. (1999), 'Designing Effective Policies for Employment Creation', in M. J. Hodges, J. J. Kirton and J. P. Daniels (eds.), *The G8's Role in the New Millennium*, Ashgate, Aldershot, pp. 159-168.

Llewellyn, J., Potter, S. and Samuelson, L. (1985), *Economic Forecasting and Policy: the International Dimenson*, Routledge and Kegan Paul, London.

Lockwood, M., Donlan, E., Joyner, K. and Simms, A. (1998), *Forever in Your Debt? Eight Poor Nations and the G8*, Christian Aid, London.

Major, J. (1999), *The Autobiography*, Harper Collins, London.

Marjolin, R. (1989), *Architect of European Unity: Memoirs 1911-1986*, Weidenfeld and Nicholson, London, translated by William Hall from *Le Travail d'une Vie*, Robert Laffont, Paris, 1986.

Maud, H. (1998), 'The Commonwealth's Edinburgh Economic Declaration', *The Round Table*, no. 346, pp. 191-198.

Organisation for Economic Cooperation and Development (OECD) (1985), *The Costs and Benefits of Protection*, Paris.

OECD (1986), *Labour Market Flexibility: Report by a High-Level Group of Experts Chaired by Professor Dahrendorf*, Paris.

OECD (1987), *National Policies and Agricultural Trade*, Paris.

OECD (1991), *Agricultural Policies, Markets and Trade: Monitoring and Outlook 1991*, Paris.

OECD (1999), *Economic Outlook*, no. 65, Paris.

Putnam, R. D. (1988), 'Diplomacy and Domestic Politics; the Logic of Two-Level Games', *International Organization*, vol. 42, no. 4, pp. 427-460.

Putnam, R. D. and Bayne, N. (1984), *Hanging Together: the Seven-Power Summits*, Heinemann for Royal Institute of International Affairs, London.

Putnam, R. D. and Bayne, N. (1987), *Hanging Together: Cooperation and Conflict in the Seven-Power Summits*, SAGE, London.

Putnam, R. D. and Henning, C. R. (1989), 'The Bonn Summit of 1978: A Case Study in Coordination', in R. N. Cooper and others (eds.), *Can Nations Agree? Issues in International Economic Cooperation*, The Brookings Institution, Washington.

Roberts, A. and Kingsbury, B. (1993), *United Nations, Divided World*, Clarendon Press, Oxford.

Schott, J. J. (1994), *The Uruguay Round: An Assessment*, Institute for International Economics, Washington.

Shonfield, A. (1976a), *International Economic Relations of the Western World, 1957-1971*, vol. 1, Oxford University Press for Royal Institute of International Affairs.

Shonfield, A. (1976b), 'Can the Western Economic System Stand the Strain', *The World Today*, vol. 34, no. 5, p. 172.

Shonfield, A. (1980), 'The Politics of the Mixed Economy', *International Affairs*, vol. 56, no. 1, p. 11.

Silberston, Z. (1984), *The Multi-Fibre Agreement and the UK Economy*, Her Majesty's Stationery Office, London.

Spero, J. and Hart, J. (1997), *The Politics of International Economic Relations*, fifth edition, Routlege, London and New York.

Staple, G. (1999), 'Combating Transnational Financial Crime' in M. J. Hodges, J. J. Kirton and J. P. Daniels (eds.), *The G8's Role in the New Millennium*, Ashgate, Aldershot, pp. 169-179.

Strange, S. (1995), 'The Limits of Politics', *Government and Opposition*, vol. 30, no. 3, pp. 291-311.

Strange, S. (1996), *The Retreat of the State: the Diffusion of Power in the World Economy*, Cambridge University Press, Cambridge.

Sullivan, S. (1997), *From War to Wealth: Fifty Years of Innovation*, Organisation for Economic Cooperation, Paris.

Thatcher, M. (1993), *The Downing Street Years*, HarperCollins, London.

Urquhart, B. and Childers, E. (1990-1994), *A World in Need of Leadership - Tomorrow's United Nations; Towards a More Effective United Nations; and Renewing the United Nations System*, Dag Hammarskold Foundation, Uppsala.

Watt, D. (1984), *Next Steps for Summitry: Report of the Twentieth Century Fund International Conference on Economic Summitry*, Priority Press, New York.

Winham, G. L. (1992), *The Evolution of International Trade Agreements*, University of Toronto Press, Toronto and London.

Wolfe, R. (1998), *Farm Wars: the Political Economy of Agriculture and the International Trade Regime*, Macmillan, Basingstoke.

World Bank (1993), *World Development Report 1993*, Oxford University Press for World Bank, London.

World Bank (1997), *World Development Indicators 1997*, World Bank, Washington.

Index